The Communist Manifesto

"In a world of growing inequality, where the wealth of elites condemns hundreds of millions of people to lives of poverty and despair, where greed and the insatiable pursuit of even greater profit has put life itself on the planet in peril, the words of Marx and Engels emblazoned in *The Communist Manifesto* have never rung more true: 'The proletarians have nothing to lose but their chains. They have a world to win.' Longtime socialist Phil Gasper brings one of the world's most important texts to life in new and important ways in this updated, annotated version. For everyone from new readers to those who have held onto their copies for years, Gasper brings fresh insights in a brand new context to the world's most famous pamphlet, at a time when its rousing call to action has never been more important."

—**Keeanga-Yamahtta Taylor**, author of *From #BlackLivesMatter to Black Liberation*

"An indispensable guide to an indispensable document. The new edition of this outstanding, trailblazing work could not be more welcome."

—**China Miéville**, author of *A Spectre, Haunting: On the Communist Manifesto*

Praise for the 2005 Edition

"Phil Gasper's new edition of *The Communist Manifesto* comes at a critical moment in world history, when a global capitalism that Marx described with amazing accuracy a hundred and fifty years ago shows all the signs of disarray that he predicted. What Gasper does is to remind us how relevant the *Manifesto* is to our world today. His introduction and afterword are useful guides to the *Manifesto* and to its importance in our time. His notes give us fascinating tidbits of information that a thoughtful reader of the *Manifesto* will find extremely valuable. Gasper brings alive one of the great classics of modern political thought, an indispensable addition to anyone's library."

—**Howard Zinn**, author of *A People's History of the United States*

"The more those in power reject and ignore Marx and his ideas, the more the world comes to resemble the barbaric social system Marx predicted capitalism was in the process of becoming. Therefore, Marx's ideas are becoming more and more relevant to understand what we see before us. This new edition of *The Communist Manifesto*, with its excellent informative notes and commentaries, enables the reader to appreciate this document both historically and theoretically, both in relation to its own time and in relation to the realities around us."

—**Allen Wood**, Indiana University

"Distinguished from all other English-language editions currently in print in two critical ways: (1) it is a fully annotated edition, and (2) it provides much needed corrections to the 1888 Samuel Moore translation supervised by Engels.... In addition to the text of the *Manifesto* itself and the annotations, the book includes a clear, accessible introduction by Gasper and a useful afterword. In the latter he replies to criticisms of the *Manifesto* (some emanating from the left) and demonstrates its continuing relevance. The numerous appendices to the book include all the prefaces to the *Manifesto*, Engels's 'Principles of Communism,' and a generous collection of extracts from Marx and Engels' writings."

—***Monthly Review***

The Communist Manifesto

A Road Map to History's Most Important Political Document

Revised Second Edition

Karl Marx and Frederick Engels

Edited by Phil Gasper

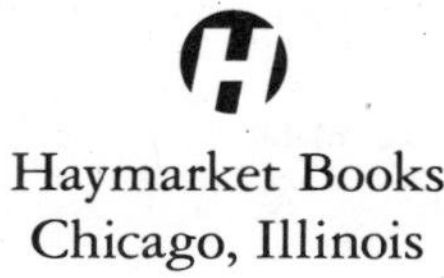

Haymarket Books
Chicago, Illinois

The Communist Manifesto:
A Road Map to History's Most Important Political Document
Revised Second Edition
By Karl Marx and Frederick Engels
Edited by Phil Gasper

This edition published 2024 by Haymarket Books
www.haymarketbooks.org

Manifesto of the Communist Party first published in 1848;
this translation first published in 1888

ISBN: 978-1-64259-978-7

Distributed to the trade in the US through Consortium Book Sales and Distribution (www.cbsd.com) and internationally through Ingram Publisher Services International (www.ingramcontent.com).

This book was published with the generous support of Lannan Foundation, Wallace Action Fund, and Marguerite Casey Foundation.

Special discounts are available for bulk purchases by organizations and institutions.
Please email info@haymarketbooks.org for more information.

Cover design by Benjamin Koditschek.

Printed in Canada by union labor.

Library of Congress Cataloging-in-Publication data is available.

10 9 8 7 6 5 4 3 2 1

For T. J.

I pondered all these things, and how men fight and lose the battle, and the thing that they fought for comes about in spite of their defeat, and when it comes turns out not to be what they meant, and other men have to fight for what they meant under another name.

William Morris, *A Dream of John Ball*

The best story I've ever heard about *The Communist Manifesto* came from Hans Morgenthau, the great theorist of international relations who died in 1980. It was the early seventies at CUNY, and he was reminiscing about his childhood in Bavaria before World War I. Morgenthau's father, a doctor in a working-class neighborhood of Coburg, often took his son along on house calls. Many of his patients were dying of TB; a doctor could do nothing to save their lives, but might help them die with dignity. When his father asked about last requests, many workers said they wanted to have the *Manifesto* buried with them when they died. They implored the doctor to see that the priest didn't sneak in and plant the Bible on them instead. . . .

As the nineties end, we find ourselves in a dynamic global society ever more unified by downsizing, de-skilling, and dread—just like the old man said. . . . At the dawn of the twentieth century, there were workers who were ready to die with *The Communist Manifesto.* At the dawn of the twenty-first, there may be even more who are ready to live with it.

Marshall Berman, *Unchained Melody*

Working people have it harder and harder these days, and we believe that things will get better when workers of the world unite.

Julia Reichert, accepting the 2019 Academy Award
for Best Documentary for *American Factory*

Contents

Preface and Acknowledgments

There are dozens of editions of *The Communist Manifesto* currently in print—do we really need another? I think a combination of three things makes this edition distinctive and worthwhile. First, it is edited by someone who is sympathetic to Marx's general political perspective and views the *Manifesto* as more than an interesting historical relic. Second, it is aimed specifically at both students reading the *Manifesto* for the first time and young political activists—fighting against corporate globalization, war, environmental destruction, and all forms of oppression—who want to know whether Marx's ideas are useful guides for them today. Third, it includes not just an introduction and a few notes on the text, but a full set of annotations, as well as study and discussion questions, an afterword on the contemporary relevance of the *Manifesto*, and a glossary. Several of the extant editions have one or even two of these features, but none has all three. The only other fully annotated version of the *Manifesto* in English that I am aware of is Hal Draper's *The Adventures of the Communist Manifesto* (1994; reissued by Haymarket Books in 2020). Draper's book is an important resource, which I often found valuable in writing my own commentary, but it is written at a level of scholarly detail that most new readers of the *Manifesto* would find intimidating. While Draper's annotations contain many penetrating insights, it is often hard to see the forest for the trees. In what follows, I hope the forest remains fully visible.

This revised second edition includes a revised Afterword, updated Further Reading suggestions, and other small changes.

Thanks to Anthony Arnove, Paul D'Amato, Julie Fain, Kim Gasper-Rabuck, and Snehal Shingavi, who provided advice and encouragement when I was working on the first edition of this book.

P. G.
January 2024

INTRODUCTION

History's Most Important Political Document

The Communist Manifesto was first published in February 1848. Why is it still worth reading a book that was written so long ago? One answer to that question is that the authors of the *Manifesto*, Karl Marx and Frederick Engels,[1] describe a world that is still recognizably our own. In the *Manifesto* they call it "bourgeois society"—in other words, a society in which the bourgeois class (defined by Engels as "the class of modern capitalists, owners of the means of social production, and employers of wage labor") is dominant—but later Marx himself would popularize the name by which it is now commonly known: capitalism. Much has changed since the mid-nineteenth century, but like Marx and Engels, we still live in a capitalist society. When they were writing, capitalism was established in relatively few places, most importantly in parts of western Europe and North America, but Marx and Engels envisioned that capitalism would eventually become a global system. Today nearly every area of the world is part of a single capitalist economic system. Precisely because Marx and Engels lived at a time when modern capitalism was young, they were able to analyze the system in a way that still seems to many to capture its essential features and its core dynamic. Here, for instance, is their dazzling description of the incessant change that capitalism brings in its wake:

> The bourgeoisie cannot exist without constantly revolutionizing the instruments of production, and thereby the relations of production, and with them the whole relations of society. Conservation of the old modes of production in unaltered form was, on the contrary, the first condition

> of existence for all earlier industrial classes. Constant revolutionizing of production, uninterrupted disturbance of all social conditions, everlasting uncertainty and agitation distinguish the bourgeois epoch from all earlier ones. All fixed, fast-frozen relations, with their train of ancient and venerable prejudices and opinions, are swept away, all new-formed ones become antiquated before they can ossify. All that is solid melts into air, all that is holy is profaned, and man is at last compelled to face with sober senses his real conditions of life and his relations with his kind. (I.18)*

Change can be exhilarating, and Marx and Engels praise the way in which capitalism has shattered narrow horizons and produced technological marvels. But they also see capitalism as a system that is increasingly running out of control, a system that concentrates wealth and power in the hands of a small minority, creates huge pools of poverty, turns life into a daily grind that prevents most people from fulfilling their potential, and experiences frequent and enormously wasteful economic crises. Capitalist development is also highly destructive of the natural environment, and economic competition between capitalist states often leads to military confrontation and war. The only solution to these potentially devastating problems, according to the *Manifesto*, is the abolition of capitalism itself and its replacement by a system in which the majority of the population democratically control society's economic resources—in other words, genuine communism.[2] Marx and Engels' proposal is, to say the least, controversial. However, a strong case can be made that the problems they diagnose have not disappeared. If the roots of these problems run as deeply as Marx and Engels contend, then radical action remains necessary. That, perhaps, is reason enough to ponder the alternative they advocate.

---

*References to passages in the *Manifesto* are by section number and paragraph number (e.g., I.12, III.26, etc.). References to passages in the preamble use "P" followed by paragraph number (e.g., P.2). References to numbered points within paragraphs are given by adding a third number (e.g., II.72.5). References to other works (listed at the end of the book) are by author and date.

Marx and Engels

Marx and Engels were both born to relatively well-to-do families in small towns in the German Rhineland—Marx in Trier in 1818, and Engels in Barmen two years later. Although the Rhineland was a province of Prussia, Napoleon's armies had occupied it until 1814, and its intellectual life had thus been deeply affected by the radical ideas of the French Revolution of 1789.[3] These ideas were very much in the air as Marx and Engels grew up.

Because of Germany's economic and political backwardness at this time, what had been acted out in practice in France came to be reflected only in abstract philosophy in Marx and Engels' homeland.[4] As Marx later put it, "In politics, the Germans have *thought* what other nations have *done*" (Marx 1844, p. 59). By the 1820s, the idealist philosophy of Hegel, with its emphasis on change—in particular historical change—had become dominant in Germany. Hegel believed that history was to be explained in terms of the development of ideas, indeed that history itself is merely a series of stages in the development of a World Spirit or Absolute Mind.[5] However, Hegel's writing was highly obscure and open to different interpretations. Conservatives interpreted him as saying that the emergence of the highly authoritarian Prussian state represented the culmination of world history. After Hegel's death in 1831, the radical Young Hegelians rejected this conclusion as absurd and instead used Hegel's emphasis on change as a justification for the democratic transformation of society. They rejected the notion of Absolute Mind as a metaphysical extravagance, but remained idealists in the sense that they held that historical progress was the result of humanity achieving self-understanding.

Both Marx and Engels were members of the Young Hegelian movement in Berlin for a time—Marx when he was a student at the University of Berlin, and Engels while he was stationed in the city for his military service. Unlike Marx, who completed a doctorate in philosophy, Engels did not pursue formal schooling very far, but he was a fine writer and had a thorough grasp of the latest philosophical ideas. Between 1839 and 1842, Engels published nearly fifty articles, including two acclaimed anonymous pamphlets in which he defended the ideas of the Young Hegelians against the reactionary philosophy of Hegel's contemporary Schelling (Engels 1842a, 1842b).

Marx and Engels were soon to break with the Young Hegelians. Initially, and independently, they were strongly influenced by the work of Ludwig Feuerbach, who rejected the idealism of the other Young Hegelians and argued that religious ideas reflected the material conditions in which they arose. Even more importantly, events took both Marx and Engels away from the abstract discussion of ideas detached from the real world. Marx received his doctorate in 1841,[6] but an academic career was ruled out, as a new period of political reaction began in Prussia and the Young Hegelians were denied university positions. Instead, Marx became the editor of a radical liberal newspaper, the *Rheinische Zeitung.* This experience was to finally lead him to settle accounts with all varieties of Hegelianism. As one commentator puts it, the "young Marx is often portrayed as having come to a revolutionary understanding of society *through* a critique of Hegel's texts on the state and society. The biographical fact, however, is that he came *to* the content of his critique of the Hegelian view of the state *through* a year and a half of rubbing his nose against the social and political facts of life, which he encountered as the crusading editor of the most extreme leftist democratic newspaper in pre-1848 Germany" (Draper 1977, p. 31). Marx himself later commented on this period of his life: "I experienced for the first time the embarrassment of having to take part in discussions on so-called material interests" (Marx 1859, p. 3).[7] In particular, following the debates in the Rhine Province's parliament,[8] where the deputies regularly voted in favor of their own material interests, led Marx to reject the Hegelian idea that the state was—or could be—above classes.

By 1843, Marx was beginning to recognize that the ideals of the French Revolution, with its call for liberty and democracy, could never be achieved in a society based on material inequality. Formal freedom and democracy might exist in such a society, but they would be subverted in the interests of those who controlled the wealth. Real freedom was impossible in a society divided into exploiters and exploited. What was needed, Marx concluded, was not formal equality before the law, but a society of genuine equality in which economic power was not in the hands of a privileged minority. What was needed, in other words, was the abolition of private property. Thus, Marx's commitment to radical democracy and human liberation led him over a period of years to communism.

Marx had already reached the materialist conclusion that the starting point for understanding human society is not the realm of ideas but actual human beings and the material conditions in which they live. However, he had not yet come to the view that the modern working class of wage laborers (the proletariat) was central to the project of transforming society. Two things finally brought him to this conclusion. The first was his move to Paris in late 1843, after the censors closed the *Rheinische Zeitung.* France was economically and politically far more advanced than Germany, and Marx came into contact for the first time with an organized working-class movement. The second factor that led Marx to recognize the importance of the working class was the influence of Engels.

Marx and Engels had met briefly in 1842, but had not gotten on very well. Shortly afterward, Engels left for England to work in his father's business in Manchester. By this time Engels already regarded himself as a communist (a year earlier than Marx), and he immediately became involved in the British working-class movement and began the research that was to culminate in his pathbreaking study *The Condition of the Working Class in England*, eventually published in 1845, which exposed the brutal exploitation of the Industrial Revolution. In late 1843, Engels also wrote an important article, "Outlines of a Critique of Political Economy" (published the following year), which contained in embryo many of the ideas that Marx and he were later to develop in greater detail. Engels' article had a great influence on Marx, turning him toward the study of political economy. It was this that led Marx to conclude that the working class was the key to the revolutionary transformation of society because of its role in the economy and its ability to shut down the entire system of production.

When Marx and Engels met again in 1844, they found themselves in complete political agreement and began a partnership that only ended with Marx's death in 1883.[9] They collaborated first on *The Holy Family* (1845), a long critique of some of the Young Hegelians, whom they had come to see as pompous windbags who refused to participate in real political activity. Shortly afterward, Marx was expelled from Paris by the authorities and moved to Brussels.

Here, he and Engels collaborated on *The German Ideology* (written in 1845–46, but never published in their lifetimes), which was intended to be both a final settling of accounts with the Young Hegelians and an exposition of Marx and Engels' own views on materialism, revolution, and communism.

The Materialist View of History

In *The German Ideology*, Marx and Engels set out systematically for the first time their materialist conception of historical change (now often called "historical materialism"), which underlies much of what they say in *The Communist Manifesto.* They criticize the Young Hegelians for wrongly holding that human progress is held back primarily by illusions, mistaken ideas, and false consciousness. In response, Marx and Engels argue

> This demand to change consciousness amounts to a demand to interpret reality in another way, i.e., to recognize it by means of another interpretation. The Young-Hegelian ideologists, in spite of their allegedly "world-shattering" statements, are the staunchest conservatives. The most recent of them have found the correct expression for their activity when they declare they are only fighting against "*phrases.*" They forget, however, that to these phrases they themselves are only opposing other phrases, and that they are in no way combating the real existing world when they are merely combating the phrases of this world. (p. 41)[10]

Instead of starting with ideas, society can only be understood, and ultimately changed, by examining the material realities on which it is based.

> The premises from which we begin are not arbitrary ones, not dogmas, but real premises from which abstraction can only be made in the imagination. They are the real individuals, their activity and the material conditions under which they live, both those which they find already existing and those produced by their activity. These premises can thus be verified in a purely empirical way. (p. 42)

The fundamental fact about real individuals is that they must engage in production in order to survive, and this shapes every other aspect of their lives.

> Men can be distinguished from animals by consciousness, by religion or anything else you like. They themselves begin to distinguish themselves from animals as soon as they begin to produce their means of subsistence, a step which is conditioned by their physical organization. By producing their means of subsistence men are indirectly producing their actual material life.
>
> The way in which men produce their means of subsistence depends first of all on the nature of the actual means of subsistence they find in existence and have to reproduce. This mode of production must not be considered simply as being the production of the physical existence of the individuals. Rather it is a definite form of activity of these individuals, a definite form of expressing their life, a definite mode of life on their part. As individuals express their life, so they are. What they are, therefore, coincides with their production, both with what they produce and with how they produce. The nature of individuals thus depends on the material conditions determining their production. (p. 42)

The material conditions of production include both the forces of production (or productive forces)—the methods and technology used in production—and what Marx and Engels call here the "form of intercourse" between individuals, or what they later call the "social relations of production." This includes the division of labor within production, which at a certain point in history gives rise to distinct social classes with their own antagonistic interests. On this basis develops the whole of the rest of society, including culture, social structures, and the institutions of the state. This is the starting point of Marx and Engels' materialist conception of history—"the 'history of humanity' must always be studied and treated in relation to the history of industry and exchange" (p. 50).

> The social structure and the State are continually evolving out of the life-process of definite individuals, but of individuals, not as they may appear in their own or other people's imagination, but as they *really* are; i.e., as they operate, produce materially, and hence as they work under definite material limits, presuppositions, and conditions independent of their will. . . .

> In direct contrast to German philosophy which descends from heaven to earth, here we ascend from earth to heaven. That is to say, we do not set out from what men say, imagine, conceive, nor from men as narrated, thought of, imagined, conceived, in order to arrive at men in the flesh. We set out from real, active men, and on the basis of their real life-process we demonstrate the development of the ideological reflexes and echoes of this life-process. The phantoms formed in the human brain are also, necessarily, sublimates of their material life-process, which is empirically verifiable and bound to material premises. Morality, religion, metaphysics, all the rest of ideology and their corresponding forms of consciousness, thus no longer retain the semblance of independence. They have no history, no development; but men, developing their material production and their material intercourse, alter, along with this their real existence, their thinking and the products of their thinking. Life is not determined by consciousness, but consciousness by life. (pp. 46–47)

However, the ideas to be found in any given society are not simply the result of material conditions in general; they are also a reflection of the interests of the dominant, exploiting class.

> The ideas of the ruling class are in every epoch the ruling ideas, i.e., the class which is the ruling material force of society, is at the same time its ruling intellectual force. The class which has the means of material production at its disposal, has control at the same time over the means of mental production, so that thereby, generally speaking, the ideas of those who lack the means of mental production are subject to it. The ruling ideas are nothing more than the ideal expression of the dominant material relationships, the dominant material relationships grasped as ideas. (p. 64)

In arguing that the ideas in people's heads have to be explained in terms of the material conditions of their lives, Marx and Engels were following in the footsteps of Ludwig Feuerbach, but they also criticized Feuerbach for ignoring how, over time, human activity changes those conditions and gives rise to new ones, leading to profound changes in the rest of society. "As far as Feuerbach is a materialist he does not deal with history, and as far as he considers history he is not a materialist. With him materialism and history diverge completely"

(p. 64). In contrast to Feuerbach's static conception, Marx and Engels point to the deep tensions that exist within societies that are divided into antagonistic classes, and that drive history forward:

> [T]he forces of production, the state of society, and consciousness can and must come into contradiction with one another, because . . . intellectual and material activity—enjoyment and labor, production and consumption—devolve on different individuals, and . . . the only possibility of their not coming into contradiction lies in the negation [i.e., abolition] in its turn of the division of labor. . . .
>
> . . . [A]ll struggles within the State, the struggle between democracy, aristocracy, and monarchy, the struggle for the franchise, etc., etc. are merely the illusory forms in which the real struggles of the different classes are fought out among one another. (pp. 52, 54)

A large part of *The German Ideology* is devoted to giving an account of European history that concretely illustrates these general ideas. In particular, Marx and Engels describe the way in which feudal society developed, and how tensions between the productive forces and the "form of intercourse" eventually led to the emergence of capitalism and the triumph of the bourgeoisie.

> This contradiction between the productive forces and the form of intercourse, which . . . has occurred several times in past history, without, however, endangering the basis, necessarily on each occasion burst out in a revolution, taking on at the same time various subsidiary forms, such as all-embracing collisions, collisions of various classes, contradiction of consciousness, battle of ideas, etc., political conflict, etc. From a narrow point of view one may isolate one of these subsidiary forms and consider it as the basis of these revolutions; and this is all the more easy as the individuals who started the revolutions had illusions about their own activity according to their degree of culture and the stage of historical development.
>
> Thus all collisions in history have their origin, according to our view, in the contradiction between the productive forces and the form of intercourse. (pp. 88–89)

Just as such contradictions emerged as feudalism developed, Marx and Engels argued that they would inevitably appear in capitalism as well. For this reason they claim that communist revolution is not a utopian ideal, but something that will be produced by actual material conditions, when circumstances "have rendered the great mass of humanity 'propertyless,' and produced, at the same time, the contradiction of an existing world of wealth and culture, both of which conditions presuppose a great increase in productive power, a high degree of its development." Without a high level of production, scarcity cannot be abolished, and the result of revolution would be that "*want* is merely made general, and with *destitution* the struggle for necessities and all the old filthy business [i.e., class exploitation] would necessarily be reproduced" (p. 56).[11] In addition, in a world of "universal competition," in which all countries are part of a single economic system, revolution cannot survive in a single country, since "each extension of intercourse would abolish local communism." They continue:

> [T]he mass of propertyless workers—the utterly precarious position of labor-power on a mass scale cut off from capital or from even a limited satisfaction and, therefore, no longer merely temporarily deprived of work itself as a secure source of life—presupposes the world market through competition. The proletariat can thus only exist *world-historically*, just as communism, its activity, can only have a "world-historical" existence. (p. 56)

The conditions for successful communist revolution thus presuppose an integrated world economy in which the mass of the population finds it increasingly difficult to secure a decent life—not a bad summary of the effects of globalization at the start of the twenty-first century.

Having set out their conception of history, Marx and Engels draw four further conclusions about the possibility and nature of communist revolution (pp. 94–95):

> (1) In the development of productive forces there comes a stage when productive forces and means of intercourse are brought into being, which, under the existing relationships, only cause mischief, and are no longer productive but destructive forces (machinery and money); and connected with this a class is called forth, which has to bear all the

> burdens of society without enjoying its advantages, which, ousted from society, is forced into the most decided antagonism to all other classes; a class which forms the majority of all members of society, and from which emanates the consciousness of the necessity of a fundamental revolution, the communist consciousness, which may, of course, arise among the other classes too through the contemplation of the situation of this class.
>
> (2) The conditions under which definite productive forces can be applied are the conditions of the rule of a definite class of society, whose social power, deriving from its property, has its practical-idealistic expression in each case in the form of the State; and, therefore, every revolutionary struggle is directed against a class, which till then has been in power.
>
> (3) In all revolutions up till now the mode of activity always remained unscathed and it was only a question of a different distribution of this activity, a new distribution of labor to other persons, whilst the communist revolution is directed against the preceding mode of activity, does away with labor, and abolishes the rule of all classes with the classes themselves, because it is carried through by the class which no longer counts as a class in society, is not recognized as a class, and is in itself the expression of the dissolution of all classes, nationalities, etc. within present society; and
>
> (4) Both for the production on a mass scale of this communist consciousness, and for the success of the cause itself, the alteration of men on a mass scale is, necessarily, an alteration which can only take place in a practical movement, a revolution; this revolution is necessary, therefore, not only because the ruling class cannot be overthrown in any other way, but also because the class overthrowing it can only in a revolution succeed in ridding itself of all the muck of ages and become fitted to found society anew.

Marx and Engels argue that the working class under capitalism occupies a unique position. Unlike the bourgeoisie under feudalism, for example, workers do not have their own form of private property to protect. In this sense, it is a "class which no longer counts as a class in society"—a class which, when it moves into activity, will not fight just for its own interests, but for the interests of humanity as a whole. As the forces of production come into conflict with capitalist relations of production, the crisis can only be permanently resolved by the abolition of private property and its replacement by communal control of the economy, creating a society in which individual lives are no longer at the mercy of impersonal market forces, and in which true freedom therefore becomes possible. However, such a transformation requires "the alteration of men on a mass scale," something that can only take place in the course of struggle itself, culminating in the revolutionary overthrow of capitalist society. Their material situation leads workers to fight to protect their interests, but in the course of doing so, their consciousness changes both to see the need to replace the whole system and to give them the confidence and vision to do so.

The Communist League and the *Manifesto*

The 1840s was a period of growing political and economic crises in Europe. In response to this situation, Marx and Engels began a Communist Correspondence Committee in 1846, which enabled them to forge ties with communists and other radicals in both Europe and the United States. Among those with whom they made close links were some of the left-wing leaders of the Chartists in Britain (the first mass working-class movement, which was fighting for a charter of democratic reforms), and leaders of the League of the Just, a radical organization of perhaps two hundred German workers, many living in exile in Paris and London. The League organized secretly and had a romantic and conspiratorial view of revolution, in which a dedicated minority would seize power on behalf of the masses; in London, however, its leading members were influenced by the growth of trade unions and by the Chartists. In early 1847, Marx and Engels decided to join the League, and in June of that year, Engels attended an international congress convened by the League in London aimed at unifying communists from several countries, with the expectation that a revolution was imminent.[12] At this conference, the League of the Just renamed itself the Communist League; reorganized itself on more open, democratic lines; and abandoned its previous abstract slogans concerning justice and equality in favor of the call "Workers of All Countries, Unite!"

The Communist League was moving quickly in the direction of Marx and Engels' ideas. The June congress produced a communist "confession of faith," written by Engels (1847a) as a series of questions and answers for discussion among the League's members in preparation for a second congress in November. In October, following further debates in the organization, Engels wrote an improved version, *Principles of Communism* (1847b), still in question-and-answer form. Shortly afterward, he wrote to Marx:

> I believe that the best thing is to do away with the catechism [question and answer] form and give the thing the title: *Communist Manifesto.* We have to bring in a certain amount of history, and the present form does not lend itself to this very well.[13]

A few days later, on November 29, the second congress of the Communist League began in London. After much debate over the next ten days, Marx and Engels finally fully won the organization over to their ideas, and Marx was commissioned to write the League's official program. Thus, *The Communist Manifesto* was born. Marx wrote it over the next several weeks in Brussels, but he drew heavily on Engels' earlier drafts, so both are rightly credited as authors of the final version. As Marx was completing the document in late January 1848, revolution was already breaking out in parts of Italy. In mid-February, it was published in German in London, with the title *Manifest der Kommunistischen Partei* (Manifesto of the Communist Party).

Within days of the *Manifesto*'s publication, revolution had spread to Paris—where the monarchy was overthrown—and, over the next few weeks, to much of the rest of Europe, including Germany. Marx, Engels, and other members of the Communist League took part in the revolutionary movement in Germany, where they hoped the bourgeoisie would overthrow feudalism and create more favorable conditions for a workers' revolution. However, in Germany, the bourgeoisie proved more concerned about the threat from the working class than the repressive status quo, and the revolution went down to defeat in 1849. Elsewhere, too, the forces of counterrevolution were eventually victorious. Marx and Engels went into exile in England, convinced that while the revolutionary moment had passed for the time being, the inexorable workings of economic and social forces would create new opportunities in the future.[14]

Socialism or Communism?

In the *Manifesto*, Marx and Engels emphatically identify themselves as communists. Elsewhere, however, they are happy to describe themselves as socialists (or sometimes "scientific socialists"). How should these terms be understood, and how are they related?

The first point to bear in mind is that at the time the *Manifesto* was written, "socialist" was often used broadly to refer to anyone concerned by capitalism's social problems, no matter what kind of solution they offered to those problems. This is how Marx and Engels use the term in Section III of the *Manifesto*. It thus makes sense for them to talk about "reactionary socialists" (who want to solve the problems by turning the clock back) and "conservative socialists" (who think the problems can be solved without fundamentally changing anything), as well as "critical-utopian socialists" (who want a new kind of society, but have no realistic strategy to achieve it). By contrast, the term "communist" clearly signified a commitment to some form of communal ownership and was the term used by radical workers themselves. For this reason, there was no question which name Marx and Engels would choose to use, as Engels himself explained in his Preface to the English edition of 1888[15]

> [W]hen it was written, we could not have called it a *socialist* manifesto. By Socialists, in 1847, were understood, on the one hand the adherents of the various Utopian systems: Owenites in England, Fourierists in France,[16] both of them already reduced to the position of mere sects, and gradually dying out; on the other hand, the most multifarious social quacks who, by all manner of tinkering, professed to redress, without any danger to capital and profit, all sorts of social grievances, in both cases men outside the working-class movement, and looking rather to the "educated" classes for support. Whatever portion of the working class had become convinced

> of the insufficiency of mere political revolutions, and had proclaimed the necessity of total social change, called itself Communist. It was a crude, rough-hewn, purely instinctive sort of communism; still, it touched the cardinal point and was powerful enough amongst the working class to produce the Utopian communism of Cabet[17] in France, and of Weitling[18] in Germany. Thus, in 1847, socialism was a middle-class movement, communism a working-class movement. Socialism was, on the {European} Continent at least, "respectable"; communism was the very opposite. And as our notion, from the very beginning, was that "the emancipation of the working class must be the act of the working class itself," there could be no doubt as to which of the two names we must take. Moreover, we have, ever since, been far from repudiating it.

As the nineteenth century progressed, "socialist" came to signify not merely concern with "the social question," but opposition to capitalism and support for some form of social ownership. While never abandoning the term "communist," Marx and Engels were also quite happy to call themselves socialists in this sense, in which "socialism" is simply a more general term than "communism."[19] What is most distinctive about the kind of socialism they supported, however, is that it can only be created through the active participation of workers themselves—or as Engels puts it in the quotation above, "the emancipation of the workers must be the act of the working class itself." American Marxist Hal Draper called this conception "socialism from below" and contrasted it with various varieties of "socialism from above," in which an elite imposes change on a passive working class.[20] Historically, most versions of self-described socialism have been varieties of "socialism from above," which from Marx and Engels' perspective was not genuine socialism at all.

Unlike the utopian socialists, who drew up intricate blueprints of post-capitalist society (which they sometimes attempted to put into practice on a small scale), Marx and Engels never speculated on the detailed organization of a future socialist or communist society. The key task for them was building a movement to overthrow capitalism. If and when that movement was successful, it would be up to the members of the new society to decide democratically how it was to be organized, in the concrete historical circumstances in which they

Continued on page 18

Marxism in a Nutshell

1. Perhaps more than any other thinker, Marx's ideas have to be separated from the actions of many of those who have claimed to act in his name. Marx hated dogmatic thinking (he once half-jokingly responded to a group of his self-described followers, "All I know is that I am no Marxist!") and saw himself as a defender of radical democracy and human freedom. He condemned capitalism because he saw it as an irrational system that denies the majority of people an opportunity to fulfill their potential. Defenders of capitalism claim that, whatever its problems, it is a system based on freedom. Marx thought this to be an illusion.

2. Marx was a **materialist** who held that to understand any society we must examine the way in which it organizes production. According to Marx, this depends on two things: (a) the **forces of production**—land, raw materials, technology, skills, and knowledge; and (b) the **social relations of production**—who controls the forces of production and how. Marx argues that (a) and (b) are related—given a certain level of development of the forces of production, only certain relations of production are possible. It is also possible for the forces and relations of production to come into conflict. The forces of production may change in such a way that the relations of production begin to hold them back, stunting their further development. Or the relations of production may evolve to the point where they become incompatible with the existing forces of production.

3. The relations of production define the **class structure** of society. For most of human history, societies have been sharply divided into different classes, with those at the top controlling most of the wealth and those at the bottom doing most of the work that produces the wealth. This exploitative relationship is the basis of class conflict. In slave societies, slaveholders control the wealth while slaves do the work. In feudal societies, lords don't own peasants, but they are legally entitled to most of the wealth that peasants produce. Despite the fact that under modern capitalism slavery is illegal and there are no longer laws determining the place of individuals within society, according to Marx we still live in a class society in which capitalists (the **bourgeoisie**) control most of the wealth that workers (the **proletariat**) produce. Even if everyone in a capitalist society began equal, competition would soon result in some controlling much more than others and the majority having only their **labor power** to sell.

4. For this reason, Marx argues that capitalism is not based on exchange between equals. To avoid poverty, workers are forced to sell their labor power to capitalists. Capitalists will only buy it if they think they can get more out of the worker than she receives in wages. So, at root, just as are slave and feudal societies, capitalism is based on **exploitation**. Capitalists want to pay their workers as little as possible and to make them work as hard as possible. Partly for this reason, most workers don't find their jobs fulfilling—work is **alienating** rather than rewarding.

5. The forces and relations of production together make up the **economic base** of society. According to Marx, this economic base shapes the rest of society, particularly its political and legal **superstructure.** The class that has economic dominance also has dominance elsewhere. It controls the political state and (consciously or unconsciously) uses its economic power to shape society's main institutions and ideas—social, legal, religious, philosophical, artistic, etc.—to support its interests, thus propagating an **ideology** that supports the status quo. In capitalist societies, the economic power of the bourgeoisie undermines genuine democracy. Ruling classes also have an interest in promoting divisions in the working class, such as those based on race, gender, and nationality.

6. Marx condemns capitalism as an exploitative and alienating system, but also as an irrational one. While capitalism has created technological wonders and greatly raised the level of production, it has also created huge **inequalities.** In a world that produces more than enough food for everyone, half the world's population does not get enough to eat. Capitalism also regularly fails on its own terms, with frantic booms regularly giving way to economic slumps that destroy many businesses and throw millions out of work. According to Marx, such **economic crises** are inevitable features of capitalism.

7. Economist Adam Smith argued that the pursuit of individual self-interest is the best way of promoting the public good. However, there are many circumstances in which the pursuit of self-interest leaves everybody worse off. For instance, if one business notices an unmet demand, it may invest in new production in order to increase its profits, but other businesses, acting independently, may do the same, creating a huge glut of new goods that come onto the market at the same time. Because production under capitalism is essentially uncoordinated, such **crises of overproduction**, as Marx called them, are common and can throw the whole economy into a tailspin. Nor is there any easy way to avoid such problems, since if individual companies try to play it safe, they risk being driven out of business by more aggressive rivals. As society's productive forces grow, they come into increasing conflict with capitalist relations of production, and the crises get worse. Marx has a **dialectical** understanding of class society, because he sees internal contradictions and conflicts eventually producing dramatic changes.

8. Capitalism is not only disrupted by regular economic crises, Marx also believes that it results in **environmental destruction and war**. By its nature, capitalism is based on continuous expansion, which repeatedly comes into conflict with the natural environment. Global warming is an ominous contemporary example—in order to do something about it, we would need to sharply reduce our consumption of fossil fuels. However, since many of the most powerful corporations (including oil, coal, and auto companies) make huge profits from such consumption, little has been done to develop alternative, renewable energy sources. Since powerful states defend the economic interests of their own capitalist classes, Marx also believes that capitalist competition is at the root of war. Big corporations look to the states with which they are associated to help them control markets and gain access to resources.

9. According to Marx, capitalism is exploitative, alienating, undemocratic, irrational, environmentally destructive, and prone to war. But it also creates the possibility of an alternative. Capitalism creates a huge urban working class, which Marx believes has enormous potential power if it can overcome its divisions to organize and struggle for its interests collectively. Over the long run, capitalism cannot provide a satisfactory life for the vast majority of people who live under it. In fighting to improve their circumstances, workers ultimately find themselves running up against the limits of what capitalism can grant them. If they are able to use their collective strength to bring the system to a halt by general strikes and mass demonstrations, they can carry out a popular **revolution** that unseats the capitalists from power and creates a new social order, based on democratic **workers' control** of the economy and society.

10. Marx says comparatively little about what this alternative—**socialism** or **communism**—will look like, but he envisages a society based on cooperation rather than competition, in which the economy is democratically controlled and there is much greater social equality. With the elimination of class antagonisms, the material basis for all forms of oppression would disappear. In particular, full **women's liberation** would become a reality. Market mechanisms would gradually give way to forms of democratic planning that respect the environment, production would be organized to meet human needs and wants, not to make profits for a minority, and work would be organized to be fulfilling, not a hated chore. Whether such an alternative to capitalism is possible is perhaps the most important question facing humanity in the twenty-first century. Early in the twentieth century, the Polish-German revolutionary Rosa Luxemburg described the alternatives facing humanity as socialism or barbarism. Ultimately, that may be our choice.

Continued from page 15

found themselves. Marx did comment in a more general way about what could be expected to happen in the aftermath of a successful workers' revolution.[21] In the *Critique of the Gotha Program* (1875),[22] Marx notes that because a communist society will not develop "on its own foundations" but will emerge from capitalist society, it will therefore be "in every respect, economically, morally, and intellectually, still stamped with the birthmarks of the old society from whose womb it emerges." At this early stage of its development, although some goods and services (such as housing and health care) would be provided to everyone, and although no one would grow rich at the expense of others, work would be rewarded in proportion to a person's contribution. Only later, when work has been reorganized to become truly fulfilling, so that "labor has become not only a means of life but life's prime want," and when the level of production has consequently increased, will it be possible to go beyond market incentives and reward people not in accordance with their individual contribution, but in accordance with what they need to flourish.[23] Some people have come to refer to the first phase of postcapitalist society that Marx describes as "socialism," and to the higher phase that will follow it as "communism." When used in this sense, "socialism" is not a more general term than "communism," but the name for a stage in the development of full communism.

Objections and Responses

More has been written about Marx's ideas than those of any other individual thinker, and from the moment he first presented them, they have been subject to fierce criticism. This is hardly surprising. As Marx and Engels wrote in the *Manifesto*, "The ruling ideas of each age have ever been the ideas of its ruling class" (II.59). Anyone who challenges those ideas can expect to be sharply attacked by defenders of the status quo.[24] Marxism has been declared dead many times, but time and again it has proved to be more resilient than its critics have claimed.

Of the many objections raised against Marxism, some rest on myths and misunderstandings, while others deserve more serious consideration. Marx never claimed to have spoken the final word on anything. His favorite motto was "doubt everything," and he put forward his views in a scientific spirit, reconsidering and changing them in the light of new evidence.[25] Nevertheless, he never abandoned his core ideas, which have continued to prove remarkably fruitful as tools for understanding society and inspiring movements for radical social change.[26]

It is obviously not possible to consider here all the objections that have been raised against Marxism, but some brief comments on a few of the more common may be useful.

(1) "*Marx's theories have failed in practice.*" This is surely the most widespread objection to Marxism, particularly since the collapse of the former Soviet Union and other so-called socialist regimes in Eastern Europe. However, this argument only makes sense if these countries were genuinely socialist in Marx's sense. It is true that in all these countries the means of production were state owned, but state ownership of the economy was never Marx and Engels' criterion of socialism. In chapter 3 of *Socialism: Utopian and Scientific* (1880), Engels wrote:

> [S]ince Bismarck went in for State-ownership of industrial establishments, a kind of spurious Socialism has arisen ... that without more ado declares *all* State-ownership, even of the Bismarckian sort, to be socialistic. Certainly, if the taking over by the State of the tobacco industry is socialistic, then Napoleon and Metternich must be numbered among the founders of Socialism.[27]

For Marx and Engels, socialism meant workers running society—as Marx put it, a society in which "the material conditions of production are the co-operative property of the workers themselves."[28] While the state owned the economy in the Soviet bloc countries, the state itself was not controlled by the working class, but by a privileged bureaucratic elite who controlled the surplus wealth created by the workers. Moreover, these bureaucratic rulers were driven by economic and military competition with the rest of the world to reinvest the surplus and to expand production in a continuous cycle of accumulation. If this analysis is correct, then what failed in Eastern Europe was not any kind of socialism, but a variety of bureaucratic state capitalism.[29]

(2) *"Marx's views are in conflict with human nature."* The argument that human beings are by nature competitive, selfish, and aggressive is one of the oldest arguments against socialism. In recent years, it has been made in scientific terms by sociobiologists and evolutionary psychologists. Harvard biologist E. O. Wilson, for example, once joked about Marxism, "Wonderful theory. Wrong species." Psychologist Steven Pinker claims, "The standard Marxist theory of human nature has probably been refuted by many sources of evidence, including the anthropological record and Darwinian theory."[30] However, the evidence for such claims is highly dubious. Biologically, the most distinctive human feature is our large and flexible brain, and the most striking feature of human behavior throughout history is its enormous changeability, not its rigidity. Capitalism tends to encourage competitive, selfish, and aggressive behavior, but even under capitalism, people frequently exhibit cooperation, solidarity, and compassion. In circumstances that encouraged such characteristics, they would likely be exhibited more often. This is what Marx and Engels meant in *The German Ideology* by "the alteration of men on a mass scale." Such changes, they believed, would begin as the result of the activity of workers themselves, fighting collectively to improve their lives, and in turn altering the circumstances in which they live. Nothing about our biology or psychology says that this is impossible, indeed, quite the contrary. As evolutionary biologist Stephen Jay Gould once put it:

> Violence, sexism, and general nastiness *are* biological since they represent one subset of a possible range of behaviors. But peacefulness, equality, and kindness are just as biological—and we may see their influence increase if we can create social structures that permit them to flourish. (Gould 1977, p. 257)

(3) *"Capitalism has changed since Marx's day and his criticisms are no longer relevant."* This objection can take a variety of forms, from the claim that the working class is disappearing, to the claim that living standards in the advanced capitalist countries today are much higher than in the nineteenth century, to the claim that the worst excesses of capitalism can be controlled by government intervention. I discuss these issues at some length in the Afterword to this book. Suffice it to say

that Marx and Engels' argument is not that it is impossible for living standards to rise under capitalism, or that some of its problems cannot be ameliorated for periods of time by various forms of state action, but that none of these measures can change the underlying nature of the system, and that new crises—whether economic, social, or environmental—cannot be indefinitely postponed. As they note at the beginning of the *Manifesto*, the class struggle may be hidden or it may be open. In periods when it is hidden, it may appear to some to have disappeared entirely. But if Marx and Engels are right, that will prove to be an illusion.

Synopsis of the *Manifesto*

It may be helpful to give a brief outline of the *Manifesto*. In the preamble, Marx and Engels announce their intention to dispel the myths about communism and to state its actual ideas and goals. Section I begins by emphasizing the historical importance of class and class struggle, then goes on to explain the rise of the bourgeoisie, the dominant class in the economically most advanced societies. Marx and Engels argue that the bourgeoisie came to power as a result of a growing contradiction between the forces and relations of production in feudal society. Though the bourgeoisie has played a historically progressive role, a similar contradiction is emerging in modern society, which will eventually lead to the bourgeoisie's own downfall at the hands of the proletariat. Marx and Engels describe the development of the proletariat and explain why it is capable of playing a revolutionary role. They argue that the victory of the proletariat will bring about the end of class exploitation.

Section II starts by describing the relation of organized Communists to the rest of the working class. According to Marx and Engels, the Communists do not set themselves up as rivals to other genuine working-class organizations, but are simply the most politically advanced and militant section of the workers' movement. The central idea of communism is the abolition of bourgeois private property (which Marx and Engels distinguish from the abolition of all property). Much of the rest of this section responds to various objections to communism. Finally, Marx and Engels set out the program that might be implemented by a successful workers' revolution.

In section III, Marx and Engels criticize other tendencies identified as socialist. "Feudal socialism" was an unsuccessful attempt by sections of the old landed aristocracy to promote its own agenda by manipulating working-class grievances. "Petty-bourgeois socialism" was put forward by sections of the middle class that objected to modern industry destroying small businesses. "True socialism" was a German variant of petty-bourgeois socialism that ignored historical circumstances and substituted moralism for class politics. All these were reactionary (or backward-looking) ideologies. "Bourgeois socialism" is an attempt to solve capitalism's social problems without fundamentally changing the economic system. Finally, various forms of "critical-utopian socialism" make valuable criticisms of capitalism, but because they see workers merely as victims, they have no serious strategy for transforming society.

In the brief final section, Marx and Engels explain the relation of Communist to non–working-class opposition parties. Communists support all progressive movements, but at the same time refuse to hide their political differences. Marx and Engels believed the struggle against feudalism in Germany was of particular importance because if successful, it would lead almost immediately to a workers' revolution. Communists bring the issue of private property to the forefront in every struggle and refuse to hide their aims. The *Manifesto* ends with a rousing call for revolution and international solidarity.

The *Manifesto* in Outline

Preamble

1–4 The purpose of the *Manifesto*.

Section I: Bourgeois and Proletarians

1–3 The historical importance of class.
4–5 Class in modern bourgeois society (capitalism).
6–12 The historical development of the bourgeoisie.
13–18 The revolutionary role of the bourgeoisie.
19–21 Capitalism as an international system.
22–24 Capitalism's drive to centralization, concentration, and technological growth.
25–28 The contradictions of feudal society compared to the contradictions of capitalism.

29–30 The role of the proletariat.
31–35 Exploitation and the degradation of work under capitalism.
36–43 The historical development of the proletariat.
44–46 The revolutionary role of the proletariat compared to other non-bourgeois classes.
47–51 Why the proletariat represents the interests of the vast majority.
52 Why the bourgeoisie is no longer fit to rule.
53 How the bourgeoisie produces its own gravediggers.

Section II: Proletarians and Communists

1–7 The relation of Communists to the working class and the workers' movement.
8–17 Communism and the abolition of bourgeois private property.
18–20 The nature of capital.
21–24 Wage-labor under capitalism.
25–32 Response to the objection that communism will destroy freedom and individuality.
33–34 Response to the objection that communism will destroy the incentive to work.
35–36 Response to the objection that communism will destroy culture.
37–38 Bourgeois ideas are historically limited, not eternal laws of nature.
39–45 Response to the objection that communism will abolish the family.
46–51 Response to the objection that communism will create a "community of women."
52–56 Response to the objection that communism will destroy countries and nationality.
57–67 Response to religious, philosophical, and ideological criticisms of communism.
68–72 The immediate goals of a workers' revolution.
73–74 The goal of a classless society.

Section III: Socialist and Communist Literature

1–11 Criticism of feudal socialism.
12–18 Criticism of petty-bourgeois socialism.
19–35 Criticism of "true" socialism.
36–43 Criticism of bourgeois socialism.
44–57 Criticism of critical-utopian socialism and communism.

Section IV: Position of the Communists in Relation to the Various Existing Opposition Parties

1–4 The relation of Communists to non–working-class opposition parties.
5–7 The special importance of Germany.
8–12 Communists and revolution.

Notes

1. Engels (like Marx) spent most of his adult life in England and chose to anglicize his name from "Friedrich" to "Frederick." Marx also occasionally anglicized his first name as "Charles."
2. I say "genuine" communism because it bears little resemblance to countries that have typically been identified as communist, such as the former Soviet Union.
3. The French Revolution of 1789 overthrew the feudal, absolute monarchy of King Louis XVI and proclaimed for "liberty, equality, fraternity." Napoleon seized power in a military coup in 1795, after a bitter conflict between the revolution's radical and moderate leaders. Over the next decade and a half, he conquered much of western Europe, eventually declaring himself Emperor. In this contradictory way, many of the revolution's progressive ideas were spread to other countries.
4. Germany was not united as a single country until much later in the nineteenth century. At this time, the German population was still divided between dozens of small states, of which Prussia was by far the largest.
5. Hegel's writings are notoriously difficult to understand. On one reading, he sees the entire universe as a conscious being gradually moving toward self-understanding. For an elementary introduction to Hegel's ideas, see Singer 1983.
6. Marx's thesis was a comparison of the materialist philosophies of the ancient Greek philosophers Democritus and Epicurus. See Marx 1841.
7. Marx means that he previously knew nothing about these important issues.
8. "The proceedings of the *Rhenish Landtag* on thefts of wood and parceling of landed property, the official polemic, which Herr von Schaper, then *Oberpräsident* of the Rhine Province, opened against the *Rheinische Zeitung* on the conditions of the Moselle peasantry, and finally debates on free trade and protective tariffs provided the first occasions for occupying myself with economic questions" (Marx 1859, p. 3).
9. Engels died in 1895. He frequently downplayed his contributions to the partnership, but while it is certainly true that Marx played the dominant role, Engels was an original and important thinker in his own right who frequently played a crucial role in stimulating Marx's ideas (as well as providing Marx with vital financial support for many years).
10. Page references are to C. J. Arthur (ed.), *The German Ideology* (New York: International Publishers, 1970).
11. Marx and Engels' brief comments provide the basis for a materialist explanation of the failure of the Russian Revolution of 1917, more than seventy years later. In an economically backward country, the revolution did not have the resources to build socialism by itself. With the failure of revolutions in other countries, Russia was left isolated and impoverished, and "all the old filthy business" eventually returned. See Harman 1967.
12. Marx was unable to travel from Brussels due to lack of money.
13. Engels to Marx, November 23–24, 1847 (quoted in Struik 1971, p. 60).
14. The Communist League itself fell apart after the defeat of the German Revolution, but many of its members, including Marx and Engels, played prominent roles in the International Working Men's Association (later called the "First International") in the 1860s and 1870s.
15. Reprinted in Appendix A. Footnotes in the quotation that follows are the editor's.
16. Followers respectively of Robert Owen (1771–1851), who set up a model mill town in Britain, and Charles Fourier (1772–1837), who described a socially harmonious ideal society in elaborate detail.
17. Étienne Cabet (1788–1856) wrote a novel describing an ideal communist community, which he and his followers later unsuccessfully attempted to put into practice.
18. Wilhelm Weitling (1808–1871) was a German tailor who played a leading role in the League of the Just before it was influenced by Marx and Engels' views.

19. Marxists have also used other terms to describe themselves. In the late nineteenth century, Marx's followers typically called themselves "social democrats." Today, however, this label has come to designate support for social reforms that attempt to make capitalism more humane rather than replace it entirely. Given the association of "communism" with regimes such as the former Soviet Union, some contemporary Marxists prefer to call themselves "revolutionary socialists."
20. See Draper 1966.
21. Marx and Engels also drew lessons from the actual experience of workers' struggles. In particular, they drew important lessons from the Paris Commune of 1871, when workers controlled the city for two months. See Marx 1871, and Marx and Engels' Preface to the 1872 edition of the *Manifesto* (reprinted in Appendix A).
22. This work consists of Marx's critical commentary on a draft program produced by the United Workers' Party of Germany.
23. At this stage, society would operate with the principle, "From each according to his ability, to each according to his needs!" *Critique of the Gotha Program* (Marx 1875).
24. Of course, Marx has also had many critics on the Left, including anarchists, feminists, non-Marxist socialists, and, more recently, postmodernists. There isn't space to consider these criticisms here, but see the suggestions for further reading at the end of this book.
25. Several of these changes are noted in the annotations to the *Manifesto*. For Marx's motto, see Marx's "Confession" (1865).
26. Perhaps an analogy with Marx's contemporary Charles Darwin is apt. While Darwin inevitably made many mistakes, his central idea of evolution by natural selection remains the foundation of modern biology.
27. Engels, *Socialism: Utopian and Scientific*, part III, note 4 (1880). Otto von Bismarck was the conservative chancellor of Germany from 1871 to 1890. Napoleon I established a state monopoly over the tobacco trade in France in 1810. Prince Klemens von Metternich did the same in Austria at around the same time. Engels continues: "If the Belgian State, for quite ordinary political and financial reasons, itself constructed its chief railway lines; if Bismarck, not under any economic compulsion, took over for the State the chief Prussian lines, simply to be the better able to have them in hand in case of war, to bring up the railway employees as voting cattle for the Government, and especially to create for himself a new source of income independent of parliamentary votes—this was, in no sense, a socialistic measure, directly or indirectly, consciously or unconsciously. Otherwise, the Royal Maritime Company, the Royal porcelain manufacture, and even the regimental tailor of the army would also be socialistic institutions."
28. Marx, *Critique of the Gotha Program*, part I (1875). Not everyone accepts the state-capitalist analysis of these economies. The key point is that they did not in any way fit Marx and Engels' conception of socialism. For more, see Hudis 2013.
29. See Arnove 2000. Of all these countries, only the Soviet Union experienced a genuine workers' revolution. For a Marxist explanation of the defeat of this revolution in the 1920s and the emergence under Stalin of a state capitalist regime, see Arnove 2000 and Binns 2003. For discussion of the continued relevance of the concept of state capitalism in the post-Soviet era, see Molyneux 2021.
30. For references, see Gasper 2004, 2005. For further discussion, see Kamin, Lewontin, and Rose 2017 and Prinz 2012.

The Annotated *Communist Manifesto*

Preamble

¶1 A specter is haunting Europe—the specter of communism. All the powers of old Europe have entered into a holy alliance to exorcise this specter: Pope and Czar, Metternich and Guizot, French Radicals, and German police-spies.

¶2 Where is the party in opposition that has not been decried as communistic by its opponents in power? Where the opposition that has not hurled back the branding reproach of communism, against the more advanced opposition parties, as well as against its reactionary adversaries?

¶3 Two things result from this fact.

I. Communism is already acknowledged by all European powers to be itself a power.

II. It is high time that Communists should openly, in the face of the whole world, publish their views, their aims, their tendencies, and meet this nursery tale of the specter of communism with a manifesto of the party itself.

1. Marx and Engels' examples represent the geographical and ideological diversity of their opponents. Prince Metternich was Austria's reactionary foreign minister for more than thirty years. François Guizot was a moderate French politician who became premier in 1847. The French Radicals opposed monarchy but supported capitalism.

2. Marx had personal experience of such attacks even before he had become a communist himself. Under his editorship, the radical liberal newspaper *Rheinische Zeitung*, published in Cologne, had been accused of communist sympathies in 1842.

3. Marx and Engels are probably exaggerating the importance of the communist movement, which was still quite small at this time. Nevertheless, European political leaders in the 1840s were certainly terrified of the possibility of revolution. Within days of the *Manifesto*'s publication, a revolutionary upsurge overthrew the government in France and swept across much of the rest of Europe. Although most of these revolutions were

¶4 To this end, Communists of various nationalities have assembled in London and sketched the following manifesto, to be published in the English, French, German, Italian, Flemish, and Danish languages.

defeated, many Communists, including Marx and Engels, played prominent roles in them.[1]

4. The reference here is to a meeting of the Communist League (formerly the League of the Just)—composed largely of German émigrés living in London and Paris—that commissioned the *Manifesto* in December 1847. It was originally published in German and soon translated into English and Swedish, but it did not become available in other languages until the 1870s.

I.
Bourgeois and Proletarians*

¶1 The history of all hitherto existing society** is the history of class struggles.

¶2 Freeman and slave, patrician and plebeian, lord and

*By bourgeoisie is meant the class of modern capitalists, owners of the means of social production and employers of wage labor. By proletariat, the class of modern wage laborers who, having no means of production of their own, are reduced to selling their labor power in order to live. [Engels, 1888 English edition]

**That is, all written history. In 1847, the pre-history of society, the social organization existing previous to recorded history, was all but unknown. Since then, [August von] Haxthausen [1792–1866] discovered common ownership of land in Russia, [Georg Ludwig von] Maurer [1790–1872] proved it to be the social foundation from which all Teutonic races started in history, and, by and by, village communities were found to be, or to have been, the primitive form of society everywhere from India to Ireland. The inner organization of this primitive communistic society was laid bare, in its typical form, by [Lewis Henry] Morgan's [1818–61] crowning discovery of the true nature of the gens and its relation to the tribe. With the dissolution of the primeval communities, society begins to be differentiated into separate and finally antagonistic classes. I have attempted to retrace this process of dissolution in: Der Ursprung der Familie, des Privateigenthumus und des Staats [The Origin of the Family, Private Property and the State], 2nd edition, Stuttgart, 1886. [Engels, 1888 English edition]

1. The view that most human societies are divided into social classes with antagonistic interests is central to Marx and Engels' outlook.

2. Marx and Engels list some of the major social groups that existed in ancient slave societies and in medieval European feudalism. Their comment at the end of the paragraph that class struggle may lead either to revolution or to "common ruin" is evidence that they did not accept the deterministic idea that society develops as a result of historical forces independent of human decisions and action.

Study and discussion questions for this section begin on page187.

serf, guild-master* and journeyman, in a word, oppressor and oppressed, stood in constant opposition to one another, carried on an uninterrupted, now hidden, now open fight, a fight that each time ended either in a revolutionary reconstitution of society at large, or in the common ruin of the contending classes.

¶3 In the earlier epochs of history, we find almost everywhere a complicated arrangement of society into various orders, a manifold gradation of social rank. In ancient Rome we have patricians, knights, plebeians, slaves; in the Middle Ages, feudal lords, vassals, guild-masters, journeymen, apprentices, serfs; in almost all of these classes, again, subordinate gradations.

¶4 The modern bourgeois society that has sprouted from the ruins of feudal society has not done away with class antagonisms. It has but established new classes, new conditions of oppression, new forms of struggle in place of the old ones.

¶5 Our epoch, the epoch of the bourgeoisie, possesses, however, this distinctive feature: it has simplified the class antagonisms. Society as a whole is more and more splitting up into two great hostile camps, into two great classes directly facing each other: bourgeoisie and proletariat.

¶6 From the serfs of the Middle Ages sprang the chartered burghers of the earliest towns. From these burgesses the first elements of the bourgeoisie were developed.

---

*Guild-master, that is, a full member of a guild, a master within, not a head of a guild. [Engels, 1888 English edition]

4. By "modern bourgeois society," Marx and Engels mean capitalism, in which the bourgeoisie—made up of those who own society's means of production and employ wage labor—is the dominant, exploiting class. (See Engels' first footnote.)

5. The proletariat is the modern working class—those who earn a wage by working for others. Marx and Engels are not saying that all classes apart from the bourgeoisie and proletariat will vanish. For more on the tendency of class structure to become polarized under capitalism, see I.15, I.35, and I.44. (See Engels' first footnote again.)

6. Marx and Engels start to explain how the bourgeoisie first emerged in feudal society, and how it eventually became the dominant class. Serfs were peasants who were required to work for feudal lords. Burghers (or burgesses) were the non-aristocratic middle class in the towns, often merchants or manufacturers.

¶7 The discovery of America, the rounding of the Cape, opened up fresh ground for the rising bourgeoisie. The East-Indian and Chinese markets, the colonization of America, trade with the colonies, the increase in the means of exchange and in commodities generally, gave to commerce, to navigation, to industry, an impulse never before known, and thereby, to the revolutionary element in the tottering feudal society, a rapid development.

¶8 The feudal system of industry, under which industrial production was monopolized by closed guilds, now no longer sufficed for the growing wants of the new markets. The manufacturing system took its place. The guild-masters were pushed on one side by the manufacturing middle class; division of labor between the different corporate guilds vanished in the face of division of labor in each single workshop.

¶9 Meantime the markets kept ever growing, the demand ever rising. Even manufacture no longer sufficed. Thereupon, steam and machinery revolutionized industrial production. The place of manufacture was taken by the giant, modern industry, the place of the industrial middle class by industrial millionaires, the leaders of whole industrial armies, the modern bourgeois.

¶10 Modern industry has established the world market, for which the discovery of America paved the way. This market has given an immense development to commerce, to navigation, to communication by land. This development has, in its turn, reacted on the extension of industry; and in proportion as industry,

7. The New World was, of course, "discovered" by Columbus in 1492. The Cape of Good Hope at the southern tip of Africa was rounded by Portuguese navigator Bartolomeu Dias four years earlier, opening up the possibility of a sea route to the East. The emerging bourgeoisie was a "revolutionary element" because its economic interests increasingly put it in fundamental conflict with the existing feudal order.

8. Feudal economic relations give way to early capitalism. The first capitalist societies developed in Holland and England in the seventeenth century, following revolutions that overthrew the previous ruling classes.

9. Marx and Engels describe the Industrial Revolution, which first began in Britain in the second half of the eighteenth century. They are using "manufacture" in the original sense of production by hand.

10. Marx and Engels discuss capitalism's global tendencies and the way in which expanded markets stimulate the development of technology and industry in greater detail later in this section. Here, their main point is that these changes led to the disappearance of the remnants of feudalism.

commerce, navigation, railways extended, in the same proportion the bourgeoisie developed, increased its capital, and pushed into the background every class handed down from the Middle Ages.

¶11 We see, therefore, how the modern bourgeoisie is itself the product of a long course of development, of a series of revolutions in the modes of production and of exchange.

¶12 Each step in the development of the bourgeoisie was accompanied by a corresponding political advance of that class. An oppressed class under the sway of the feudal nobility, an armed and self-governing association in the medieval commune,* here independent urban republic (as in Italy and Germany), there taxable "third estate" of the monarchy (as in France), afterwards, in the period of manufacturing proper, serving either the semi-feudal or the absolute monarchy as a counterpoise against the nobility and, in fact, cornerstone of the great monarchies in general—the bourgeoisie has at last, since the establishment of modern industry and of the world market, conquered for itself, in the modern representative state, exclusive political

11. In *Capital* Volume I, Marx explains the bourgeoisie's rise in England as due to advances in agricultural methods and manufacturing technology, the forced expulsion of the rural population to the cities, the expropriation of Church land, and brutal colonial exploitation, which generated vast wealth.

12. Marx and Engels describe how, as the bourgeoisie's economic importance increased, so did its political power, until it eventually established itself as a new ruling class (although in Marx's day, the bourgeoisie still generally ruled in alliance with sections of the old landowning classes).

According to Marx and Engels, governments in capitalist countries act to promote the interests of the economically dominant capitalist class, even though this class is made up of only a tiny minority of the population.[2] Compare I.26.

---

*"Commune" was the name taken in France by the nascent towns even before they had conquered from their feudal lords and masters local self-government and political rights as the "Third Estate." Generally speaking, for the economical development of the bourgeoisie, England is here taken as the typical country; for its political development, France. [Engels, 1888 English edition]

This was the name given their urban communities by the townsmen of Italy and France, after they had purchased or conquered their initial rights of self-government from their feudal lords. [Engels, 1890 German edition]

sway. The executive of the modern state is but a committee for managing the common affairs of the whole bourgeoisie.

¶13 The bourgeoisie, historically, has played a most revolutionary part.

¶14 The bourgeoisie, wherever it has got the upper hand, has put an end to all feudal, patriarchal, idyllic relations. It has pitilessly torn asunder the motley feudal ties that bound man to his "natural superiors," and has left remaining no other nexus between man and man than naked self-interest, than callous "cash payment." It has drowned the most heavenly ecstasies of religious fervor, of chivalrous enthusiasm, of philistine sentimentalism, in the icy water of egotistical calculation. It has resolved personal worth into exchange value, and in place of the numberless indefeasible chartered freedoms, has set up that single, unconscionable freedom—free trade. In one word, for exploitation, veiled by religious and political illusions, it has substituted naked, shameless, direct, brutal exploitation.

¶15 The bourgeoisie has stripped of its halo every occupation hitherto honored and looked up to with reverent awe. It has converted the physician, the lawyer, the priest, the poet, the man of science, into its paid wage laborers.

¶16 The bourgeoisie has torn away from the family its sentimental veil, and has reduced the family relation to a mere money relation.

¶17 The bourgeoisie has disclosed how it came to pass that the brutal display of vigor in the Middle Ages, which reactionaries so much admire, found its fitting

13. Marx and Engels explain this role in the next few paragraphs. See especially I.18.

14. As capitalist societies develop, market relations tend to replace other, more traditional and paternalistic bonds between individuals. The bourgeoisie thinks of freedom in economic terms, i.e., as free trade—the ability to exchange goods and services without restriction. Because economic motivations are not hidden, and because they are less hemmed in by other considerations than in the past, Marx and Engels claim that exploitation is both more open and more intense under capitalism. Corporate guilds under feudalism were granted royal charters spelling out their special privileges and freedoms. Capitalism sweeps away restrictions on commerce and replaces limited feudal freedoms with free trade.

15. In capitalist economies, many previously privileged professionals come to be treated in the same way as ordinary wage laborers. Here, as in some other places, Marx and Engels describe a tendency as if it were a completed process, mainly for rhetorical effect.

16. Some modern economists (such as Nobel laureate Gary Becker) analyze the family in just such market terms—i.e., as a contractual relationship in which the different parties each pursue personal gain.

17. The "brutal display of vigor" mentioned here is presumably a reference to medieval militarism, which is contrasted to the lethargy of the feudal nobility with complement in the most slothful indolence. It has been the first to show what man's activity can bring about. It has accomplished wonders far surpassing Egyptian pyramids, Roman aqueducts, and Gothic cathedrals; it has conducted expeditions that put in the shade all former exoduses of nations and crusades.

¶18 The bourgeoisie cannot exist without constantly revolutionizing the instruments of production, and thereby the relations of production, and with them the whole relations of society. Conservation of the old modes of production in unaltered form was, on the contrary, the first condition of existence for all earlier industrial classes. Constant revolutionizing of production, uninterrupted disturbance of all social conditions, everlasting uncertainty and agitation distinguish the bourgeois epoch from all earlier ones. All fixed, fast-frozen relations, with their train of ancient and venerable prejudices and opinions, are swept away, all new-formed ones become antiquated before they can ossify. All that is solid melts into air, all that is holy is profaned, and man is at last compelled to face with sober senses his real conditions of life and his relations with his kind.

¶19 The need of a constantly expanding market for its products chases the bourgeoisie over the whole surface of the globe. It must nestle everywhere, settle everywhere, establish connections everywhere.

¶20 The bourgeoisie has through its exploitation of the world market given a cosmopolitan character to production and consumption in every country. To the great chagrin of reactionaries, it has drawn from under

respect to its economic activity. The stagnation of the Middle Ages is often exaggerated, but it is certainly true that capitalism's economic and technological achievements since the Industrial Revolution tower over everything that came before.

18. This is one of the most rhetorically brilliant passages in a work filled with rhetorically brilliant passages. The instruments of production are the tools and technology used at a particular time. The relations of production are the complex ways in which individuals and groups are interconnected in economic activity, crucially including those who own or control the instruments (or means) of production. Market competition is the underlying cause for continual technological innovation under capitalism, but these rapid changes affect not just the economy and class relations, but the entire fabric of society—from culture, customs, and morals to the structure of the family. Such changes can be exhilarating and liberating, but they can also be profoundly disorienting and alienating, as life becomes more of a rat race, and more dominated by economic imperatives.

19. The search for new markets, raw materials, and cheap labor drives capitalists around the world. Marx and Engels were the first to notice the process that today is called "globalization."

20. Globalization has numerous contradictory consequences. Among the positive results, from Marx and Engels' perspective, is that the economic basis for narrow-minded nationalism is undermined as production and consumption the feet of industry the national ground on which it stood. All old-established national industries have been destroyed or are daily being destroyed. They are dislodged by new industries, whose introduction becomes a life and death question for all civilized nations, by industries that no longer work up indigenous raw material, but raw material drawn from the remotest zones; industries whose products are consumed, not only at home, but in every quarter of the globe. In place of the old wants, satisfied by the productions of the country, we find new wants, requiring for their satisfaction the products of distant lands and climes. In place of the old local and national seclusion and self-sufficiency, we have intercourse in every direction, universal inter-dependence of nations. And as in material, so also in intellectual production. The intellectual creations of individual nations become common property. National one-sidedness and narrow-mindedness become more and more impossible, and from the numerous national and local literatures, there arises a world literature.

¶21 The bourgeoisie, by the rapid improvement of all instruments of production, by the immensely facilitated means of communication, draws all, even the most barbarian, nations into civilization. The cheap prices of its commodities are the heavy artillery with which it batters down all Chinese walls, with which it forces the barbarians' intensely obstinate hatred of foreigners to capitulate. It compels all nations, on pain of extinction, to adopt the bourgeois mode of production; it compels them to introduce what it calls civilization

assume an increasingly international character. The same process is reflected in the cultural realm. Increased mobility and contact between people of different national backgrounds gives rise to new forms of art, music, literature, even cuisine, which fuse together the contributions of many different countries and cultures.

21. The leading capitalist countries are driven to extend their economic system to the less-developed parts of the world. (Nineteenth-century anthropologists used the term "barbarian" to describe members of preliterate societies. Marx and Engels did not use it with the negative connotations it has since acquired.) Today, "free trade" agreements open up poor countries to imports and investment from the advanced economies, giving multinational corporations access to cheap labor. Marx and Engels are also making a reference to the Opium War between Britain and China (1839–42), which forced the Chinese to open their economy to British imports (including opium).[3]

into their midst, i.e., to become bourgeois themselves. In one word, it creates a world after its own image.

¶22 The bourgeoisie has subjected the country to the rule of the towns. It has created enormous cities, has greatly increased the urban population as compared with the rural, and has thus rescued a considerable part of the population from the isolation of rural life. Just as it has made the country dependent on the towns, so it has made barbarian and semi-barbarian countries dependent on the civilized ones, nations of peasants on nations of bourgeois, the East on the West.

¶23 The bourgeoisie keeps more and more doing away with the scattered state of the population, of the means of production, and of property. It has agglomerated population, centralized the means of production, and has concentrated property in a few hands. The necessary consequence of this was political centralization. Independent or but loosely connected provinces, with separate interests, laws, governments, and systems of taxation, became lumped together into one nation, with one government, one code of laws, one national class-interest, one frontier, and one customs tariff.

¶24 The bourgeoisie, during its rule of scarce one hundred years, has created more massive and more colossal productive forces than have all preceding generations together. Subjection of nature's forces to man, machinery, application of chemistry to industry and agriculture, steam navigation, railways, electric telegraphs, clearing of whole continents for cultivation, canalization of rivers, whole populations conjured out of the ground—what earlier century had even a presentiment

22. Capitalism creates centers of economic activity that dominate less central areas. Within advanced and less-advanced countries, large urban centers develop. Internationally, the more developed economies dominate the less developed ones.

23. Economic development and centralization leads to the emergence of nation-states with centralized governments and unified legal systems. At the time the *Manifesto* was written, this process was still incomplete even in Western Europe. Italy became a unified nation only in the 1860s. Germany was not unified until the 1870s.

24. Marx and Engels return to the theme first raised in I.17 above: the incredible technological revolution that capitalist relations of production have brought about.

that such productive forces slumbered in the lap of social labor?

¶25 We see then: the means of production and of exchange, on whose foundation the bourgeoisie built itself up, were generated in feudal society. At a certain stage in the development of these means of production and of exchange, the conditions under which feudal society produced and exchanged, the feudal organization of agriculture and manufacturing industry, in one word, the feudal relations of property became no longer compatible with the already developed productive forces; they became so many fetters. They had to be burst asunder; they were burst asunder.

¶26 Into their place stepped free competition, accompanied by a social and political constitution adapted to it, and the economic and political sway of the bourgeois class.

¶27 A similar movement is going on before our own eyes. Modern bourgeois society, with its relations of production, of exchange and of property, a society that has conjured up such gigantic means of production and of exchange, is like the sorcerer who is no longer able to control the powers of the nether world whom he has called up by his spells. For many a decade past, the history of industry and commerce is but the history of the revolt of modern productive forces against modern conditions of production, against the property relations that are the conditions for the existence of the bourgeoisie and of its rule. It is enough to mention the commercial crises that by their periodical return put on its trial, each time more threateningly, the exis-

25. Capitalism first emerged when feudal production relations became an obstacle to the bourgeoisie's economic interests and its need to develop new methods of production and exchange. The overthrow of feudalism became the precondition for such developments to take place. More generally, the idea that society's productive forces will eventually come into conflict with its relations of production is a key theme in Marx and Engels' materialist perspective. Gradual changes eventually create economic and social contradictions that can only be solved by revolutionary upheaval. Compare I.27.

27. Having described the rise of capitalist society, Marx and Engels now shift to a discussion of the developments that they believe will lead to its downfall. Just as feudal relations of production became incompatible with the bourgeoisie's rapid development of society's productive forces, capitalist relations of production come into conflict with the massive productive forces that these relations have themselves brought into existence. Capitalism is driven by competition between individual units of production for markets. As the forces of production become more complex and the units of production become larger, economic booms become more frantic and economic slumps more severe. In particular, because market competition is uncoordinated, rival capitalist companies will each invest more and more to meet expected demand, eventually leading to a glut of products that cannot be sold at a profit. Companies respond by cutting production and laying off workers, further

tence of the entire bourgeois society. In these crises a great part not only of the existing products, but also of the previously created productive forces, are periodically destroyed. In these crises there breaks out an epidemic that in all earlier epochs would have seemed an absurdity—the epidemic of overproduction. Society suddenly finds itself put back into a state of momentary barbarism; it appears as if a famine, a universal war of devastation, had cut off the supply of every means of subsistence; industry and commerce seem to be destroyed; and why? Because there is too much civilization, too much means of subsistence, too much industry, too much commerce. The productive forces at the disposal of society no longer tend to further the development of the conditions of bourgeois property; on the contrary, they have become too powerful for these conditions, by which they are fettered, and so soon as they overcome these fetters, they bring disorder into the whole of bourgeois society, endanger the existence of bourgeois property. The conditions of bourgeois society are too narrow to comprise the wealth created by them. And how does the bourgeoisie get over these crises? On the one hand by enforced destruction of a mass of productive forces; on the other by the conquest of new markets, and by the more thorough exploitation of the old ones. That is to say, by paving the way for more extensive and more destructive crises, and by diminishing the means whereby crises are prevented.

¶28 The weapons with which the bourgeoisie felled feudalism to the ground are now turned against the bourgeoisie itself.

reducing demand and plunging the whole economy into recession. In precapitalist societies, crises resulted from a shortage of vital goods, but under capitalism, the crises are typically the result of producing too much. Millions lose their jobs and are thrown into poverty, even though there is much vital work to be done, and more than enough wealth exists to provide everyone with a decent standard of living. Instead, valuable resources are destroyed or wasted until it eventually becomes profitable to invest in new production again, setting the stage for new and more severe crises in the future. As the *Manifesto* was being written, European capitalism was in the midst of its third major slump in just over twenty years.

28. In other words, the relentless expansion of capitalist production eventually becomes the system's biggest weakness.

¶29 But not only has the bourgeoisie forged the weapons that bring death to itself; it has also called into existence the men who are to wield those weapons—the modern working class—the proletarians.

¶30 In proportion as the bourgeoisie, i.e., capital, is developed, in the same proportion is the proletariat, the modern working class, developed—a class of laborers, who live only so long as they find work, and who find work only so long as their labor increases capital. These laborers, who must sell themselves piecemeal, are a commodity like every other article of commerce, and are consequently exposed to all the vicissitudes of competition, to all the fluctuations of the market.

¶31 Owing to the extensive use of machinery and to the division of labor, the work of the proletarians has lost all individual character and, consequently, all charm for the workman. He becomes an appendage of the machine, and it is only the most simple, most monotonous, and most easily acquired knack, that is required of him. Hence, the cost of production of a workman is restricted, almost entirely, to the means of subsistence that he requires for his maintenance, and for the propagation of his race. But the price of a commodity, and therefore also of labor, is equal to its cost of production. In proportion, therefore, as the repulsiveness of the work increases, the wage decreases. Nay more, in proportion as the use of machinery and division of labor increases, in the same proportion the burden of toil also increases, whether by prolongation of the working hours, by increase of the work exacted in a given time, or by increased speed of machinery, etc.

29. Just as feudal economies encouraged the development of a powerful bourgeoisie whose interests came into conflict with the old system, capitalism produces a working class with the power to overthrow bourgeois society.

30. At the time that Marx and Engels were writing, the proletariat was a relatively new class, very different from previous oppressed classes. In earlier societies, slaves were regarded as instruments of production, while peasants and artisans often owned some of the tools, land, and raw materials used to produce. Modern workers own no economic resources apart from their capacity to perform work. Note that the working class consists of everyone forced to sell their labor power, not just factory workers.

31. In his *Economic and Philosophic Manuscripts* (written in 1844, but unpublished in his lifetime), Marx identifies the nature of work under capitalism as one aspect of what he calls "alienation." Rather than rewarding and challenging, most work in capitalist society is a tedious and hated chore. As work becomes deskilled and less interesting, it also becomes more burdensome and less well paid. Marx and Engels appeal to the labor theory of value—according to which the value of a commodity is equal to the average quantity of labor needed to produce it—to explain this. Since it requires less work to produce an unskilled worker than a skilled one, the economic value of the former is lower than that of the latter, and hence the skilled worker receives a higher wage.

¶32 Modern industry has converted the little workshop of the patriarchal master into the great factory of the industrial capitalist. Masses of laborers, crowded into the factory, are organized like soldiers. As privates of the industrial army, they are placed under the command of a perfect hierarchy of officers and sergeants. Not only are they slaves of the bourgeois class, and of the bourgeois state, they are daily and hourly enslaved by the machine, by the overlooker, and, above all, by the individual bourgeois manufacturer himself. The more openly this despotism proclaims gain to be its end and aim, the more petty, the more hateful, and the more embittering it is.

¶33 The less the skill and exertion of strength implied in manual labor, in other words, the more modern industry becomes developed, the more is the labor of men superseded by that of women. Differences of age and sex have no longer any distinctive social validity for the working class. All are instruments of labor, more or less expensive to use, according to their age and sex.

¶34 No sooner is the exploitation of the laborer by the manufacturer, so far, at an end, that he receives his wages in cash, than he is set upon by the other portions of the bourgeoisie, the landlord, the shopkeeper, the pawnbroker, etc.

¶35 The lower strata of the middle class—the small tradespeople, shopkeepers, and retired tradesmen generally, the handicraftsmen and peasants—all these sink gradually into the proletariat, partly because their diminutive capital does not suffice for the scale on

32. For many under capitalism, work is organized in enormous regimented and hierarchical workplaces. Marx and Engels talk about factories, but today the same is true of work in many other environments, including large offices. Labor laws, where they exist, are hard to enforce, and bosses and managers frequently behave like petty dictators. This paragraph is the first place in the *Manifesto* where Marx and Engels use the term "capitalist."

33. Mechanization makes it easier for capitalism to draw women, and even children, into the paid workforce, at wages lower than those paid to men. The percentage of women in the workforce has historically varied as a result of economic, political, and ideological factors, but today in the United States, nearly 50 percent of those employed are women, and women still only earn 75 percent of what men are paid.

34. Workers are not only exploited by their employers, but swindled outside the workplace when they buy the necessities of life.

35. A section of the middle class (or "petty bourgeoisie")—those whose position in the economy places them below the capitalists but above the workers—is pushed down into the growing ranks of the proletariat. Marx and Engels are talking here about one part of the middle class—they are not claiming that the entire class will disappear. In the past one hundred years, with the expansion of professional occupations and managerial positions, a "new middle class" has which modern industry is carried on, and is swamped in the competition with the large capitalists, partly because their specialized skill is rendered worthless by new methods of production. Thus the proletariat is recruited from all classes of the population.

¶36 The proletariat goes through various stages of development. With its birth begins its struggle with the bourgeoisie. At first the contest is carried on by individual laborers, then by the workpeople of a factory, then by the operatives of one trade, in one locality, against the individual bourgeois who directly exploits them. They direct their attacks not against the bourgeois conditions of production, but against the instruments of production themselves; they destroy imported wares that compete with their labor, they smash to pieces machinery, they set factories ablaze, they seek to restore by force the vanished status of the workman of the Middle Ages.

¶37 At this stage, the laborers form an incoherent mass scattered over the whole country, and broken up by their mutual competition. If anywhere they unite to form more compact bodies, this is not yet the consequence of their own active union, but of the union of the bourgeoisie, which class, in order to attain its own political ends, is compelled to set the whole proletariat in motion, and is moreover yet, for a time, able to do so. At this stage, therefore, the proletarians do not fight their enemies, but the enemies of their enemies, the remnants of absolute monarchy, the landowners, the non-industrial bourgeois, the petty bourgeoisie. Thus the whole historical movement is concentrated in

grown up alongside what remains of the old one. Compare III.13.

36. From the birth of modern capitalism, workers have struggled against their exploitation. Here, and in the next few paragraphs, Marx and Engels describe how this develops from a conflict between individuals to one between entire classes. In early nineteenth-century Britain, agricultural workers inspired by Ned Ludd smashed machinery that was throwing them out of work. The term "Luddite" has come to refer to people who oppose new technology, but in an economic system in which technological developments make many people's lives worse rather than better, such opposition may be quite rational.

37. To the extent that the proletariat acts collectively in early capitalism, Marx and Engels claim that it does so as a result of the bourgeoisie drawing it into activity on the bourgeoisie's own behalf, to combat those classes and remnants of classes whose interests are opposed to those of industrial capitalism. Compare I.41.

the hands of the bourgeoisie; every victory so obtained is a victory for the bourgeoisie.

¶38 But with the development of industry, the proletariat not only increases in number, it becomes concentrated in greater masses, its strength grows, and it feels that strength more. The various interests and conditions of life within the ranks of the proletariat are more and more equalized, in proportion as machinery obliterates all distinctions of labor, and nearly everywhere reduces wages to the same low level. The growing competition among the bourgeois, and the resulting commercial crises, make the wages of the workers ever more fluctuating. The unceasing improvement of machinery, ever more rapidly developing, makes their livelihood more and more precarious; the collisions between individual workmen and individual bourgeois take more and more the character of collisions between two classes. Thereupon, the workers begin to form combinations (trades' unions) against the bourgeois; they club together in order to keep up the rate of wages; they found permanent associations in order to make provision beforehand for these occasional revolts. Here and there, the contest breaks out into riots.

¶39 Now and then the workers are victorious, but only for a time. The real fruit of their battles lies not in the immediate result, but in the ever expanding union of the workers. This union is helped on by the improved means of communication that are created by modern industry and that place the workers of different localities in contact with one another. It was just this contact that was needed to centralize the numerous local

38. At a later stage, however, with the emergence of giant industry, wage laborers increasingly unite to defend their own interests. Modern industry concentrates workers together in large numbers, while technological developments reduce the differences between them and reduce job security. Wages may increase during booms, but are pushed down again during slumps. Workers form unions to keep wages up through collective action and to accumulate funds to finance strikes. (Marx and Engels were among the first leftists to view the emergence of unions favorably and to see it as a crucial step on the road to revolutionary change.) The class struggle can also express itself in the form of riots against various forms of capitalist exploitation and oppression. In the history of capitalism, such uprisings have been provoked by everything from the high price of basic commodities to police brutality and racism.

39. While workers sometimes win their immediate demands for better wages or improved working conditions, these victories are only temporary so long as relations of class exploitation continue to exist. The most important achievement of these struggles is the increased organization and coordination of the working class as a whole, which is facilitated by dramatic improvements in communication and transportation. When Marx and Engels say, "every class struggle is a political struggle," they mean class-wide struggles at the national level. Such conflicts place demands not just on individual employers but on the state itself, and necessarily raise the question of who controls society.

struggles, all of the same character, into one national struggle between classes. But every class struggle is a political struggle. And that union, to attain which the burghers of the Middle Ages, with their miserable highways, required centuries, the modern proletarians, thanks to railways, achieve in a few years.

¶40 This organization of the proletarians into a class, and consequently into a political party, is continually being upset again by the competition between the workers themselves. But it ever rises up again, stronger, firmer, mightier. It compels legislative recognition of particular interests of the workers, by taking advantage of the divisions among the bourgeoisie itself. Thus the Ten Hours Bill in England was carried.

¶41 Altogether, collisions between the classes of the old society further in many ways the course of development of the proletariat. The bourgeoisie finds itself involved in a constant battle. At first with the aristocracy; later on with those portions of the bourgeoisie itself whose interests have become antagonistic to the progress of industry; at all times with the bourgeoisie of foreign countries. In all these battles it sees itself compelled to appeal to the proletariat, to ask for its help, and thus to drag it into the political arena. The bourgeoisie itself, therefore, supplies the proletariat with its own elements of political and general education, in other words, it furnishes the proletariat with weapons for fighting the bourgeoisie.

¶42 Further, as we have already seen, entire sections of the ruling classes are, by the advance of industry, precipitated into the proletariat, or are at least threatened

40. In 1848, there were few political parties in the modern sense. Marx and Engels use the expression "political party" to mean a movement concerned with political as well as economic issues. Economic competition between workers is an important barrier to working-class unity, but Marx and Engels are confident that it will be overcome. The Ten Hours Bill, passed in 1847 after long struggle, limited the working day to ten hours for women and children.

41. Compare I.37. In the process of drawing the proletariat into political struggles, the bourgeoisie provides workers with the education they will need to fight against capitalism successfully.

42. This is perhaps a reference to I.35, where it was stated that "the proletariat is recruited from all classes of the population," although fragments of the ruling class were not specifically mentioned.

in their conditions of existence. These also supply the proletariat with educational elements.

¶43 Finally, in times when the class struggle nears the decisive hour, the process of dissolution going on within the ruling class, in fact within the whole range of old society, assumes such a violent, glaring character that a small section of the ruling class cuts itself adrift and joins the revolutionary class, the class that holds the future in its hands. Just as, therefore, at an earlier period, a section of the nobility went over to the bourgeoisie, so now a portion of the bourgeoisie goes over to the proletariat, and in particular, a portion of the bourgeois ideologists, who have raised themselves to the level of comprehending theoretically the historical movement as a whole.

¶44 Of all the classes that stand face to face with the bourgeoisie today, the proletariat alone is a genuinely revolutionary class. The other classes decay and go under in the face of modern industry; the proletariat is its special and essential product.

¶45 The lower middle class, the small manufacturer, the shopkeeper, the artisan, the peasant, all these fight against the bourgeoisie, to save from ruin their existence as fractions of the middle class. They are therefore not revolutionary, but conservative. Nay, more, they are reactionary, for they try to roll back the wheel of history. If by chance they are revolutionary, they are only so in view of their impending transfer into the proletariat, they thus defend not their present, but their future interests, they desert their own standpoint to place themselves at that of the proletariat.

43. The previous paragraphs describe two ways in which the proletariat acquires the educated skills needed for political struggle and revolution. A third, according to Marx and Engels, occurs in the turmoil of prerevolutionary situations, when a small part of the bourgeoisie—or at least "a portion of the bourgeois ideologists"—defects politically to the side of the working class, just as a section of the aristocracy had earlier allied itself with the bourgeoisie.

44. While other non-bourgeois classes that existed in Marx and Engels' day went into decline with the development of industry, capitalism could not develop without giving rise to a huge class of wage laborers, whose position in the economy gives it the power to make a revolution.

45. The *Manifesto* identifies the petty bourgeoisie as a generally reactionary force (although their imminent descent into the proletariat may make elements of the middle class revolutionary). In fact, Engels had already rejected this view in favor of the idea that workers have common interests with sections of the peasantry and middle classes and should look for allies among them. Marx (who wrote the final draft of the *Manifesto*) soon came over to Engels' view, due to the experience of the 1848 revolutions. The middle class is not uniformly reactionary or progressive, but can be pulled in both directions, and often plays a contradictory role.

¶46 The "dangerous class," the social scum, that passively rotting mass thrown off by the lowest layers of old society, may here and there be swept into the movement by a proletarian revolution; its conditions of life, however, prepare it far more for the part of a bribed tool of reactionary intrigue.

¶47 In the conditions of the proletariat, those of old society at large are already virtually swamped. The proletarian is without property; his relation to his wife and children has no longer anything in common with the bourgeois family-relations; modern industrial labor, modern subjection to capital, the same in England as in France, in America as in Germany, has stripped him of every trace of national character. Law, morality, religion, are to him so many bourgeois prejudices, behind which lurk in ambush just as many bourgeois interests.

¶48 All the preceding classes that got the upper hand sought to fortify their already acquired status by subjecting society at large to their conditions of appropriation. The proletarians cannot become masters of the productive forces of society except by abolishing their own previous mode of appropriation, and thereby also every other previous mode of appropriation. They have nothing of their own to secure and to fortify; their mission is to destroy all previous securities for, and insurances of, individual property.

¶49 All previous historical movements were movements of minorities, or in the interest of minorities. The proletarian movement is the self-conscious, independent movement of the immense majority, in the

46. The German term for the group that Marx and Engels are talking about is "Lumpenproletariat" (literally the "proletariat in rags"). Today, it is sometimes referred to as the "underclass"—a section of the population that is permanently or semipermanently excluded from the workforce, and which often supports itself by criminal activity.

47. Marx and Engels are describing tendencies that they believe exist under capitalism, although they write here as if these tendencies have already come to fruition.

48. Earlier revolutions replaced one dominant exploiting class with another. Although the mode of exploitation changed, exploitation itself remained. But proletarian revolution, according to Marx and Engels, will lead to the abolition of exploitation, because this is the only way in which workers can take collective control of the economy. The goal is not to eliminate all forms of individual ownership, but to end private control of society's key economic resources. See II.12–14 below.

49. In 1848, the proletariat was still a minority in most capitalist countries. Nevertheless, it could lead the majority toward revolution. Marx and Engels reject the view that socialist revolution can be the work of a minority acting on behalf of the majority. Revolution will only bring liberation if those to be liberated participate in it. The final sentence hints at Marx and Engels' later view that a successful workers' revolution will need to replace the existing state interest of the immense majority. The proletariat, the lowest stratum of our present society, cannot stir, cannot raise itself up, without the whole superincumbent strata of official society being sprung into the air.

¶50 Though not in substance, yet in form, the struggle of the proletariat with the bourgeoisie is at first a national struggle. The proletariat of each country must, of course, first of all settle matters with its own bourgeoisie.

¶51 In depicting the most general phases of the development of the proletariat, we traced the more or less veiled civil war raging within existing society, up to the point where that war breaks out into open revolution, and where the forcible overthrow of the bourgeoisie lays the foundation for the sway of the proletariat.

¶52 Hitherto, every form of society has been based, as we have already seen, on the antagonism of oppressing and oppressed classes. But in order to oppress a class, certain conditions must be assured to it under which it can, at least, continue its slavish existence. The serf, in the period of serfdom, raised himself to membership in the commune, just as the petty bourgeois, under the yoke of feudal absolutism, managed to develop into a bourgeois. The modern laborer, on the contrary, instead of rising with the progress of industry, sinks deeper and deeper below the conditions of existence of his own class. He becomes a pauper, and pauperism develops more rapidly than population and wealth. And here it becomes evident that the bourgeoisie is unfit any longer to be the ruling class in society, and to impose its conditions of existence upon society as an

with radically new institutions. Compare II.68.

50. Elsewhere (e.g., II.5.1, II.55, and IV.12), Marx and Engels emphasize that a successful workers' movement must be international in scope. But workers in each country must first win power from their own ruling class. Compare II.53.

51. A workers' revolution would end capitalist control of society and allow the proletariat to win political power for itself and its allies. Like all previous social transformations, this can only come about through the threat or use of force, because the ruling class will not relinquish its privileges in any other way.

52. While Marx and Engels are correct that capitalism produces, and even requires, high levels of poverty (despite the fact that enough is produced to provide the basics of life for everyone), their argument for revolution does not depend on the claim that the working class as a whole will be pushed into pauperism. In his later economic writings, Marx explicitly rejected this view, and the *Manifesto* has already noted (I.38) that workers organize into unions precisely to keep their wages up. Nevertheless, over the long run, as economic crises throw society into turmoil, capitalism cannot provide a decent existence for the majority of the population. (For more on the medieval commune mentioned in the third sentence, see Engels' footnote to I.12.)

overriding law. It is unfit to rule because it is incompetent to assure an existence to its slave within his slavery, because it cannot help letting him sink into such a state, that it has to feed him, instead of being fed by him. Society can no longer live under this bourgeoisie, in other words, its existence is no longer compatible with society.

¶53 The essential condition for the existence and for the sway of the bourgeois class is the formation and augmentation of capital; the condition for capital is wage labor. Wage labor rests exclusively on competition between the laborers. The advance of industry, whose involuntary promoter is the bourgeoisie, replaces the isolation of the laborers, due to competition, by their revolutionary combination, due to association. The development of modern industry, therefore, cuts from under its feet the very foundation on which the bourgeoisie produces and appropriates products. What the bourgeoisie therefore produces, above all, are its own grave-diggers. Its fall and the victory of the proletariat are equally inevitable.

53. The final paragraph of Section I expands on the theme first introduced in I.29—the very workings of capitalism gives rise to a class that has both the interest and the power to overthrow it. The final sentence in which proletarian victory is described as "inevitable" is often taken as evidence that Marx and Engels hold a deterministic view of human history. Against this, Marx and Engels say at the beginning of this section (I.2) that there is more than one possible outcome to class struggle. It thus seems more reasonable to read the paragraph's concluding words as a rhetorical flourish aimed at spurring on the *Manifesto*'s readers, rather than as the expression of a metaphysical theory of history as a deterministic process.

II.
Proletarians and Communists

¶1 In what relation do the Communists stand to the proletarians as a whole?

¶2 The Communists are not a special party in relation to the other working-class parties.

¶3 They have no interests separate and apart from those of the proletariat as a whole.

¶4 They do not set up any special principles of their own, by which to shape and mold the proletarian movement.

¶5 The Communists are distinguished from the other working-class parties by this only:

1. In the national struggles of the proletarians of the different countries, they point out and bring to the front the common interests of the entire proletariat, independently of all nationality.

2. In the various stages of development, which the struggle of the working class against the bourgeoisie has to pass through, they always and everywhere represent the interests of the movement as a whole.

1. Having laid out a historical and social analysis, Marx and Engels turn to the political role of Communists.

2. By "party," Marx and Engels mean both political tendencies and organizations such as the trade unions (modern political parties did not yet exist). Communists do not set themselves up as rivals to existing working-class organizations, such as the Chartists in Britain.[4]

4. Marx and Engels are not saying that Communists do not have their own views (which is obviously false), but that they do not require the rest of the workers' movement to accept their views before they participate in it.

5. Communists see themselves as representing the interests of the whole working class, not the interests of only one segment. Marx and Engels believe that in the course of class struggle the workers' movement will arrive at communist

Study and discussion questions for this section begin on page 189.

¶6 The Communists, therefore, are on the one hand, practically, the most advanced and resolute section of the working-class parties of every country, that section, which pushes forward all others; on the other hand, theoretically, they have over the great mass of the proletariat the advantage of clearly understanding the line of march, the conditions, and the ultimate general results of the proletarian movement.

¶7 The immediate aim of the Communists is the same as that of all the other proletarian parties: formation of the proletariat into a class, overthrow of the bourgeois supremacy, conquest of political power by the proletariat.

¶8 The theoretical conclusions of the Communists are in no way based on ideas or principles that have been invented, or discovered, by this or that would-be universal reformer.

¶9 They merely express, in general terms, actual relations springing from an existing class struggle, from a historical movement going on under our very eyes. The abolition of existing property relations is not at all a distinctive feature of communism.

¶10 All property relations in the past have continually been subject to historical change consequent upon the change in historical conditions.

¶11 The French Revolution, for example, abolished feudal property in favor of bourgeois property.

¶12 The distinguishing feature of communism is not the abolition of property generally, but the abolition of bourgeois property. But modern bourgeois private

conclusions as the result of its own experiences. So, the key task for Communists is to help organize and to participate in struggle, rather than to win converts to their own perspective. Some later Marxists (in particular, the Russian revolutionary Vladimir Lenin) concluded that the obstacles to working-class unity are greater than Marx and Engels recognize, requiring a more deliberate effort to propagate communist ideas and to gather the most class-conscious workers in their own organization.[5]

6. The differences between Marx, Engels, and Lenin mentioned above are matters of emphasis and degree. Here, Marx and Engels describe the role of Communists as in effect the vanguard (the leading units in an army) of the working class, an idea later associated with Lenin.

7. Winning political power for the proletariat is the goal of any working-class party worthy of the name (though many have not been worthy of the name). This is the first aim that must precede any further transformation of society in a socialist direction. Compare II.73.

8. Marx and Engels distinguish their own ideas from those of utopian reformers, whose plans for reorganizing society amount to building "castles in the air" (III.55).

9. By contrast, Marx and Engels claim that communist ideas grow out of and express the actual class struggle. (See the commentary on II.5.) Communism calls for the institution of new forms of property, but it is hardly the first political movement to do this.

10. Some defenders of capitalism claim that the property relations it embodies are property is the final and most complete expression of the system of producing and appropriating products that is based on class antagonisms, on the exploitation of the many by the few.

¶13 In this sense, the theory of the communists may be summed up in the single sentence: Abolition of private property.

¶14 We communists have been reproached with the desire of abolishing the right of personally acquiring property as the fruit of a man's own labor, which property is alleged to be the groundwork of all personal freedom, activity, and independence.

¶15 Hard-won, self-acquired, self-earned property! Do you mean the property of the petty artisan and of the small peasant, a form of property that preceded the bourgeois form? There is no need to abolish that; the development of industry has to a great extent already destroyed it, and is still destroying it daily.

¶16 Or do you mean modern bourgeois private property?

¶17 But does wage labor create any property for the laborer? Not a bit. It creates capital, i.e., that kind of property, which exploits wage labor, and which cannot increase except upon conditions of begetting a new supply of wage labor for fresh exploitation. Property, in its present form, is based on the antagonism of capital and wage labor. Let us examine both sides of this antagonism.

¶18 To be a capitalist is to have not only a purely personal, but a social position in production. Capital is a collective product, and only by the united action

somehow natural, but property forms have in fact changed enormously through history.

11. The French Revolution of 1789 overthrew King Louis XVI and ended feudalism in France.

12. The bourgeois revolutions of the seventeenth and eighteenth centuries abolished feudal property relations. Communism aims at the overthrow of capitalist property relations. Since, according to Marx and Engels, capitalism is based on the most developed system of exploitation, the abolition of capitalism will mean the end of exploitation itself.

13. "Private property" refers to private control of the economy, not to all personal possessions. See II.22.

14. Marx and Engels discuss this objection to communism at length over the next eighteen paragraphs (through II.32). Incidentally, for Marx and Engels, ownership is defined in terms of effective control, whether or not this has legal recognition.

15. Marx and Engels return to a theme raised earlier in I.35 and I.44. Capitalism steadily destroys traditional forms of small property ownership. The past generation, for instance, has witnessed the near extinction of family farms in the United States. Similarly, mega-retailers such as Walmart drive small store owners out of business.

17. Marx and Engels are responding to the criticism of communism raised in II.14. Apologists for capitalism claim that private ownership of the economy is the basis of freedom. Marx and Engels respond that, on the contrary, capitalist private property rests on the exploitation of the working of many members, nay, in the last resort, only by the united action of all members of society, can it be set in motion.

¶19 Capital is, therefore, not only a personal, it is a social power.

¶20 When, therefore, capital is converted into common property, into the property of all members of society, personal property is not thereby transformed into social property. It is only the social character of the property that is changed. It loses its class character.

¶21 Let us now take wage labor.

¶22 The average price of wage labor is the minimum wage, i.e., that quantum of the means of subsistence, which is absolutely requisite to keep the laborer in bare existence as a laborer. What, therefore, the wage laborer appropriates by means of his labor merely suffices to prolong and reproduce a bare existence. We by no means intend to abolish this personal appropriation of the products of labor, an appropriation that is made for the maintenance and reproduction of human life, and that leaves no surplus wherewith to command the labor of others. All that we want to do away with is the miserable character of this appropriation, under which the laborer lives merely to increase capital, and is allowed to live only in so far as the interest of the ruling class requires it.

¶23 In bourgeois society, living labor is but a means to increase accumulated labor. In communist society, accumulated labor is but a means to widen, to enrich, to promote the existence of the laborer.

class, and thus undermines genuine freedom for a large portion of the population.

18. Members of the capitalist class often claim that their wealth is the product of their own hard work, but without the contribution of workers, nothing would be produced at all. In the final analysis, wealth is always a social product. Capital is wealth that can be invested to make more money.

20. Marx and Engels explain the positive goal of communism—capitalist private property is to be replaced by communal ownership. This will not transform capital into something social—it has always been produced by a social process—but it means that economic wealth will no longer be based on class exploitation.

22. Marx and Engels are following the views of David Ricardo, the leading bourgeois economist of the early nineteenth century, who argued that wages under capitalism would tend to be driven down to an absolute minimum. As noted earlier (see comments on I.52), Marx later rejected this view. The key point they are making here, however, is that abolition of private property does not mean that workers will lose their personal possessions. On the contrary, in a communist society, workers would be entitled to a more generous share of society's wealth. What no one would be entitled to, however, are resources that would give them control over the labor (and thus the lives) of others (see II.32).

23. Under capitalism, labor power is just one more commodity, and a small minority controls the wealth that labor creates. Under communism, society's wealth would be used in the interests of workers.

¶24 In bourgeois society, therefore, the past dominates the present; in communist society, the present dominates the past. In bourgeois society, capital is independent and has individuality, while the living person is dependent and has no individuality.

¶25 And the abolition of this state of things is called by the bourgeois, abolition of individuality and freedom! And rightly so. The abolition of bourgeois individuality, bourgeois independence, and bourgeois freedom is undoubtedly aimed at.

¶26 By freedom is meant, under the present bourgeois conditions of production, free trade, free selling and buying.

¶27 But if selling and buying disappears, free selling and buying disappears also. This talk about free selling and buying, and all the other "brave words" of our bourgeoisie about freedom in general, have a meaning, if any, only in contrast with restricted selling and buying, with the fettered traders of the Middle Ages, but have no meaning when opposed to the communistic abolition of buying and selling, of the bourgeois conditions of production, and of the bourgeoisie itself.

¶28 You are horrified at our intending to do away with private property. But in your existing society, private property is already done away with for nine-tenths of the population; its existence for the few is solely due to its non-existence in the hands of those nine-tenths. You reproach us, therefore, with intending to do away with a form of property, the necessary condition for whose existence is the non-existence of any property for the immense majority of society.

24. In capitalist society, accumulated wealth (the past) is used to control workers, and corporations are granted the rights of persons.[6] In a communist society, workers (the present) will control the wealth. Bourgeois society celebrates individual freedom, but in reality undermines it for most people.

25. Under communism, one person would not be free to accumulate wealth by controlling the labor of others. Ending this bourgeois freedom for a minority would increase genuine freedom for the rest of society.

26. Compare I.14.

27. Freedom only exists under capitalism in comparison to feudalism, which placed tight restrictions on trade and the development of production, not in comparison to communism, which aims at the abolition of an economy based on commodity exchange. While, in theory, the law under capitalism treats everyone equally, inequality and exploitation mean that the freedom of most is restricted. As the writer Anatole France noted: "The law, in its majestic equality, forbids the rich as well as the poor to sleep under bridges." Compare II.17.

28. Recall that by "private property" Marx and Engels mean private control of economic resources (see II.22). In 1998, the wealthiest 10 percent of the population in the United States owned more than 85 percent of assets in stocks and mutual funds, 84 percent of financial securities, 91 percent of trusts, and 92 percent of all equity in private businesses.[7] Capitalism depends on the majority of the population lacking economic resources so that they are compelled to work for others.

¶29 In one word, you reproach us with intending to do away with your property. Precisely so; that is just what we intend.

¶30 From the moment when labor can no longer be converted into capital, money, or rent into a social power capable of being monopolized, i.e., from the moment when individual property can no longer be transformed into bourgeois property, into capital, from that moment, you say, individuality vanishes.

¶31 You must, therefore, confess that by "individual" you mean no other person than the bourgeois, than the middle-class owner of property. This person must, indeed, be swept out of the way, and made impossible.

¶32 Communism deprives no man of the power to appropriate the products of society; all that it does is to deprive him of the power to subjugate the labor of others by means of such appropriation.

¶33 It has been objected that upon the abolition of private property all work will cease and universal laziness will overtake us.

¶34 According to this, bourgeois society ought long ago to have gone to the dogs through sheer idleness; for those of its members who work, acquire nothing, and those who acquire anything, do not work. The whole of this objection is but another expression of the tautology that there can no longer be any wage labor when there is no longer any capital.

¶35 All objections urged against the communistic mode of producing and appropriating material products have, in the same way, been urged against the communistic mode of producing and appropriating

29. In other words, the Communists intend to end private control of the economy by the bourgeoisie.

31. Compare II.25. The bourgeoisie was at one time a middle class between the aristocracy and the peasantry. Marx and Engels seem to be using "middle class" in that historical sense here.

32. This paragraph reemphasizes the difference between personal possessions and capitalist private property (see II.22).

33. Marx and Engels now briefly turn their attention to the criticism that communism will destroy the incentive to work.

34. Under capitalism, those who work the hardest (workers at the bottom of society) gain the least,[8] while those who gain the most (owners of capital) accumulate wealth though they do nothing. In post-capitalist society, it is a truism that no one will have to work to make others rich in order to survive.

intellectual products. Just as, to the bourgeois, the disappearance of class property is the disappearance of production itself, so the disappearance of class culture is to him identical with the disappearance of all culture.

¶36 That culture, the loss of which he laments, is, for the enormous majority, a mere training to act as a machine.

¶37 But don't wrangle with us so long as you apply to our intended abolition of bourgeois property the standard of your bourgeois notions of freedom, culture, law, etc. Your very ideas are the outgrowth of the conditions of your bourgeois production and bourgeois property, just as your jurisprudence is but the will of your class made into a law for all, a will whose essential character and direction are determined by the economical conditions of existence of your class.

¶38 The selfish misconception that induces you to transform into eternal laws of nature and of reason, the social forms springing from your present mode of production and form of property—historical relations that rise and disappear in the progress of production—this misconception you share with every ruling class that has preceded you. What you see clearly in the case of ancient property, what you admit in the case of feudal property, you are of course forbidden to admit in the case of your own bourgeois form of property.

¶39 Abolition of the family! Even the most radical flare up at this infamous proposal of the communists.

36. To cite one important example, most education under capitalism is designed to produce docile workers, not creative thinkers.[9] Compare II.44.

37. Marx and Engels set out a key aspect of their materialist approach to history and society. As Marx puts it elsewhere: "The mode of production of material life conditions the general process of social, political, and intellectual life. It is not the consciousness of men that determines their existence, but their social existence that determines their consciousness."[10] But Marx and Engels do not claim that bourgeois ideas lack any independent content or have no internal logic of their own.

38. Like all earlier ruling classes, the bourgeoisie imagines that existing social relations are natural, rational, and permanent. It is obvious now that those earlier ruling classes were mistaken—their societies merely corresponded to a particular stage in the development of production—but the bourgeoisie is unable to recognize this in its own case. Portraying the existing order as natural is an important part of ruling-class ideology, aimed at convincing others that there is no alternative. Compare II.62–65.

¶40 On what foundation is the present family, the bourgeois family, based? On capital, on private gain. In its completely developed form, this family exists only among the bourgeoisie. But this state of things finds its complement in the practical absence of the family among the proletarians, and in public prostitution.

¶41 The bourgeois family will vanish as a matter of course when its complement vanishes, and both will vanish with the vanishing of capital.

¶42 Do you charge us with wanting to stop the exploitation of children by their parents? To this crime we plead guilty.

¶43 But, you will say, we destroy the most hallowed of relations when we replace home education by social.

¶44 And your education! Is not that also social, and determined by the social conditions under which you educate, by the intervention, direct or indirect, of society, by means of schools, etc.? The communists have not invented the intervention of society in education; they do but seek to alter the character of that intervention, and to rescue education from the influence of the ruling class.

¶45 The bourgeois clap-trap about the family and education, about the hallowed co-relation of parent and child, becomes all the more disgusting, the more, by the action of modern industry, all family ties among the proletarians are torn asunder, and their children transformed into simple articles of commerce and instruments of labor.

40. Compare I.16 and I.47. Many early socialists, echoing ideas in Plato's *Republic*, believed that some form of communal living should replace the private family. However, Marx and Engels' main point is that capitalism itself tends to pull working-class families apart. In the 1840s, there was concern that industrial exploitation might destroy family life entirely.[11]

41. When capitalism is transcended, new social structures—including new family structures—will develop.

42. Compare II.45.

43. The idea of universal, publicly funded education was still a radical one in the mid-nineteenth century.

44. All education reflects broader social influences. What is distinctive about the Communist approach is that it aims to end the unacknowledged dominance of ruling-class ideas in education.[12]

45. In the mid-nineteenth century, child labor was common (as it still is in much of the world today, including in the United States[13]). Contemporary politicians still pose as defenders of "family values," while enacting policies that harm working families and benefit corporations. Legislation to make it more difficult to declare bankruptcy is one striking recent example.

¶46 But you communists would introduce community of women, screams the whole bourgeoisie in chorus.

¶47 The bourgeois sees in his wife a mere instrument of production. He hears that the instruments of production are to be exploited in common and, naturally, can come to no other conclusion than that the lot of being common to all will likewise fall to the women.

¶48 He has not even a suspicion that the real point aimed at is to do away with the status of women as mere instruments of production.

¶49 For the rest, nothing is more ridiculous than the virtuous indignation of our bourgeois at community of women which, they pretend, is to be openly and officially established by the communists. The communists have no need to introduce community of women; it has existed almost from time immemorial.

¶50 Our bourgeois, not content with having the wives and daughters of their proletarians at their disposal, not to speak of common prostitutes, take the greatest pleasure in seducing each other's wives.

¶51 Bourgeois marriage is in reality a system of wives in common and thus, at the most, what the communists might possibly be reproached with is that they desire to introduce, in substitution for a hypocritically concealed, an openly legalized community of women. For the rest, it is self-evident that the abolition of the present system of production must bring with it the abolition of the community of women springing from that system, i.e., of prostitution both official and unofficial.

46. The idea of holding women in common goes back to Plato's *Republic* (compare comment on II.40), but was not advocated by Marx and Engels.

47. Because women have been treated as the property of men under capitalism and earlier class societies, the bourgeoisie wrongly assumes that women will become common property in a communist society.

48. Communism will do away with women's status as property. The goal is liberation and full equality for women and men.

49. In the following paragraphs, Marx and Engels point out the hypocrisy of the bourgeoisie with respect to the morality of marriage and sexual relations.

¶52 The communists are further reproached with desiring to abolish countries and nationality.

¶53 The workers have no country. We cannot take from them what they have not got. Since the proletariat must first of all acquire political supremacy, must rise to be the leading class of the nation, must constitute itself *the* nation, it is, so far, itself national, though not in the bourgeois sense of the word.

¶54 National divisions and antagonisms between peoples are daily more and more vanishing, owing to the development of the bourgeoisie, to freedom of commerce, to the world market, to uniformity in the mode of production and in the conditions of life corresponding thereto.

¶55 The supremacy of the proletariat will cause them to vanish still faster. United action, of the leading civilized countries at least, is one of the first conditions for the emancipation of the proletariat.

¶56 In proportion as the exploitation of one individual by another is put an end to, the exploitation of one nation by another will also be put an end to. In proportion as the antagonism between classes within the nation vanishes, the hostility of one nation to another will come to an end.

¶57 The charges against communism made from a religious, a philosophical and, generally, from an ideological standpoint, are not deserving of detailed examination.

¶58 Does it require deep intuition to comprehend that man's ideas, views, and conceptions, in one word, man's consciousness, changes with every change in the

53. Workers in one country have many more interests in common with workers in other countries than with capitalists in their own country. The working-class movement in any country needs a national focus only because its first task is to overthrow its own ruling class.[14]

54. Compare I.20 and I.47. Marx and Engels emphasize one tendency that exists under capitalism, but ignore competing forces, including efforts to propagate nationalism by ruling classes to promote their own interests. Draper suggests that Marx and Engels are mainly describing the attitude workers should have toward such ideology.

55. A successful workers' revolution will need to be international in scope and eliminate national rivalries between workers. Socialism cannot survive for long in a single isolated country surrounded by hostile capitalist forces.[15]

56. Just as a successful workers' revolution will end the economic exploitation of wage labor, it will also end the colonial and imperialist exploitation of less developed countries by more developed ones.

58. Compare I.47 and II.37. In the next few paragraphs, Marx and Engels elaborate on their materialist perspective. Philosophical, religious, and ideological criticisms of communism are dismissed as expressions of existing social relations.

conditions of his material existence, in his social relations and in his social life?

¶59 What else does the history of ideas prove, than that intellectual production changes its character in proportion as material production is changed? The ruling ideas of each age have ever been the ideas of its ruling class.

¶60 When people speak of the ideas that revolutionize society, they do but express the fact that within the old society the elements of a new one have been created, and that the dissolution of the old ideas keeps even pace with the dissolution of the old conditions of existence.

¶61 When the ancient world was in its last throes, the ancient religions were overcome by Christianity. When Christian ideas succumbed in the eighteenth century to rationalist ideas, feudal society fought its death battle with the then revolutionary bourgeoisie. The ideas of religious liberty and freedom of conscience merely gave expression to the sway of free competition within the domain of knowledge.

¶62 "Undoubtedly," it will be said, "religious, moral, philosophical, and juridical ideas have been modified in the course of historical development. But religion, morality, philosophy, political science, and law constantly survived this change."

¶63 "There are, besides, eternal truths, such as freedom, justice, etc., that are common to all states of society. But communism abolishes eternal truths, it abolishes all religion, and all morality, instead of constituting them on a new basis; it therefore acts in contradiction to all past historical experience."

59. Bourgeois ideas might include the following: the best rise to the top; there isn't enough to go around; men are naturally aggressive, while women are nurturing, etc. Such ideas reinforce existing inequalities.

60. Marx and Engels are arguing that ideas are not the primary motor of social change. Ideas certainly play a crucial role in historical change, but ideas that have a significant social impact are themselves expressions of changes in underlying material conditions.

61. Christianity became the official religion of the Roman Empire in the fourth century AD, little more than a hundred years before the collapse of Rome. The development of capitalism gave rise to the Reformation (the Protestant split from the Catholic Church) in the sixteenth century, the scientific revolution in the seventeenth century, and the Enlightenment in the eighteenth century. Thus, many traditional Christian ideas (but not the religion itself, of course) have "succumbed."

62. Compare II.38.

63. The claim that communism will abolish morality is one that Engels explicitly rejected. As he later put it, "there has on the whole been progress in morality," but a "really human morality . . . becomes possible only at a stage of society that has not only overcome class antagonisms but has even forgotten them in practical life."[16]

¶64 What does this accusation reduce itself to? The history of all past society has consisted in the development of class antagonisms, antagonisms that assumed different forms at different epochs.

¶65 But whatever form they may have taken, one fact is common to all past ages, viz., the exploitation of one part of society by the other. No wonder, then, that the social consciousness of past ages, despite all the multiplicity and variety it displays, moves within certain common forms, or general ideas, which cannot completely vanish except with the total disappearance of class antagonisms.

¶66 The communist revolution is the most radical rupture with traditional property relations; no wonder that its development involves the most radical rupture with traditional ideas.

¶67 But let us have done with the bourgeois objections to communism.

¶68 We have seen above that the first step in the revolution by the working class is to raise the proletariat to the position of ruling class, to win the battle of democracy.

¶69 The proletariat will use its political supremacy to wrest, by degrees, all capital from the bourgeoisie, to centralize all instruments of production in the hands of the state, i.e., of the proletariat organized as the ruling class; and to increase the total of productive forces as rapidly as possible.

¶70 Of course, in the beginning, this cannot be effected except by means of despotic inroads on the rights of property, and on the conditions of bourgeois production; by means of measures, therefore,

65. More accurately, all past ages described in "written history" (recall Engels' footnote to I.1). The apparent "eternal" character of some ideas (for example, the sexist view that men are better suited than women to run society) may simply reflect the fact that they are common to all class societies. In a classless society, many such ideas may be rejected.

68. See I.51, II.7, and II.53. Following the short-lived Paris Commune of 1871, Marx and Engels concluded that the conquest of power would have to involve the destruction of the old bureaucratic state and its replacement by radically new institutions, based on directly elected and revocable workers' delegates, to permit real democratic control.[17]

69. Political power can change hands quickly in a revolution, but the large-scale transformation of social and economic relations will take much longer. Over time, the most important sectors of the economy will be placed under state control. Note, though, that state control by itself is not socialism—what matters is control by a democratic workers' state.[18]

70. Transformation of the economy will require coercive steps, because the bourgeoisie will not willingly agree to surrender its economic power. No individual economic measure will by itself create a new mode of production, and each alone may appear unsustainable, but together they will create a momentum that will in time bring about the replacement of capitalism by socialism.

which appear economically insufficient and untenable, but which, in the course of the movement, outstrip themselves, necessitate further inroads upon the old social order, and are unavoidable as a means of entirely revolutionizing the mode of production.

¶71 These measures will of course be different in different countries.

¶72 Nevertheless, in the most advanced countries, the following will be pretty generally applicable.

1. Abolition of property in land and application of all rents of land to public purposes.

2. A heavy progressive or graduated income tax.

3. Abolition of all right of inheritance.

4. Confiscation of the property of all emigrants and rebels.

5. Centralization of credit in the hands of the state, by means of a national bank with state capital and an exclusive monopoly.

6. Centralization of the means of communication and transport in the hands of the state.

7. Extension of factories and instruments of production owned by the state; the bringing into cultivation of waste lands, and the improvement of the soil generally in accordance with a common plan.

8. Equal liability of all to labor. Establishment of industrial armies, especially for agriculture.

71. In 1872, Marx and Engels added, "no special stress is laid on the revolutionary measures proposed at the end of Section II."[19]

72. Marx and Engels list here a set of demands formulated by the Communist League, which would move the economy in a socialist direction.

1. Marx and Engels later drew a distinction between large landowners (whose property would be seized) and small ones (whose property would not).

2. A tax is progressive when those who are better off pay at a higher rate.

3. Ending inheritance would promote greater economic and social equality.

4. The targets here are those who flee the country or support counter-revolution.

5. The abolition of private banks would be a further limitation on the freedom of capital.

6. The reference to communication was added in Moore's translation following the introduction of the telephone.

7. State ownership of factories would be a further limitation of capitalist property relations. Marx and Engels also raise environmental issues here, which they discuss extensively elsewhere.[20] Capitalist accumulation destroys the natural environment, creating problems that can only be solved by socialist planning.

8. Everyone will be required to work if capable. By an industrial army, Marx

9. Combination of agriculture with manufacturing industries; gradual abolition of the distinction between town and country by a more equable distribution of the population over the country.

10. Free education for all children in public schools. Abolition of children's factory labor in its present form. Combination of education with industrial production, etc.

¶73 When, in the course of development, class distinctions have disappeared, and all production has been concentrated in the hands of a vast association of the whole nation, the public power will lose its political character. Political power, properly so called, is merely the organized power of one class for oppressing another. When the proletariat during its contest with the bourgeoisie is compelled, by the force of circumstances, to organize itself as a class; when, by means of a revolution, it makes itself the ruling class and, as such, sweeps away by force the old conditions of production; then it will, along with these conditions, have swept away the conditions for the existence of class antagonisms and of classes generally, and will thereby have abolished its own supremacy as a class.

¶74 In place of the old bourgeois society, with its classes and class antagonisms, we shall have an association in which the free development of each is the condition for the free development of all.

and Engels mean a program of public employment.

9. Here, again, Marx and Engels raise environmental issues.

10. Compare II.42 and II.43. The final sentence proposes including work experience as part of a well-rounded education. Draper notes that this idea was later taken up by the progressive-school movement.[21]

73. For Marx and Engels, the state is always an instrument for imposing the rule of one class on the rest of society, and politics is an expression of this class domination. When the working class seizes state power, it will itself become the new ruling class, a role it must take to prevent the bourgeoisie from returning to power.[22] However, a workers' revolution will, at the same time, create the conditions for the abolition of exploitation and thus the end of class distinctions themselves. When this point is reached, there will be no more social classes, no more state (in the sense of a set of institutions that enforce the rule of one class), and no more politics (in the sense of a struggle between different classes). The members of such a society would be able to settle their differences through genuine democratic discussion, debate, and decision making.

74. Marx and Engels place individual freedom at the center of their vision of postcapitalist society.

III.

Socialist and Communist Literature

1. REACTIONARY SOCIALISM

A. Feudal Socialism

¶1 Owing to their historical position, it became the vocation of the aristocracies of France and England to write pamphlets against modern bourgeois society. In the French revolution of July 1830, and in the English reform agitation, these aristocracies again succumbed to the hateful upstart. Thenceforth, a serious political contest was altogether out of the question. A literary battle alone remained possible. But even in the domain of literature, the old cries of the restoration period had become impossible.*

¶2 In order to arouse sympathy, the aristocracy was obliged to lose sight, apparently, of its own interests, and to formulate its indictment against the bourgeoisie in the interest of the exploited working class alone. Thus the aristocracy took their revenge by singing lampoons on their new master, and whispering in his

*Not the English Restoration 1660 to 1689, but the French Restoration 1814 to 1830. [Engels, 1888 English edition]

In the early nineteenth century, "socialism" was used very broadly to refer to any concern with the social problems produced by capitalism. "Reactionary socialists" wanted to solve these problems by returning to an earlier form of society.

1. In 1830, the French bourgeoisie overthrew the Bourbon dynasty (restored after Napoleon's defeat in 1814) and replaced it with a constitutional monarchy, represented by the "Citizen King" Louis Philippe. The 1832 Reform Act in Britain modestly expanded voting eligibility and abolished some of the more blatantly biased aspects of the parliamentary system, strengthening bourgeois influence in the House of Commons. These developments marked the final subordination of the landed aristocracy to the bourgeoisie.

2. Compare II.4. A lampoon is a satirical attack. The "coming catastrophe" will be the culmination of capitalism's growing social problems.

Study and discussion questions for this section begin on page 191.

ears sinister prophesies of coming catastrophe.

¶3 In this way arose feudal socialism: half lamentation, half lampoon; half echo of the past, half menace of the future; at times, by its bitter, witty, and incisive criticism, striking the bourgeoisie to the very heart's core, but always ludicrous in its effect, through total incapacity to comprehend the march of modern history.

¶4 The aristocracy, in order to rally the people to them, waved the proletarian alms-bag in front for a banner. But the people, so often as it joined them, saw on their hindquarters the old feudal coats of arms, and deserted with loud and irreverent laughter.

¶5 One section of the French Legitimists and "Young England" exhibited this spectacle.

¶6 In pointing out that their mode of exploitation was different to that of the bourgeoisie, the feudalists forget that they exploited under circumstances and conditions that were quite different and that are now antiquated. In showing that, under their rule, the modern proletariat never existed, they forget that the modern bourgeoisie is the necessary offspring of their own form of society.

¶7 For the rest, so little do they conceal the reactionary character of their criticism that their chief accusation against the bourgeoisie amounts to this: that under the bourgeois *régime* a class is being developed that is destined to cut up root and branch the old order of society.

¶8 What they upbraid the bourgeoisie with is not so much that it creates a proletariat, as that it creates a *revolutionary* proletariat.

3. The feudal socialism of the aristocrats both mourns and ridicules bourgeois society. It looks back wistfully to the past, while warning of the "coming catastrophe" to which bourgeois society is headed. What the feudal socialists fail to see is that historical changes have made a return to the past impossible.

4. An alms-bag is used to collect charitable donations for the poor. Marx and Engels' point is that the aristocracy professed concern for working-class poverty in an unsuccessful attempt to win support from the proletariat.

5. The Legitimists were right-wing opponents of Louis Philippe (see comment on III.1). "Young England" was a faction of the British Tory Party that looked back to precapitalist society as a time of social harmony, and played a role in the passage of the Ten Hours Bill. (See I.40.)

6. See I.6–8 for Marx and Engels' description of how the bourgeoisie emerged in feudal society, and why feudal relations of production became obsolete. Feudalists are those who defend feudal values and ideas.

7. Marx and Engels are suggesting that the emergence of a revolutionary proletariat is part of the "coming catastrophe" that the feudalists warn against (see III.2).

8. What concerns the feudalists is not so much the exploitation of the proletariat, but that this exploitation may provoke revolution.

¶9 In political practice, therefore, they join in all coercive measures against the working class; and in ordinary life, despite their highfalutin phrases, they stoop to pick up the golden apples dropped from the tree of industry, and to barter fidelity, love, and honor for traffic in wool, beetroot-sugar, and potato spirits.*

¶10 As the parson has ever gone hand in hand with the feudalist, so has clerical socialism with feudal socialism.

¶11 Nothing is easier than to give Christian asceticism a socialist tinge. Has not Christianity declaimed against private property, against marriage, against the state? Has it not preached in the place of these, charity and poverty, celibacy and mortification of the flesh, monastic life and Mother Church? Religious socialism is but the holy water with which the priest consecrates the heart-burnings of the aristocrat.

9. Regardless of their pretentious statements criticizing bourgeois society, the feudalists abandon their principles and take every opportunity to reap the economic rewards of the new system.

11. According to Marx and Engels, clerical or religious socialism is, like feudal socialism, a backward-looking doctrine.

"Mortification of the flesh" means denial of one's physical appetites.

B. Petty-Bourgeois Socialism

¶12 The feudal aristocracy was not the only class that was ruined by the bourgeoisie, not the only class whose conditions of existence pined and perished in the atmosphere of modern bourgeois society. The medieval

The petty bourgeoisie consists of people whose economic situation places them between capitalists and workers. By describing an ideology as petty bourgeois, Marx and Engels are saying that it reflects the mental outlook or material interests of such people. The description is not simply an insult.

12. Marx and Engels are thinking particularly of mid-nineteenth-century Germany.

---

*This applies chiefly to Germany, where the landed aristocracy and squirearchy have large portions of their estates cultivated for their own account by stewards, and are, moreover, extensive beetroot-sugar manufacturers and distillers of potato spirits. The wealthier British aristocracy are, as yet, rather above that; but they, too, know how to make up for declining rents by lending their names to floaters of more or less shady joint-stock companies. [Engels, 1888 English edition]

burgesses and the small peasant proprietors were the precursors of the modern bourgeoisie. In those countries which are but little developed, industrially and commercially, these two classes still vegetate side by side with the rising bourgeoisie.

¶13 In countries where modern civilization has become fully developed, a new class of petty bourgeois has been formed, fluctuating between proletariat and bourgeoisie, and ever renewing itself as a supplementary part of bourgeois society. The individual members of this class, however, are being constantly hurled down into the proletariat by the action of competition and, as modern industry develops, they even see the moment approaching when they will completely disappear as an independent section of modern society, to be replaced in manufactures, agriculture, and commerce by labor overseers and stewards.

¶14 In countries like France, where the peasants constitute far more than half of the population, it was natural that writers who sided with the proletariat against the bourgeoisie should use, in their criticism of the bourgeois *régime*, the standard of the peasant and petty bourgeois, and from the standpoint of these intermediate classes should take up the cudgels for the working class. Thus arose petty-bourgeois socialism. Sismondi was the head of this school, not only in France but also in England.

¶15 This school of socialism dissected with great acuteness the contradictions in the conditions of modern production. It laid bare the hypocritical apologies of economists. It proved, incontrovertibly, the disastrous

13. Compare I.35. As noted there, Marx and Engels are not claiming that the middle class as a whole will disappear, even though individual members of the petty bourgeoisie are forced to become wage-workers, and even though the class as a whole may be significantly restructured. In fact, Marx and Engels here correctly foresee the emergence of a "new middle class" of managers, balanced between capital and labor.

14. Jean-Charles-Léonard Simonde de Sismondi (1773–1842) was a Swiss political economist who argued that economic crises are unavoidable under capitalism, and who advocated state intervention to protect small producers from being swallowed up by larger ones.

15. Here is one example of this kind of criticism of capitalism, from Sismondi: "Exertion today is separated from its recompense; it is not the same man that first works, and then reposes; but it is because the one works that the other rests. . . . The indefinite multiplication of the productive powers of labor can then only have for result the increase of luxury and enjoyment of the idle rich."[23]

effects of machinery and division of labor; the concentration of capital and land in a few hands; overproduction and crises; it pointed out the inevitable ruin of the small burghers and peasants, the misery of the proletariat, the anarchy in production, the crying inequalities in the distribution of wealth, the industrial war of extermination between nations, the dissolution of old moral bonds, of the old family relations, of the old nationalities.

¶16 In its positive aims, however, this form of socialism aspires either to restoring the old means of production and of exchange, and with them the old property relations and the old society, or to cramping the modern means of production and of exchange within the framework of the old property relations that have been, and were bound to be, exploded by those means. In either case, it is both reactionary and utopian.

¶17 Its last words are: corporate guilds for manufacture; patriarchal relations in agriculture.

¶18 Ultimately, when stubborn historical facts had dispersed all intoxicating effects of self-deception, this form of socialism ended in a miserable fit of the blues.

16. By "utopian," Marx and Engels mean a vision of a new kind of society that in some way ignores material conditions. The schemes of the petty-bourgeois socialists are unrealizable because social circumstances had changed too much by the mid-nineteenth century to make it possible to turn the clock back.

17. In other words, petty-bourgeois socialism, like feudal socialism, looks to the past for solutions.

C. German or "True" Socialism

¶19 The socialist and communist literature of France, a literature that originated under the pressure of a bourgeoisie in power, and that was the expression of the struggle against this power, was introduced into Germany at a time when the bourgeoisie in that country had just begun its contest with feudal absolutism.

"True" socialism is actually a variety of petty-bourgeois socialism. See III.31–34.

19. Germany lagged behind France and Britain politically and economically in the first half of the nineteenth century.

¶20 German philosophers, would-be philosophers, and *beaux esprits*, eagerly seized on this literature, only forgetting that when these writings immigrated from France into Germany, French social conditions had not immigrated along with them. In contact with German social conditions, this French literature lost all its immediate practical significance and assumed a purely literary aspect. It was bound to appear to be idle speculation about the true society, about the realization of human nature. Thus, to the German philosophers of the eighteenth century, the demands of the first French Revolution were nothing more than the demands of "practical reason" in general, and the utterance of the will of the revolutionary French bourgeoisie signified, in their eyes, the laws of pure will, of will as it was bound to be, of true human will generally.

¶21 The work of the German *literati* consisted solely in bringing the new French ideas into harmony with their ancient philosophical conscience, or rather, in annexing the French ideas without deserting their own philosophic point of view.

¶22 This annexation took place in the same way in which a foreign language is appropriated, namely, by translation.

¶23 It is well known how the monks wrote silly lives of Catholic saints *over* the manuscripts on which the classical works of ancient heathendom had been written. The German *literati* reversed this process with the profane French literature. They wrote their philosophical nonsense beneath the French original. For instance, beneath the French criticism of the economic functions of money, they wrote "alienation of humanity,"

20. "Beaux esprits" literally means "fine minds"—in other words, cultivated or educated people. In Germany, where the bourgeoisie was not yet in power, intellectuals interpreted socialism as a humanistic ideal, abstracted from the realities of class struggle in capitalism—something that could be achieved by appealing to people's better natures. In this, they were following in the footsteps of the German philosopher Immanuel Kant (1724–1804), who published his *Critique of Practical Reason* (which attempts to provide the rational basis for moral principles and a just society) in 1788, on the eve of the great French Revolution. Kant viewed the French bourgeoisie as motivated by rational morality, rather than by their own material interests.

21. The German "true" socialists attempted to merge Kantian and socialist ideas, thereby depriving socialism of its class perspective.

22. In Germany, socialist ideas were "translated" into philosophical language.

23. German philosophers replaced the concrete ideas of French socialism with philosophical generalities. Earlier in the 1840s, Marx and Engels had each retraced this path in the opposite direction, moving from the abstractions of Hegelian philosophy to the study of political economy.[24]

and beneath the French criticism of the bourgeois state they wrote "dethronement of the category of the general," and so forth.

¶24 The introduction of these philosophical phrases at the back of the French historical criticisms, they dubbed "philosophy of action," "true socialism," "German science of socialism," "philosophical foundation of socialism," and so on.

¶25 The French socialist and communist literature was thus completely emasculated. And, since it ceased in the hands of the German to express the struggle of one class with the other, he felt conscious of having overcome "French one-sidedness" and of representing, not true requirements, but the requirements of truth; not the interests of the proletariat, but the interests of human nature, of man in general, who belongs to no class, has no reality, who exists only in the misty realm of philosophical fantasy.

¶26 This German socialism, which took its schoolboy task so seriously and solemnly, and extolled its poor stock-in-trade in such mountebank fashion, meanwhile gradually lost its pedantic innocence.

¶27 The fight of the German and, especially, of the Prussian bourgeoisie against feudal aristocracy and absolute monarchy, in other words, the liberal movement, became more earnest.

¶28 By this, the long wished-for opportunity was offered to "true socialism" of confronting the political movement with the socialist demands, of hurling the traditional anathemas against liberalism, against representative government, against bourgeois competition, bourgeois freedom of the press, bourgeois legislation, bourgeois

25. The German "true" socialists replaced a class perspective with an appeal to humanity in general. However, humanity in general does not exist in the real world, where everyone is a member of one class or another.

26. A "mountebank" is a charlatan or trickster, such as a peddler of quack medicines.

27. In the 1840s, the German bourgeoisie began to challenge the landowners and their structures of feudal power. The "liberal movement" fought for basic democratic rights, including representative government and free speech.

28. The demands of the bourgeois movement in Germany in the 1840s were, in Marx and Engels' view, politically and socially progressive. They needed to be supported, even though they did not go far enough. Instead, by criticizing the German bourgeoisie as if (like its French counterpart) it had already won its political demands, the "true" socialists combined moralism (appeal to abstract moral principles) with ultraleftism (making a supposedly left-wing critique without taking into account the actual social and political circumstances). In practice, this verbal leftism covered over conservative cowering before the status quo.

liberty and equality, and of preaching to the masses that they had nothing to gain, and everything to lose, by this bourgeois movement. German socialism forgot, in the nick of time, that the French criticism, whose silly echo it was, presupposed the existence of modern bourgeois society, with its corresponding economic conditions of existence, and the political constitution adapted thereto, the very things whose attainment was the object of the pending struggle in Germany.

¶29 To the absolute governments, with their following of parsons, professors, country squires, and officials, it served as a welcome scarecrow against the threatening bourgeoisie.

¶30 It was a sweet finish after the bitter pills of flogging and bullets with which these same governments, just at that time, dosed the German working-class risings.

¶31 While this "true" socialism thus served the governments as a weapon for fighting the German bourgeoisie, it, at the same time, directly represented a reactionary interest, the interest of German philistines. In Germany, the petty-bourgeois class, a relic of the sixteenth century, and since then constantly cropping up again under various forms, is the real social basis of the existing state of things.

¶32 To preserve this class is to preserve the existing state of things in Germany. The industrial and political supremacy of the bourgeoisie threatens it with certain destruction; on the one hand, from the concentration of capital; on the other, from the rise of a revolutionary proletariat. "True" socialism appeared to kill these two birds with one stone. It spread like an epidemic.

29. By criticizing the bourgeoisie, the "true" socialists effectively became tools of the feudalists.[25]

31. "Philistines" refers to the smug and ignorant middle class, which Marx and Engels see as providing the social base for the existing German regimes. Compare I.45.

32. Since "true" socialism appealed to humanity in general and lacked a class perspective, it could criticize both the bourgeoisie and the proletariat for advancing their own particular interests. In this way, its advocates advanced their own concealed middle-class interests.

¶33 The robe of speculative cobwebs, embroidered with flowers of rhetoric, steeped in the dew of sickly sentiment, this transcendental robe in which the German socialists wrapped their sorry "eternal truths," all skin and bone, served to wonderfully increase the sale of their goods amongst such a public.

¶34 And on its part, German socialism recognized, more and more, its own calling as the bombastic representative of the petty-bourgeois philistine.

¶35 It proclaimed the German nation to be the model nation, and the German petty philistine to be the typical man. To every villainous meanness of this model man, it gave a hidden, higher, socialistic interpretation, the exact contrary of its real character. It went to the extreme length of directly opposing the "brutally destructive" tendency of communism, and of proclaiming its supreme and impartial contempt of all class struggles. With very few exceptions, all the so-called socialist and communist publications that now circulate in Germany belong to the domain of this foul and enervating literature.*

33. Marx and Engels save particular venom for the proponents of "true" socialism, who they see as providing left-wing cover for feudalism.

34. "Bombastic" means pompous.

35. According to Marx and Engels, the "true" socialists idealized German society while rejecting class struggle, which they viewed as "brutally destructive." This political current disappeared after the upheaval of the 1848 revolutions (see comment to P.3).

"Enervating" means weakening or deadening.

2. CONSERVATIVE OR BOURGEOIS SOCIALISM

¶36 A part of the bourgeoisie is desirous of redressing social grievances in order to secure the continued existence of bourgeois society.

Recall that Marx and Engels are using "socialism" very broadly to mean any program of social reform.

36. A section of the ruling class always believes that ameliorating some of the problems of the working class will make revolution less likely.

---

*The revolutionary storm of 1848 swept away this whole shabby tendency and cured its protagonists of the desire to dabble further in Socialism. The chief representative and classical type of this tendency is Herr Karl Grün. [Engels, 1890 German edition]

¶37 To this section belong economists, philanthropists, humanitarians, improvers of the condition of the working class, organizers of charity, members of societies for the prevention of cruelty to animals, temperance fanatics, hole-and-corner reformers of every imaginable kind. This form of socialism has, moreover, been worked out into complete systems.

¶38 We may cite Proudhon's *Philosophie de la Misère* as an example of this form.

¶39 The socialistic bourgeois want all the advantages of modern social conditions without the struggles and dangers necessarily resulting therefrom. They desire the existing state of society minus its revolutionary and disintegrating elements. They wish for a bourgeoisie without a proletariat. The bourgeoisie naturally conceives the world in which it is supreme to be the best; and bourgeois socialism develops this comfortable conception into various more or less complete systems. In requiring the proletariat to carry out such a system, and thereby to march straightaway into the social New Jerusalem, it but requires in reality that the proletariat should remain within the bounds of existing society, but should cast away all its hateful ideas concerning the bourgeoisie.

¶40 A second and more practical, but less systematic, form of this socialism sought to depreciate every revolutionary movement in the eyes of the working class by showing that no mere political reform, but only a change in the material conditions of existence, in economical relations, could be of any advantage to them. By changes in the material conditions of existence, this

37. Marx and Engels reserve special criticism for any conception of socialism in which the working class is considered a passive receptacle for the schemes of others, rather than the active creator of its own liberation.

38. The French writer Pierre Joseph Proudhon (1803–65) was a founder of anarchism (opposition to all government), but at this time was known for his advocacy of credit unions. His *Philosophy of Poverty* was published in 1847. Marx wrote a stinging response to his ideas in *The Poverty of Philosophy* (1847).

39. New Jerusalem is the heaven on earth promised in the New Testament's book of Revelation.

40. This version of bourgeois socialism attempts to dismiss political reforms by falsely counterposing them to economic ones, while interpreting the latter to mean simply a more efficient form of administration. Even if the economic demands had been more radical, it is wrong to counterpose economic and political demands. Greater political freedom, for example, makes it easier to win economic changes.

form of socialism, however, by no means understands abolition of the bourgeois relations of production, an abolition that can be effected only by a revolution, but administrative reforms, based on the continued existence of these relations; reforms, therefore, that in no respect affect the relations between capital and labor but, at the best, lessen the cost, and simplify the administrative work, of bourgeois government.

¶41 Bourgeois socialism attains adequate expression when, and only when, it becomes a mere figure of speech.

¶42 Free trade: for the benefit of the working class. Protective duties: for the benefit of the working class. Prison reform: for the benefit of the working class. This is the last word and the only seriously meant word of bourgeois socialism.

¶43 It is summed up in the phrase: the bourgeois is a bourgeois—for the benefit of the working class.

41. Marx and Engels seem to mean that bourgeois social reform is a deception that does not really improve the situation of the working class.

42. Capitalist politicians today still claim their policies will benefit workers. Nineteenth-century prison reform was supposed to be humane, but according to Charles Dickens, it resulted in psychological torture worse than the physical punishment it replaced.[26]

3. CRITICAL-UTOPIAN SOCIALISM AND COMMUNISM

¶44 We do not here refer to that literature which, in every great modern revolution, has always given voice to the demands of the proletariat, such as the writings of Babeuf and others.

¶45 The first direct attempts of the proletariat to attain its own ends, made in times of universal excitement, when feudal society was being overthrown, necessarily failed, owing to the then undeveloped state of the proletariat, as well as to the absence of the economic

By "utopian," Marx and Engels mean speculations about postcapitalist society not based on an analysis of the social forces capable of bringing change. The utopians nevertheless produced powerful critiques of capitalism (see III.54).

44. François-Noël "Gracchus" Babeuf (1760–97) advocated egalitarian communism at the time of the great French Revolution. He led a failed uprising by the "conspiracy of equals" in 1796, intended to bring about a classless society.

conditions for its emancipation, conditions that had yet to be produced, and could be produced by the impending bourgeois epoch alone. The revolutionary literature that accompanied these first movements of the proletariat had necessarily a reactionary character. It inculcated universal asceticism and social leveling in its crudest form.

¶46 The socialist and communist systems properly so called, those of Saint-Simon, Fourier, Owen, and others, spring into existence in the early undeveloped period, described above, of the struggle between proletariat and bourgeoisie (see Section I. Bourgeois and Proletarians).

¶47 The founders of these systems see, indeed, the class antagonisms, as well as the action of the decomposing elements, in the prevailing form of society. But the proletariat, as yet in its infancy, offers to them the spectacle of a class without any historical initiative or any independent political movement.

¶48 Since the development of class antagonism keeps even pace with the development of industry, the economic situation, as they find it, does not as yet offer to them the material conditions for the emancipation of the proletariat. They therefore search after a new social science, after new social laws that are to create these conditions.

¶49 Social action is to yield to their personal inventive action, historically created conditions of emancipation to fanciful ones, and the gradual, spontaneous class-organization of the proletariat to an organization of society specially contrived by these inventors. Future

45. Marx and Engels may be referring to the Diggers (or True Levelers), Ranters, and other early communist and radical movements during the period of the English Revolution in the mid-seventeenth century. These movements were "reactionary" only in the sense that their egalitarianism was based on the idea of returning to a simpler form of life.[27]

46. Count Claude-Henri de Saint-Simon (1760–1825) advocated scientific social planning. Charles Fourier (1772–1837) described in detail an ideal community called a "phalanstery." Robert Owen (1771–1858) was a successful British industrialist who set up a mill town designed to benefit the workers in New Lanark, Scotland.

47. The early socialists mentioned in the previous paragraph understood class divisions, but saw workers as the passive victims of exploitation, not as a class capable of actively fighting for its own liberation.

48. Workers are capable of overthrowing capitalism only when economic developments have welded them together as a class. Because these conditions had not yet come about, the utopians attempted to end exploitation by finding "new social laws" (i.e., theories that would explain how to bypass reality).

49. Instead of seeing a working-class movement as central to the socialist transformation of society, the utopians see the key as making propaganda for their ideal communities, or even beginning to establish them on a small scale.

history resolves itself, in their eyes, into the propaganda and the practical carrying out of their social plans.

¶50 In the formation of their plans, they are conscious of caring chiefly for the interests of the working class as being the most suffering class. Only from the point of view of being the most suffering class does the proletariat exist for them.

¶51 The undeveloped state of the class struggle, as well as their own social status, causes socialists of this kind to consider themselves far superior to all class antagonisms. They want to improve the condition of every member of society, even that of the most favored. Hence, they habitually appeal to society at large, without the distinction of class; nay, by preference, to the ruling class. For how can people, when once they understand their system, fail to see in it the best possible plan of the best possible state of society?

¶52 Hence, they reject all political, and especially all revolutionary, action; they wish to attain their ends by peaceful means, and endeavor, by small experiments necessarily doomed to failure, and by the force of example, to pave the way for the new social gospel.

¶53 Such fanciful pictures of future society, painted at a time when the proletariat is still in a very undeveloped state and has but a fanciful conception of its own position, correspond with the first instinctive yearnings of that class for a general reconstruction of society.

¶54 But these socialist and communist publications contain also a critical element. They attack every principle of existing society. Hence they are full of the

50. Compare III.47.

51. Because they believed their plans would appeal to everyone, the utopians looked for support from everyone, particularly (because of their resources) capitalists. Fourier reportedly advertised in vain for a wealthy patron to finance the establishment of the community he advocated.

52. Marx and Engels may be talking more about the later followers of these tendencies than about the founders. See III.55.

53. Marx and Engels offer a materialist analysis of utopian socialism, seeing it as a reflection of the proletariat's relatively low level of class organization in the early nineteenth century.

54. Marx and Engels praise the early socialists for their thoroughgoing critiques of capitalism. Their positive proposals, however, required the abolition of class antagonisms, which because of the relatively low level of class struggle at the time they were writing, they did not clearly understand. Nevertheless, Marx and Engels view some of the utopians' proposals as useful in helping us to imagine what a future socialist society might look like, even though the utopians did not understand how it could be created. On town and country, see II.72.9. On the family, see II.39–41. By "the conversion of the functions of the state into a mere superintendence of production" is meant replacing the repressive role of the state with the purely administrative task of managing the economy.

most valuable materials for the enlightenment of the working class. The practical measures proposed in them, such as the abolition of the distinction between town and country, of the family, of the carrying on of industries for the account of private individuals, and of the wage system, the proclamation of social harmony, the conversion of the functions of the state into a mere superintendence of production, all these proposals point solely to the disappearance of class antagonisms, which were, at that time, only just cropping up, and which, in these publications, are recognized in their earliest, indistinct, and undefined forms only. These proposals, therefore, are of a purely utopian character.

¶55 The significance of critical-utopian socialism and communism bears an inverse relation to historical development. In proportion as the modern class struggle develops and takes definite shape, this fanciful standing apart from the contest, these fanciful attacks on it, lose all practical value and all theoretical justification. Therefore, although the originators of these systems were, in many respects, revolutionary, their disciples have, in every case, formed mere reactionary sects. They hold fast by the original views of their masters, in opposition to the progressive historical development of the proletariat. They, therefore, endeavor, and that consistently, to deaden the class struggle and to reconcile the class antagonisms. They still dream of experimental realization of their social utopias, of founding individual "*phalanstères*," of establishing "Home Colonies," of setting up a "Little Icaria"*—

55. As the level of class struggle develops, utopian ideas become less relevant. While the original utopian socialists were revolutionaries because of their trenchant criticisms of capitalism, their later followers were hostile to the organized working class and thus objectively reactionary. For example, Charles Nordhoff, in his sympathetic 1875 presentation *The Communistic Societies of the United States*, rails against trade unions as "particular, mischievous, and hateful," and denounces them for exposing society to "lasting disorders and attacks upon property." Nordhoff hoped that the utopian communities could act as a safety valve for workers, and thereby convince them to escape wage labor rather than organize on a class basis. The later utopians formed sects, because they separated themselves from the working-class movement on the basis of their own distinctive doctrines. They attempted to set up communities where their social ideals could be realized, but which soon failed.

A duodecimo edition is a miniature or pocket-sized version. On "New Jerusalem," see III.39.

duodecimo editions of the New Jerusalem—and to realize all these castles in the air, they are compelled to appeal to the feelings and purses of the bourgeois. By degrees, they sink into the category of the reactionary or conservative socialists depicted above, differing from these only by more systematic pedantry, and by their fanatical and superstitious belief in the miraculous effects of their social science.

¶56 They therefore violently oppose all political action on the part of the working class; such action, according to them, can only result from blind unbelief in the new gospel.

¶57 The Owenites in England and the Fourierists in France, respectively oppose the Chartists and the *Réformistes*.

56. The utopian sects were hostile to the struggle for political reforms, which they saw as opposed to concern with social issues. For Marx and Engels, the two cannot be separated.

57. The Chartists, the world's first mass working-class movement, fought for political reforms in Britain, including universal male suffrage and annual parliaments. The *Réformistes* were the left wing of the French republican movement.[28]

---

*Phalanstères were Socialist colonies on the plan of Charles Fourier; Icaria was the name given by Cabet to his Utopia and, later on, to his American communist colony. [Engels, 1888 English edition]

"Home Colonies" were what Owen called his communist model societies. Phalanstères was the name of the public palaces planned by Fourier. Icaria was the name given to the Utopian land of fancy, whose communist institutions Cabet portrayed. [Engels, 1890 German edition]

IV.

Position of the Communists in Relation to the Various Existing Opposition Parties

¶1 Section II has made clear the relations of the Communists to the existing working-class parties, such as the Chartists in England and the Agrarian Reformers in America.

¶2 The Communists fight for the attainment of the immediate aims, for the enforcement of the interests of the working class; but in the movement of the present, they also represent and take care of the future of that movement. In France, the Communists ally themselves with the Social Democrats* against the conservative and radical bourgeoisie, reserving, however, the right to take up a critical position in regard to phrases and illusions traditionally handed down from the great Revolution.

¶3 In Switzerland, they support the Radicals, without losing sight of the fact that this party consists of antag-

---

*The party then represented in Parliament by Ledru-Rollin, in literature by Louis Blanc, in the daily press by *La Réforme.* The name of Social-Democracy signifies, with these its inventors, a section of the democratic or republican party [in the sense of a political movement, not an organized party—ed.] more or less tinged with socialism. [Engels, English edition 1888]

1. See II.2–7. On the Chartists, see III.57. The National Reform Association in the United States campaigned for land redistribution, the ten-hour day, abolition of slavery, etc., in the 1840s.

2. Compare II.5. The French Social Democrats were the same as the Réformistes mentioned in III.57. In IV.3, they are called Democratic Socialists, i.e., socialists (in the broad sense) who supported the movement for political reforms. (Marx and Engels rapidly became disillusioned with this current, which was swept to power in the 1848 Revolution and rapidly moved to the right.) The "great Revolution" means the French Revolution of 1789.

3. Like their French counterparts, the Swiss Radicals moved to the right following the 1848 Revolution. The main point, however, is that Communists critically support all movements making demands that can strengthen working-class

Study and discussion questions for this section begin on page 192.

onistic elements, partly of Democratic Socialists, in the French sense, partly of radical bourgeois.

¶4 Among the Poles, they support the party that insists on an agrarian revolution as the prime condition for national emancipation, that party which fomented the insurrection of Cracow in 1846.

¶5 In Germany, they fight with the bourgeoisie whenever it acts in a revolutionary way, against the absolute monarchy, the feudal squirearchy, and the petty-bourgeoisie.

¶6 But they never cease, for a single instant, to instill into the working class the clearest possible recognition of the hostile antagonism between bourgeoisie and proletariat, in order that the German workers may straightway use, as so many weapons against the bourgeoisie, the social and political conditions that the bourgeoisie must necessarily introduce along with its supremacy, and in order that, after the fall of the reactionary classes in Germany, the fight against the bourgeoisie itself may immediately begin.

¶7 The Communists turn their attention chiefly to Germany, because that country is on the eve of a bourgeois revolution that is bound to be carried out under more advanced conditions of European civilization, and with a much more developed proletariat than that of England was in the seventeenth, and of France in the eighteenth century, and because the bourgeois revolution in Germany will be but the prelude to an immediately following proletarian revolution.

¶8 In short, the Communists everywhere support every revolutionary movement against the existing social and political order of things.

self-activity. The tactic of forming temporary alliances with other social forces for immediate aims, even though those forces may have other goals hostile to workers' interests, is a precursor of what was later called the "united front."[29]

4. Poles were fighting the division of their country by Russia, Prussia, and Austria. The Cracow insurrection was defeated by Russia and Austria within a few weeks, but created enormous support for Polish independence throughout Europe.

5. Marx and Engels still believed the bourgeoisie would play a revolutionary role in feudal Germany. See III.27–28. The 1848 Revolution was to reveal that German capitalists were more worried by the working class than by feudalism.

6. At this time, Marx and Engels saw the victory of the bourgeoisie against the absolutist feudal state as the necessary prelude to socialist revolution. As Engels put it in the *Principles of Communism*: "Since the communists cannot enter upon the decisive struggle between themselves and the bourgeoisie until the bourgeoisie is in power, it follows that it is in the interest of the communists to help the bourgeoisie to power as soon as possible in order the sooner to be able to overthrow it."[30]

7. Marx and Engels believed that bourgeois revolution in Germany would be followed almost immediately by a working-class revolution. After the events of 1848—in which German capitalists were more worried by the workers' movement than by the old

¶9 In all these movements they bring to the front, as the leading question in each, the property question, no matter what its degree of development at the time.

¶10 Finally, they labor everywhere for the union and agreement of the democratic parties of all countries.

¶11 The Communists disdain to conceal their views and aims. They openly declare that their ends can be attained only by the forcible overthrow of all existing social conditions. Let the ruling classes tremble at a communist revolution. The proletarians have nothing to lose but their chains. They have a world to win.

¶12 WORKERS OF ALL COUNTRIES, UNITE!

absolutist state—they concluded that even the struggle for democratic rights had to be led by the proletariat, and that a bourgeois-democratic revolution would be part of a single process culminating in a socialist revolution. This is the theory of "permanent revolution," later associated with Russian revolutionary Leon Trotsky, but advocated first by Marx and Engels.[31]

8. Socialists support all progressive movements, whether or not those movements have socialist politics. Compare II.5.

9. Compare II.6 and II.12. By "the property question," Marx and Engels mean how society's economic resources will be controlled. Communists participate in all progressive movements, whatever their politics, while continuing to argue for working-class self-emancipation.

10. Communists seek to build alliances between all genuinely progressive forces.

11. Compare P.3. In saying that "proletarians have nothing to lose but their chains," Marx and Engels mean in the revolution that they believed was imminent. They are not claiming that workers under capitalism never possess anything of value. Revolution is necessary because the old ruling class will not give up its power in any other way. Compare I.51.

12. Compare II.53–56.

Notes

1. I capitalize the word "Communist" when referring to organizations that designate(d) themselves in this way (and the members of such organizations), and use "communist," lowercase, when referring to the general ideas of communism (and one who accepts them).
2. See Domhoff 2006 and Parenti 2010.
3. China was obviously not a preliterate culture, but it was regarded as inferior by the nineteenth-century British bourgeoisie.
4. The Chartist movement in Britain was the first mass workers' movement anywhere in the world. The Chartists organized large demonstrations in support of a charter of electoral reforms in the 1830s and 1840s. See also III.57 and IV.1.
5. For a comparison of Marx's and Lenin's views on these questions, see Molyneux 2003.
6. See Bakan 2004.
7. Wolff 2000.
8. See Ehrenreich 2001.
9. See Bowles and Gintis 2011.
10. See the extract from Marx 1859 in Appendix C.
11. The ruling class was worried that the production of a healthy new generation of workers might be seriously disrupted. For the effects of capitalism on the modern working-class family, see Rubin 1976.
12. For examples of the way in which ruling-class ideology pervades education, see Loewen 2018.
13. See the Child Labor Coalition website at http://www.stopchildlabor.org.
14. It should also be noted that, although the *Manifesto* says little about it, Marx and Engels believed the fight for national freedom against colonial or imperialist domination was generally progressive. For example, they supported Irish independence from England and national independence for Poland, which in the nineteenth century was controlled by Russia, Prussia, and Austria (see IV.4).
15. Lenin, the leader of the Russian Revolution of 1917, repeated the same argument in 1920: "We always staked our play upon an international revolution and this was unconditionally right. . . . We always emphasized the fact that in one country it is impossible to accomplish such a work as a socialist revolution." Quoted in Trotsky 1930, volume 3, appendix 2, "Socialism in a separate country."
16. Engels 1877, part I, chapter 9, "Eternal Truths." For Marx and Engels' views about religion, see Siegel 2005, chapter 2.
17. See Marx and Engels' preface to the 1872 German edition.
18. Elsewhere, Marx and Engels mention other ways in which the working class can exert control over the economy, including workers' associations and cooperatives.
19. Preface to the 1872 German edition.
20. See Burkett 2014 and Foster 2000.
21. In the United States, this movement was particularly associated with the philosopher John Dewey in the late nineteenth and early twentieth century. See Rippa 1997.
22. See Marx 1874 for elaboration of this point.
23. Quoted in Marx 1867, chapter 25, "The General Law of Capitalist Accumulation," section 4.
24. The writings of the German philosopher G. W. F. Hegel (1770–1831) were a major early influence on both Marx and Engels.
25. According to Dirk Struik (1971, p. 50), "the Prussian government actually used 'true socialist' arguments to convince the workers that feudal reaction was their true ally against the bourgeoisie."
26. Dickens 1842.
27. See Hill 1972 for an account of these movements.
28. For further discussion of utopian socialism, see Engels 1880.
29. See, for instance, Leon Trotsky, "On the United Front," in Trotsky 1924.
30. See Appendix B.
31. See Marx and Engels 1850.

Additional Materials

AFTERWORD

Is the *Manifesto* Still Relevant?

In 1998, the 150th anniversary of *The Communist Manifesto*—first published in London in February 1848—was widely noted. New editions of Karl Marx and Friedrich Engels' little pamphlet were issued, academic conferences about it were held around the world, articles discussing it were published in left-wing journals, and even the mainstream media paid some attention to the *Manifesto*'s birthday.

Only a few years earlier, following the collapse of the Soviet Union and its Eastern European empire, commentators across the political spectrum had declared Marxism to be dead. By contrast, much of the commentary on this anniversary was surprisingly favorable.[1] "Apart from Charles Darwin's *Origin of Species*," wrote the *Los Angeles Times* in an introduction to a symposium on Marx, the *Manifesto* "is arguably the most important work of nonfiction written in the 19th century." In his contribution to the same discussion, the conservative sociologist Daniel Bell praised the *Manifesto*'s description of capitalism as "a stunning, prescient statement."[2] An article in the *Washington Post* called Marx "an astute critic of capitalism."[3] Steven Marcus, professor of humanities at Columbia University, described the *Manifesto* in the *New York Times* as a "masterpiece" with "enduring insights into social existence."[4] Perhaps most interesting of all was a lengthy article published in the *New Yorker* a few weeks earlier in which staff writer John Cassidy announced "The Return of Karl Marx" and reported a conversation with an investment banker:

> To my surprise, he brought up Karl Marx. "The longer I spend on Wall Street, the more convinced I am that Marx was right," he

> said. . . . "I am absolutely convinced that Marx's approach is the best way to look at capitalism."

Later in the article, Cassidy explained why Marx may be "The Next Thinker":

> Many of the contradictions that he saw in Victorian capitalism and that were subsequently addressed by reformist governments have begun reappearing in new guises, like mutant viruses. . . . [Marx] wrote riveting passages about globalization, inequality, political corruption, monopolization, technical progress, the decline of high culture, and the enervating nature of modern existence—issues that economists are now confronting anew, sometimes without realizing that they are walking in Marx's footsteps.[5]

In fact, in recent years, more than one mainstream commentator has rediscovered Marx. In a 2005 book on globalization, for instance, right-of-center *New York Times* columnist Thomas Friedman quotes at length the passage in the *Manifesto* that describes how, under the impact of capitalist development, "[a]ll that is solid melts into air" (I.18) and declares that he is "in awe at how incisively Marx detailed the forces that were flattening the world during the rise of the Industrial Revolution, and how much he foreshadowed the way these same forces would keep flattening the world right up to the present."[6]

The financial crash of 2008, which brought the world economy to its knees, also saw a revival of interest in Marx's ideas in some mainstream publications. Articles began to reappear in mainstream media sources around the world talking about the return of Karl Marx. *Time* magazine even put the author of *The Communist Manifesto* on the cover of its European (though notably not its US) edition in early 2009 with the headline "What Would Marx Think?" The article inside drew attention to Marx's "trenchant diagnosis of the underlying problems of a market economy that is surprisingly relevant even today" and that "is almost uncannily prescient about globalization's costs and benefits."[7] Fourteen years later, with the global economy facing new crises in the post-COVID world, the German newsweekly *Der Spiegel* also put Marx on its cover, this time with the headline "Hatte Marx doch recht?" (Was Marx right after all?).[8]

All this attention to Marx's ideas in general and *The Communist Manifesto* in particular is certainly welcome. But—and of course there is a "but"—with few exceptions, such commentators have restricted their praise of the *Manifesto* to what it says about the nature and workings of the capitalist system. Yet Marx and Engels did not write the *Manifesto* as a piece of abstract economic analysis. It was intended as a revolutionary call to action—an explanation not only of what is wrong with society but of how it can be transformed to create "an association, in which the free development of each is the condition for the free development of all" (II.74). Central to this strategy for change is their claim that in the modern working class—the proletariat—capitalism has produced "its own grave-diggers" (I.53). In other words, Marx and Engels argue that capitalism has created a group of people with both the capacity and the interest to fight for the overthrow of the existing system and the emancipation of all humanity.

The claim that the proletariat is a revolutionary class is the heart and soul of *The Communist Manifesto*, yet it is precisely this claim that most observers—including some on the left—emphatically reject. The radical economist Edward S. Herman (1925–2017), for example, identified "two Karl Marxes." One Marx, according to Herman, "was an exceptionally intelligent and learned observer and analyst of capitalism" whose economic theories remain essential. The other "was the activist and enlightenment optimist, who foresaw an imminent collapse of a brutal capitalism and the ushering in of a classless state and utopia. This Marx was seriously mistaken."[9] The British historian and longtime socialist Eric Hobsbawm (1917–2012), in an introduction to an anniversary edition of the *Manifesto*, stated bluntly that "if at the end of the millennium we must be struck by the acuteness of the *Manifesto*'s vision of . . . a massively globalized capitalism, the failure of another of its forecasts is equally striking. It is now evident that the bourgeoisie has not produced 'above all . . . its own grave-diggers' in the proletariat."[10] And the left-wing academic Hans Magnus Enzensberger (1929–2022) argued, "The strength of the *Manifesto* is in its analysis and not in the remedies it offers" and that "the strength of Marxism lies in its ruthless negativity."[11]

It is, however, surely not the "ruthless negativity" of the *Manifesto* that has made it the second best-selling book of all time or that continues to ensure it a wide audience today.[12] It is precisely because Marx and Engels argue that society can be radically changed that the *Manifesto* has inspired its readers down the decades.

But how seriously should their argument be taken today? Almost a quarter of a century after the *Manifesto*'s first publication, Marx and Engels wrote in a new preface that while "here and there, some detail might be improved," the basic ideas of the *Manifesto* retained their relevance.

> However much the state of things may have altered during the last twenty-five years, the general principles laid down in the *Manifesto* are, on the whole, as correct today as ever [even though the] practical application of the principles will depend, as the *Manifesto* itself states, everywhere and at all times, on the historical conditions for the time being existing.[13]

I will try to explain why, in my view, Marx and Engels' judgment remains essentially correct today. It is, to be sure, easy enough to comb through the *Manifesto* to find the occasional rhetorical exaggeration, mistake, or failed prediction.[14] But its "general principles"—and above all, its call for revolutionary change—are, if anything, even more relevant to the world today than they were in the middle of the nineteenth century.

Capitalism

The *Manifesto* begins by discussing capitalism or, as Marx and Engels refer to it throughout, "bourgeois society."[15] By this, they mean societies, like our own, in which the bourgeoisie—"the class of modern capitalists, owners of the means of social production and employers of wage labor"— is the dominant economic, social, and political group.[16] What is striking about the opening pages of the *Manifesto* is how contemporary its description of capitalism sounds. Marx and Engels portray an immensely dynamic system that has a relentless drive to expand and that has developed society's productive capacities to levels undreamed of in earlier centuries. The source of this dynamism stems from the fact that capitalists produce for the market. In the sixteenth and seventeenth centuries, the huge expansion of trade brought about by voyages of discovery and subsequent European colonization allowed an emerging urban commercial class, particularly in England, to elbow aside the old "feudal system of industry, under which industrial production was monopolized by closed guilds" (I.8) and replace it with a system based on wage labor and "free competition" (I.26). In turn, competition created a relentless drive to conquer new markets, to expand production, and to find ways to produce more for less. This is why, they write, "[t]he bourgeoisie cannot exist without constantly revolutionizing the instruments of production" (I.18) and why, even by the mid-nineteenth century, its technical achievements had dwarfed those of earlier ruling classes.

In passages describing these achievements, Marx and Engels make clear why they regard the emergence of capitalism as a historically progressive development. The bourgeoisie

> has been the first to show what man's activity can bring about. It has accomplished wonders far surpassing Egyptian pyramids, Roman aqueducts, and Gothic cathedrals; it has conducted expeditions that put in the shade all former exoduses of nations and crusades. (I.17)

A little later, they return to the same theme:

> The bourgeoisie, during its rule of scarce one hundred years, has created more massive and more colossal productive forces than have all preceding generations together. Subjection of nature's forces to man, machinery, application of chemistry to industry and agriculture, steam navigation, railways, electric telegraphs, clearing of whole continents for cultivation, canalization of rivers, whole populations conjured out of the ground—what earlier century had even a presentiment that such productive forces slumbered in the lap of social labor? (I.24)

Of course, the past 175 years have witnessed technological developments that have far outstripped even these achievements, from the electric dynamo, the telephone, and the internal combustion engine, to radio and television, air travel, computers, satellites, biotechnology, cell phones, robots, and artificial intelligence. But what Marx and Engels describe is recognizably our own world, characterized as it is by a seemingly never-ending stream of technological innovations and scientific miracles.

Capitalism's drive to expand results not only in a huge increase in society's productive capacity but also in the expansion of the system itself as capitalist relations of production are imposed on every portion of the globe, leading to the integration of the whole world into a single economic system. As many recent commentators have noted, the *Manifesto*'s account of these processes is an almost uncanny picture of the modern global economy.

> The need of a constantly expanding market for its products chases the bourgeoisie over the whole surface of the globe. It must nestle everywhere, settle everywhere, establish connections everywhere.
>
> The bourgeoisie has through its exploitation of the world market given a cosmopolitan character to production and consumption in every country. To the great chagrin of reactionaries, it has drawn from under the feet of industry the national ground on which it stood. All old-established national industries have been destroyed or are daily being destroyed. They are dislodged by new industries, whose introduction becomes a life and death question for all civilized nations, by industries that no longer work up indigenous raw material, but raw material drawn from the remotest zones; industries whose products are consumed, not only at home, but in every quarter of the globe. . . . In place of the old local and national seclusion and self-sufficiency, we have intercourse in every direction, universal inter-dependence of nations. (I.19–20)

What is perhaps most remarkable about this description is that it fits the contemporary world far more closely than it does the world of the mid-nineteenth century.[17] Marx and Engels did not have a crystal ball, but in the *Manifesto*, they uncovered the underlying dynamic of the capitalist mode of production and extrapolated it into the future. This is the source of both the book's most brilliant predictions and some of its occasional errors.[18]

The opening pages of the *Manifesto* applaud capitalism for the material benefits it makes possible and for its tendency to undermine reactionary and insular ideas.[19] However, despite that, the *Manifesto* is primarily an indictment of capitalism. In comparison with earlier forms of society, capitalism is enormously dynamic and progressive. At the same time, for all its differences with the societies that it superseded, capitalism remains a system of class exploitation in which a dominating ruling class controls the wealth produced by the mass of the population. Indeed, precisely because of its dynamism and relentless drive to expand, capitalism is frequently even more dehumanizing and brutal than anything that came before it.

In a society in which the stock market rises each time new layoffs are announced and in which the average CEO earns 399 times as much as an ordinary worker, it is not hard to see that capitalism remains a system of sharp class divisions.[20] This economic inequality reduces democracy to a sham, ensuring that "[t]he executive of the modern state is but a committee for managing the common affairs of the whole bourgeoisie" (I.12).[21] Apologists for the system sometimes claim that, with the advent of such things as mutual funds and pension schemes, we are becoming a shareholder society in which wealth is more evenly distributed. But in fact, the concentration of wealth in the United States has reached record levels. According to a report issued by the Congressional Budget Office (CBO) in September 2022, the richest 1 percent of the US population controls more than one-third of the country's wealth, the top 10 percent controls 72 percent, while the bottom 50 percent controls only 2 percent. The lowest 25 percent has negative wealth, that is, more debt than assets, with outstanding student loans accounting for the majority of the debt.[22] If we exclude the value of principal residences, the disparities are even greater. In 2019, the three wealthiest US billionaires by themselves owned more than the bottom 50 percent of the population did, and in the years since, they have gotten even richer.[23] While most of the population became poorer during the height of the COVID pandemic, US billionaires saw their wealth increase by about $1.7 trillion, or 60 percent, from early 2020 to early 2022.[24]

Significant and long-standing differences between racial and ethnic groups also persist. According to the CBO, "In 2019, White families' median wealth was 6.5 times that of Black families, 5.5 times that of Hispanic families, and 2.7 times that of Asian and other families." Globally, the figures are even more astonishing. The world's ten richest men own more than the bottom 3.1 billion people do.[25] Fewer than five hundred people around the world own more than the combined income of more than half the planet's population. Nor is it hard to understand how the rich have acquired their wealth. To cite just one statistic, in the mid-1960s, wages for manufacturing jobs in the United States were equal to 46 percent of the value added in production, while this figure had dropped to 36 percent by 1990.[26] According to the Economic Policy Institute, "From 1979 to 2020, net productivity rose 61.8%, while the hourly pay of typical workers grew far slower—increasing only 17.5% over four decades (after adjusting for inflation)."[27] The capitalist class, in other words, is squeezing out more surplus value than ever from those who work for them, and even those who regard themselves as middle class are often just a single paycheck away from poverty.[28]

But capitalism is not just about inequality. The system itself has a kind of Midas touch—everything it encounters is turned into a commodity, an item to be bought or sold in the marketplace.[29] This applies to labor (or more precisely to labor power—the ability to work) as much as to anything else:

> [L]aborers, who must sell themselves piecemeal, are a commodity, like every other article of commerce, and consequently exposed to all the vicissitudes of competition, to all the fluctuations of the market. (I.30)

Market competition enforces strict labor discipline on the workforce, turning work into a stressful, tedious, and often humiliating burden for most of the population.

> Owing to the extensive use of machinery and to division of labor, the work of the proletarians has lost all individual character and, consequently, all charm for the workman. He becomes an appendage of the machine, and it is only the most simple, most monotonous, and most easily acquired knack, that is required of him. . . . Masses of laborers, crowded into the factory, are organized like soldiers . . . under the command of a perfect hierarchy of officers and sergeants. . . . [T]hey are daily and hourly enslaved by the machine, by the overlooker, and, above all, by the individual bourgeois manufacturer himself. The more openly this despotism proclaims gain to be its end and aim, the more petty, the more hateful, and the more embittering it is. (I.31–32)

At best, work becomes an unpleasant necessity. At worst, individuals can be physically or mentally destroyed by it. According to the economist Juliet Schor, "Thirty percent of [American] adults say that they experience high stress nearly every day; even higher numbers report high stress once or twice a week. . . . Americans are literally working themselves to death—as jobs contribute to heart disease, hypertension, gastric problems, depression, exhaustion, and a variety of other ailments."[30]

Life under capitalism is a rat race, not only inside the workplace but out of it as well. In a society constantly on the move, social relations are turned upside down. Capitalism encourages greed, competition, and aggression. It degrades human relations until they are frequently based on little more than "naked self-interest" and "callous 'cash payment'" (I.14). And while its supporters prattle on endlessly about "family values," capitalism itself rips families apart.[31]

> The bourgeois clap-trap about the family and education, about the hallowed co-relation of parent and child, becomes all the more disgusting, the more, by the action of modern industry, all family ties among the proletarians are torn asunder, and their children transformed into simple articles of commerce and instruments of labor. (II.45)[32]

Vast numbers of people are thus denied a truly human existence.

Capitalism's ceaseless drive to expand not only destabilizes all social relations—but also, sooner or later, undermines the conditions for economic growth itself. Marx and Engels argue that capitalism increasingly exhibits a tendency to run out of control. It is a system in which highly destructive economic crises are unavoidable and that has thus become fundamentally irrational.

> Modern bourgeois society, with its relations of production, of exchange and of property, a society that has conjured up such gigantic means of production and of exchange, is like the sorcerer who is no longer able to control the powers of the nether world whom he has called up by his spells. (I.27)

In a world threatened by pollution, global warming, and the destruction of ecosystems as the result of uncontrolled capitalist growth, this image perhaps has a special resonance.[33] In the twenty-first century, the search for profits threatens to destroy everything in its path, including the natural environment.

The *Manifesto* does not contain a fully worked-out economic theory—Marx was later to provide that in *Capital*[34]—but it does provide a description of recurring capitalist crises that fits the modern world remarkably well.

> For many a decade past, the history of industry and commerce is but the history of the revolt of modern productive forces against modern conditions of production, against the property relations that are the conditions for the existence of the bourgeoisie and of its rule. It is enough to mention the commercial crises that by their periodical return put on its trial, each time more threateningly, the existence of the entire bourgeois society. In these crises a great part not only of the existing products, but also of the previously created productive forces, are periodically destroyed. (I.27)

The periodic crises that the *Manifesto* describes have continued to plague capitalism ever since, despite repeated claims that they have become a thing of the past. In the past fifty years, for example, the United States and other large capitalist nations experienced sharp downturns in 1974–75, 1980–82, 1990–91, and 2001–02. The 2008 financial crisis, which continues to reverberate, was the biggest shock to the world economy since the Great Depression of the 1930s.[35] With each recovery, the ruling class declares that future prosperity is assured, only to be surprised by the occurrence of the next slump. The economic crisis in Asia in the late 1990s, for example, was totally unforeseen by bourgeois economists, who, until it happened, were still confidently predicting strong economic growth for the region.[36] The situation was similar before the 2008 crisis, as David McNally recounts:

> Clinging to the so-called Efficient Market Hypothesis (EMH), which insists that markets always behave rationally, the leading lights of the economic profession repeatedly proclaimed that systemic crises were no longer possible. "The central problem of depression-prevention has been solved," announced Nobel laureate Robert Lucas, in his 2003 presidential address to the American Economic Association. Meanwhile, the originator of EMH, Eugene Fama, haughtily dismissed those who predicted a financial crisis, telling an interviewer, "The word 'bubble' drives me nuts"—just as one of the greatest financial bubbles in history was exploding.[37]

Marx and Engels not only describe the pattern of periodic crises under capitalism but also explain the special form that crises take. In earlier societies, crises were the result of shortages in vital goods, but in the modern world, precisely the opposite is the case.

> In these crises there breaks out an epidemic that in all earlier epochs would have seemed an absurdity—the epidemic of overproduction. Society suddenly finds itself put back into a state of momentary barbarism; it appears as if a famine, a universal war of devastation, had cut off the supply of every means of subsistence; industry and commerce seem to be destroyed; and why? Because there is too much civilization, too much means of subsistence, too much industry, too much commerce. (I.27)

Capitalism is a system of competition between independent producers, each trying to make a profit by outselling its rivals. Since production is uncoordinated and since each capitalist wants to grab as large a part of the market as possible, each will attempt to produce to meet the available demand. By the time the goods reach the market, there may be a huge imbalance between supply and demand. If the oversupply is severe enough, it will force many producers out of business and raise unemployment, thus further increasing the gap between supply and demand. The resulting crisis forces millions into poverty even though more than enough material resources exist to meet their needs. People go hungry while food remains unsold or is destroyed, and they go homeless while buildings remain empty.

The recent history of the real estate development and construction industries in the United States, Britain, Japan, and elsewhere provides a sad example of this process at work. Encouraged by high property prices in the mid-1980s, developers launched a massive program of office-block construction that led to substantial oversupply by the end of the decade. The resulting fall in prices caused widespread bankruptcies, which put serious pressure on the financial system and was partially responsible for triggering a severe recession in the early 1990s. The crisis in Asia in the late 1990s followed a similar pattern, with high levels of investment leading to huge overproduction of electrical goods, steel, petrochemicals, cars, and ships. This is the underlying explanation for the financial and currency crises that overwhelmed the region in 1998.[38] Similarly, the global financial crisis in 2008 was triggered by the collapse of a housing bubble that had been produced by cheap money policies introduced to rescue the United States and world economies from the crises of the late 1990s and early 2000s.

Capitalist society has raised production to the point where everybody could be provided with a decent life—enough to eat, a comfortable place to live, health care, educational and recreational opportunities, and much more. Yet capitalism not only is unable to spread such material benefits equitably but also can no longer control the productive forces it has produced.[39] As Marx and Engels put it, "The conditions of bourgeois society are too narrow to comprise the wealth created by them" (I.27). Each successive crisis can be overcome only "by paving the way for more extensive and more destructive crises" (I.27). The problem is rooted in the nature of capitalism itself.

Private ownership and the anarchy of marketplace competition are no longer compatible with large-scale economic production integrated at the social and global levels. But is there a satisfactory alternative?

The working class

In the opening pages of the *Manifesto*, Marx and Engels offer a searing and stunningly accurate indictment of capitalist society. They describe how the system works, who benefits from it, and why it repeatedly plunges into crisis. However, they go on to argue that capitalism itself creates the material and social conditions for a far more rational kind of society—a society in which exploitation and oppression have been ended and all human beings can live rewarding and fulfilling lives. In the first place, as we have just noted, capitalism has raised the level of production to the point where, for the first time in history, poverty and hunger can be eliminated and an adequate standard of living can be shared by every human being. For this to happen, though, wealth and social power must be taken away from the tiny minority who currently possess them. But this minority will not give up its advantages willingly. Like ruling classes down the ages, it will do all in its power to protect its privileges. Since it controls the key state institutions—the government, the courts, the army, and the police—this creates a problem. Is there a social force with the capacity to challenge such a formidable opponent?

The lynchpin of the *Manifesto*'s argument is that capitalism itself has brought the requisite social force into existence:

> [N]ot only has the bourgeoisie forged the weapons that bring death to itself; it has also called into existence the men who are to wield those weapons—the modern working class—the proletarians. (I.29)

As capitalism develops, it socializes the labor process, bringing workers together in large urban centers and in bigger and bigger units of production. At the same time, the pressures of economic life tend to push workers together to fight back against their exploitation. And because of their key economic position, workers have the collective power to bring production to a halt by going on strike. It is this that gives the working class the ability to challenge the domination of the bourgeoisie.

Most workers do not begin with the goal of making a revolution, but as they are forced to engage in the class struggle to protect their own interests, "the collisions between individual workmen and individual bourgeois take more and more the character of collisions between two classes" (I.38) and begin to assume a political character. The economic class struggle thus has a tendency to become a struggle by the working class as a whole to win political power from the bourgeoisie. Eventually, this fight intensifies to such a pitch that it "breaks out into open revolution, and . . . the forcible overthrow of the bourgeoisie lays the foundation for the sway of the proletariat" (I.51).

> What the bourgeoisie therefore produces, above all, is its own gravediggers. Its fall and the victory of the proletariat are equally inevitable. (I.53)[40]

The *Manifesto*'s language is powerful, but can the dramatic scenario it outlines really be taken seriously today? Critics of Marx and Engels often focus on the rhetorical flourish ("equally inevitable") with which Section I ends, accusing them of holding some kind of metaphysical theory of history in which the triumph of socialism is preordained. But this is by no means what Marx and Engels mean.[41] To suppose otherwise is not simply uncharitable, it also ignores what the *Manifesto* states in its opening paragraphs. There, Marx and Engels note that class struggle may end in more than one way: "either in a revolutionary reconstitution of society at large, or in the common ruin of the contending classes" (I.2). As Hobsbawm noted, "[C]ontrary to widespread assumptions," the *Manifesto* "is not a determinist document" but rather "a document of choices, of political possibilities rather than probabilities, let alone certainties."[42] The question is not whether working-class revolution is inevitable but whether it is a realistic possibility in the twenty-first century.

Critics of Marxism raise two main objections to the claim that the working class has the potential to lead a revolution. The first is that the working class is becoming weaker, not stronger. Marx and Engels argued, "Society as a whole is more and more splitting up into two great hostile camps, into two great classes directly facing each other: bourgeoisie and proletariat" (I.5). Against this, many critics claim that the working class is in decline, becoming an ever-smaller part of the population in the most advanced economies. Thus, according to Enzensberger, the *Manifesto*'s "class analysis has turned out to be wide off the mark. . . . The demand for [industrial] labor has declined in a dramatic way, and the classical working class is dwindling rapidly." Daniel Bell agreed: "[T]he industrial proletariat has been shrinking in every advanced industrial society, while the economies are moving into a post-industrial state."[43]

This common objection rests on a number of fundamental confusions. In the first place, the key role that Marx and Engels assign to the working class depends not simply on its numbers but on its key position within the economy—its ability to shut down production and to galvanize various other sectors of society. Even where the working class is a minority, it still has the potential to play this role. Second, and more importantly, the argument profoundly misunderstands what Marx and Engels meant by the "working class." It is certainly true that in the advanced capitalist economies, the proportion of the workforce employed in manual labor has declined substantially in the present century. In 1950, manual workers constituted 41 percent of the workforce in the United States, for example, but their proportion had shrunk to less than 18 percent by 2021.[44] But Marx and Engels did not define the working class in terms of the specific work its members do. In particular, the membership of the working class is not restricted to manual, industrial, or manufacturing workers. Rather, it consists of all those who survive only by selling their ability to work. In their words, it is "a class of laborers, who live only so long as they find work, and who find work only so long as their labor increases capital" (I.30).[45] This definition applies not just to blue-collar factory workers but also to the vast majority of people who work in the service sector and in white-collar jobs. It makes sense to define the working class in this way because workers in all these areas are subject to similar sorts of economic pressures, no matter the precise nature of their work. Indeed, one of the most important trends of the past one hundred years has been the way in which members of the workforce who at one time regarded themselves as outside the working class—clerical workers, nurses, teachers, and others—have increasingly found themselves subject to the same harsh workplace discipline as traditional factory employees.[46] As a result, many workers in these occupations have joined unions and shown an increasing willingness to go on strike.

If we understand the working class in the way that Marx and Engels defined it, far from disappearing, it is now bigger than ever before. In the more developed capitalist countries, workers and their families constitute the vast majority of the population. In the United States, for instance, the figure is probably around 75 percent. If anything, the picture is even more dramatic in other parts of the world. When the *Manifesto* was first published, most of the world's population consisted of peasants engaged in agricultural production. Today, the spread of capitalism has created a huge working class in nearly every country in the world, from Asia to Africa to Latin America.[47] Marx and Engels have been proved right: "In proportion as the bourgeoisie, i.e., capital, is developed, in the same proportion is the proletariat, the modern working class, developed" (I.30).

But even if the working class is growing, does it still have the capacity to make revolutionary change? In his introduction to the *Manifesto*, Hobsbawm contended that Marx and Engels' argument no longer applies, if it ever did. According to Hobsbawm, they base their belief in the revolutionary potential of workers on the assumption that capitalism will bring about "the inevitable pauperization of the laborers"—an assumption that even in the 1840s "was not totally convincing."[48] In the 1990s, Hobsbawm found this assumption even less convincing.

> [G]iven the enormous economic potential of capitalism so dramatically expounded in the *Manifesto* itself—why was it inevitable that capitalism could not provide a livelihood, however miserable, for most of its working class or, alternatively, that it could not afford a welfare system? That "pauperism develops even more rapidly than population and wealth"? If capitalism had a long life before it—as became obvious very soon after 1848—this did not have to happen, and indeed it did not.[49]

In other words, workers are not likely to become revolutionary because capitalism is able to offer them enough (even if, perhaps, only just enough) to keep them relatively satisfied.

But the *Manifesto*'s prediction of working-class revolution does not depend on the claim that capitalism will inevitably drive workers' wages down to a bare physical subsistence level. It is true that Marx and Engels do make this claim more than once in the *Manifesto*. For example, they state:

> The average price of wage labor is the minimum wage, i.e., that quantum of the means of subsistence, which is absolutely requisite to keep the laborer in bare existence as a laborer. What, therefore, the wage laborer appropriates by means of his labor merely suffices to prolong and reproduce a bare existence. (II.22)

Obviously, this statement is at best an exaggeration, at least for the most developed capitalist economies. It is worth noting in passing, however, that Marx and Engels were not putting forward a doctrine of their own invention but repeating the then orthodox view of the bourgeois economists. In any event, they were soon to reject this view, coming to recognize that for periods of time, wages can show sustained growth under capitalism.[50] However, they were to make several points about such wage growth that explain why it does not undermine their basic argument. First, rising wages are quite compatible with a relative decline in the share of income going to the working class. Second, since basic needs are socially determined, rising wages do not necessarily eliminate poverty. Third, and most important of all, when capitalism goes into crisis, working-class living standards come under sustained attack, as they have in the United States and elsewhere over the past fifty years.[51] At a time when the ruling class is slashing welfare provisions in every advanced capitalist country and when workers around the world are being forced to work harder simply to stay in the same place, Hobsbawm's argument is unconvincing.

It is the fact that capitalism cannot avoid devastating crises, not the claim that wages can never rise or the claim that all workers are inevitably turned into paupers, that explains why Marx and Engels see workers as constituting a revolutionary class. The point has been well made by Hal Draper:

> Capitalism cannot, in the long run, solve the economic problem of providing a human life for the mass of the people. . . . This proposition is the basis of the class approach of Marxism. Without it you have no class approach, and cannot have one. If it is not true, there is no reason not to be a good liberal. . . .
>
> . . . The demand for more becomes revolutionary when it goes beyond the capabilities of the system to provide the "more." That is the link between the fight for reforms and social revolution from a Marxist perspective. It depends on the root idea that the economic problems of the system cannot be solved within the system. . . . All that Marx claims is that in the course of the fight for "more" out of the system—regardless of what it costs the system—the struggle becomes, in the end, a revolutionary struggle.[52]

The working class is not at all moments of its existence on the verge of revolution. For long periods of time, many workers may be satisfied with their lot under capitalism. But what Marx and Engels understood was that this state of affairs cannot last forever. The chaotic, turbulent, unplanned development of capitalist economies eventually throws whole societies into turmoil and turns even the most modest of working-class demands into a challenge to the system as a whole.

Moreover, the working class is in a position to fight for its demands even if the bourgeoisie declines to meet them. As Marx and Engels put it, "[W]ith the development of industry, the proletariat not only increases in number, it becomes concentrated in greater masses, its strength grows, and it feels that strength more" (I.38). This process is not a smooth one. It has many ups and downs. The *Manifesto* notes that the "organization of the proletarians into a class, and consequently into a political party, is continually being upset again by the competition between the workers themselves" (I.40). The ruling class attempts to weaken the working class further by exacerbating national, racial, and other differences. But such divisions can be fought and overcome as capitalism continues to intensify the class struggle. And because of their strategic economic position, workers—whether blue collar or white collar, industrial or service—have the power to "become masters of the productive forces of society . . . by abolishing their own previous mode of appropriation, and thereby also every other previous mode of appropriation" (I.48).

Marx and Engels can certainly be faulted for having, in 1848, an overoptimistic conception of how quickly these processes would work themselves out.[53] As the Russian revolutionary Leon Trotsky argued on the *Manifesto*'s ninetieth anniversary in 1938,

> The error of Marx and Engels with regard to historical delays flowed in part from the underestimation of the subsequent possibilities inherent in capitalism, and in another part from the overestimation of the revolutionary maturity of the proletariat.[54]

Since the mid-nineteenth century, however, capitalism has repeatedly shown that it cannot avoid periodic crises and that these crises may bring the barbarism of modern warfare in their wake. Meanwhile, the working class has grown ever larger, increasing its potential power to shut down the economy and to threaten the very existence of the ruling class. Even in the United States today, where unionization rates have been declining for years as a result of a fierce employers' offensive, a clear majority of the workforce would like to join a union, and this potential still exists.[55]

The argument is not just a theoretical one. Time and time again over the last 175 years, workers in countries around the world have shown their capacity for mass action and, not infrequently, revolutionary struggle. As Ian Birchall notes,

> The Paris Commune of 1871, when workers governed the city through recallable delegates, was followed by the Russian Revolution, the first years of which, despite foreign intervention and bureaucratic distortion, offer a model of what workers' democracy could be. Workers' democracy surfaced again in Spain in 1936–37 and in Hungary in 1956. And in recent years workers' struggles have thrown up new organizations—the French action committees of 1968, the Chilean *cordones* of 1973, the Portuguese workers' commissions of 1974–75, the Iranian *Shoras* of 1979 and the rise of Solidarity in Poland in 1980.[56]

None of these great movements proved successful in the long run. None succeeded in permanently ending the rule of capital and in building a society free of exploitation and oppression. But there is no more reason to believe in the inevitability of defeat than in the inevitability of victory. The revolutionary movements of the past show the potential of mass working-class action.

In the United States, too, there is a rich tradition of working-class and socialist struggle that stretches back more than two hundred years.[57] However, the socialist tradition in the United States has been marked by deep discontinuities, with periods of mass radicalization and activism followed by decades in which socialist ideas have barely existed. In both 1912 and 1920, Eugene Debs won nearly a million votes running as the Socialist Party's candidate for president (on the latter occasion from a federal penitentiary, after being jailed for a speech opposing the First World War). But Debs' successes, and the founding of the Communist Party in 1919, were followed by the Palmer Raids and a decade of reaction in the 1920s.[58] The 1930s witnessed the explosive rise of industrial unionism, the growth of the Communist Party to close to one hundred thousand members, and calls by the most radical sections of the workers' movement for the founding of a labor party. But the anticommunist witch hunts beginning in the 1940s, together with the political weaknesses of the movement itself (in particular, its identification of Stalinist Russia with socialism), resulted in the virtual disappearance of the Left in the 1950s. Most recently, the civil rights and antiwar movements of the 1960s radicalized a generation of Blacks, students, and other activists, leading literally millions to embrace some version of revolutionary politics. At the height of the antiwar movement, shortly after four million students had participated in a nationwide campus strike to oppose the invasion of Cambodia in the spring of 1970, the *New York Times* reported that three million of them believed that a revolution was needed in the United States.[59] Militant young workers, often Black, led wildcat strikes in the postal service and auto and other industries.[60] A new women's movement called for equal pay for equal work, abortion rights, and redefining gender roles and the family. Yet within a few years, this "New Left" had almost completely disappeared. The movements of the 1960s and 1970s disintegrated and were followed by a one-sided class war against workers and decades of political corruption, corporate greed, growing militarism, and efforts to roll back the gains of the social movements.

Although none of these periods of radicalization fulfilled their potential, the defeats and disappearance of the movements thrown up by them were by no means predestined. There is nothing inherent in the social structure or political culture of the United States that doomed them to failure. Rather, the collapse of these movements was ultimately rooted in weaknesses in the political understanding and strategies of the organizations and individuals that led them. The task of socialists today is to learn the lessons of past defeats and to use them to ensure victory in the future.[61]

Will there be new upsurges in struggle in the future? According to *World Protests: A Study of Key Protest Issues in the 21st Century*, which analyzed almost three thousand protests that occurred between 2006 and 2020 in 101 countries, covering over 93 percent of the world's population, we are currently in a historic period of protest.[62] According to the *Washington Post*, the authors

> looked at demonstrations between 2006 and 2020 [and] found that the number of protest movements around the world had more than tripled in less than 15 years. Every region saw an increase, the study found, with some of the largest protest movements ever recorded—including the farmers' protests that began in 2020 in India; the 2019 protests against President Jair Bolsonaro in Brazil and ongoing Black Lives Matter protests since 2013. . . .
>
> Looking closely at more than 900 protest movements or episodes across 101 countries and territories, the authors came to the conclusion that we are living through a period of history like the years around 1848, 1917 or 1968 "when large numbers of people rebelled against the way things were, demanding change."[63]

One of the study's authors is quoted as saying, "Too many leaders in government and business are not listening. The vast majority of protests around the world advance reasonable demands already agreed upon by most governments. People protest for good jobs, a clean planet for future generations, and a meaningful say in the decisions that affect their quality of life."[64] As well as protests focused on democracy and political representation, more than half of the protests studied were in response to rising inequality. Other issues included corruption, labor conditions, and reform of public services. There were also many mobilizations for racial and ethnic justice, including the Black Lives Matter protests in the United States.[65] But the report also notes that there are a smaller number of protests with right-wing politics "focused on denying the rights of others" and scapegoating racial, sexual, and national minorities—an important reminder that in times of crisis, the Right, as well as the Left, can grow.

In addition to thousands of significant political protests, McNally has drawn attention to a large increase in major strike activity since the 2008 financial crisis: "Across the decade since the Great Recession, we have witnessed a series of enormous general strikes (Guadeloupe and Martinique, India, Brazil, South Africa, Colombia, Chile, Algeria, Sudan, South Korea, France, and many more) as well as strike waves that have helped to topple heads of state (Tunisia, Egypt, Puerto Rico, Sudan, Lebanon, Algeria, Iraq)."[66] Some of these strikes have been linked to broader popular mobilizations in places such as Hong Kong, Chile, Thailand, Ukraine, Lebanon, and Iraq. In the United States, a wave of teachers' strikes in 2018–19 raised important issues of social reproduction. McNally argues that "the new strike movements are harbingers of a period of *recomposition* of militant working-class cultures of resistance, the very soil out of which socialist politics can grow."[67] None of this suggests that the working class has disappeared or become impotent.[68]

Toward communism

At the center of the *Manifesto*'s vision is the idea of working-class self-emancipation. As Engels puts it in his preface to the English edition of 1888, "[O]ur notion, from the very beginning, was that 'the emancipation of the working class must be the act of the working class itself'" (¶ 5). Working-class self-activity and self-organization is thus the key both to successful revolution and to the new form of society such a revolution would bring about. The most common argument against socialism today is that the collapse of the Soviet Union proves that no alternative to capitalism is possible. But the societies that collapsed in the Soviet Union and Eastern Europe had nothing in common with Marx and Engels' conception of socialism. Just as in the West, workers in these countries were exploited by privileged ruling classes. And while internal markets in these countries had largely been abolished, the pressures of military and economic competition on a world scale imposed on them the familiar capitalist dynamic of accumulation and growth. The demise of these state capitalist regimes is in no way an argument against the possibility of genuine socialism.[69]

But what would such an alternative society be like? Unlike the early utopian socialists, Marx and Engels do not offer a detailed blueprint for the future.

They are not interested in drawing up "the best possible plan of the best possible state of society" (III.51) or painting "fanciful pictures of future society" (III.53). Such dreams are no more than "castles in the air" (III.55), unconnected with "the material conditions for the emancipation of the proletariat" (III.48), and it is primarily with analyzing these material conditions that Marx and Engels concern themselves. But the analysis of these conditions does permit them to formulate in general terms the principles on which a socialist society could be based.

The first and vital step is to "raise the proletariat to the position of ruling class, to win the battle of democracy" (II.68). Democratic working-class control of society in both the economic and the political realms is the defining feature of the *Manifesto*'s conception of socialism. Without real democracy, there can be no socialism. But how is democratic power to be exercised? In the *Manifesto*, Marx and Engels do not speculate about this, but in their preface to the German edition of 1872, they point to the example of the Paris Commune—"where the proletariat for the first time held political power for two whole months"—as a concrete historical example of what they had in mind:

> One thing especially was proved by the Commune, *viz.*, that "the working class cannot simply lay hold of the ready-made State machinery and wield it for its own purposes."[70]

The existing capitalist state has been perfected as a mechanism to ensure bourgeois rule. A successful revolution would have to dismantle it and replace it with institutions that foster genuine participation by the majority of the population. The Commune instituted a number of important measures. The standing army was abolished and replaced by workers' militias. Police, magistrates, and judges were appointed by the community and could be quickly recalled. All elected officials were also revocable at short notice, and most were not professional politicians but workers or working-class leaders who were paid only workers' wages. The executive and legislative functions of government were combined so the Commune was not just a talk shop. Instead, it provided a first concrete example of the way in which workers' democracy could be achieved.

In the context of workers' democracy, the new society could advance toward its ultimate goals: the elimination of private ownership of the economy and production for the market and the final abolition of all class divisions. Marx and Engels are clear that such dramatic economic and social changes, unlike the seizure of political power, can only come about "by degrees" (II.69). But through such measures as nationalization of land, banks, and large-scale industry, combined with heavy taxation of the wealthy, the new society could gradually eliminate production based on market competition and replace it with workers' control of production and democratic planning designed to meet people's needs and provide them with the opportunity to develop as free individuals. At the end point of this process, when class divisions have finally disappeared, "the public power [i.e., the state] will lose its political character" (II.73), ceasing to be a means for one class to impose its will on another and becoming instead a forum for democratically resolving disputed issues.

There is one final aspect of the *Manifesto*'s vision that is important. Marx and Engels observe, "The proletariat of each country must, of course, first of all settle matters with its own bourgeoisie" (I.50). But the emphasis here is on *first*, for a little later they add, "United action, of the leading civilized countries at least, is one of the first conditions for the emancipation of the proletariat" (II.56). Capitalism, as we have seen, is an international system. For this reason, it is impossible for a single region to break free from capitalist relations of production on its own, at least for any significant period of time. Left by itself, the pressures of military and economic competition with hostile capitalist powers will ensure that the revolution does not survive. It was the isolation of the Russian Revolution of 1917 that eventually led to the defeat of the workers' government and its replacement by a new ruling class. Thus, the only way in which a workers' revolution can ultimately survive is if it spreads to other countries, since the resources needed to abolish scarcity are available only on an international level. But precisely because the world economy is more and more characterized by "universal inter-dependence of nations" (I.20) and "improved means of communication . . . that place the workers of different localities in contact with one another" (I.39), the prospects for such a revolution are better today than at any earlier time. The *Manifesto*'s final call for international solidarity is not just an abstract moral slogan; it is an essential precondition for the transformation of society.

Conclusion

The Communist Manifesto is the founding document of the revolutionary socialist tradition. It explains in outline why a socialist revolution is necessary and how it can come about. The *Manifesto*'s critique of capitalism is more relevant than ever. Its argument for the revolutionary potential of the working class has lost none of its original force. But Marx and Engels also understood that socialism could not come about without the active intervention of self-conscious revolutionaries. Such revolutionaries "point out and bring to the front the common interests of the entire proletariat, independently of all nationality" and "always and everywhere represent the interests of the movement as a whole" (II.5). They "fight for the attainment of the immediate aims, for the enforcement of the interests of the working class; but in the movement of the present, they also represent and take care of the future of that movement" (IV.2).

Capitalist crisis is inevitable, but socialist revolution is not. Capitalism may yet bring about "the common ruin of the contending classes" (I.2). Only the active intervention of organized revolutionaries—"the most advanced and resolute section" of the working-class movement, with a clear "understanding [of] the line of march, the conditions, and the ultimate general results of the proletarian movement" (II.6)—can bring about a different outcome. An urgent task facing those who want to replace the horrors of capitalism with a genuinely democratic society that will allow every human being to live a rewarding life is thus the rebuilding of revolutionary socialist organizations. There is still a world to win.

Notes

1. Though of course not all. The *Economist* dismissed Marx as a "nineteenth century economic crank" (February 28, 1998). Sixties-radical-turned-Republican-zealot David Horowitz went further, blaming Marx for millions of deaths under former Soviet dictator Joseph Stalin and others and comparing him to Hitler (*Los Angeles Times*, February 8, 1998). In 2005, *Human Events* (which describes itself as "The National Conservative Weekly") named the *Manifesto* the most harmful book of the nineteenth and twentieth centuries. Marx's *Capital* also made the top ten. By contrast, a BBC News Online poll in 1999 overwhelmingly voted Marx "the greatest thinker of the last 1,000 years."
2. *Los Angeles Times*, February 8, 1998.
3. *Washington Post*, April 20, 1998.
4. *New York Times*, April 26, 1998.
5. *New Yorker*, October 20 and 27, 1997, p. 248.
6. Quoted in Scialabba 2005. Scialabba comments that the quotation from Marx and Engels "towers over the intellectual landscape of the rest of the book like a mountain over low hills." It is worth adding that capitalism does not always move in one direction. There is a drive toward greater

global interconnection between economies but also sometimes a tendency for protectionism and greater state control in the interests of "national security." The relationship between these contradictory dynamics was discussed at the time of the First World War by the Russian Marxist Nikolay Bukharin. See Gasper 2017.

7. Peter Gumbel, "Rethinking Marx," *Time*, February 2, 2009.
8. Thomas Schulz, Susanne Beyer, and Simon Book, "Hatte Marx doch recht?" *Der Spiegel*, December 30, 2022. Marx is wearing a wind turbine pendant, a button with the slogan "There Is No Planet B," and has numerous tattoos, including a recycling symbol and a female symbol with a fist. This Marx is an ecosocialist and a feminist.
9. Herman 1998, pp. 131–32.
10. Hobsbawm 1998, p. 18.
11. *Los Angeles Times*, February 8, 1998.
12. "Last year when a new pocket sized edition was produced in Britain the publishers were amazed that over 60,000 copies were sold" (*Socialist Review* [Britain] 215, January 1998, p. 17). The claim about total sales comes from *The Guinness Book of World Records*.
13. Preface to the German edition of 1872, paragraph 2. Reprinted in Appendix A.
14. For example, Marx and Engels write, "National divisions and antagonisms between peoples are daily more and more vanishing, owing to the development of the bourgeoisie, to freedom of commerce, to the world market, to uniformity in the mode of production and in the conditions of life corresponding thereto" (II.54). While it is true that national differences and antagonisms have far from disappeared in the modern world (although to be fair, the *Manifesto* does not say that they will die out completely under capitalism), even Marx and Engels' errors often contain important grains of truth. The economic trends they point to are real ones, and national differences have survived them only because of the vigorous intervention of the ruling class. As Birchall (1998, p. 116) notes, "Nationalism as it has developed in the modern world is not a spontaneous product of the blood; it was fought for throughout two centuries by politicians and educationists, who strove to instill a sense of nationhood where none existed naturally," and it is thus "the result of a long, hard struggle by political and cultural means to create loyalty to the nation state, and a failure by socialist internationalists to effectively counter that loyalty." For Marxist analyses of nationalism, see Löwy 1976, Harman 1992, and Finn 2023.
15. The word "capitalism" does not occur in the *Manifesto*, although Marx and Engels do use the term "capitalist" in a few places (I.32, I.35, and II.18).
16. This is Engels' definition in a footnote added to the English edition of 1888.
17. See Birchall 1998, p. 114, and Hobsbawm 1998, pp. 17–18.
18. Some of the errors arise when Marx and Engels project a single tendency in a unilinear direction without taking into account the complicating effects of possible countertendencies.
19. As Marshall Berman (1998, p. 255) noted, the praise is sometimes "so extravagant, it skirts the edge of awe."
20. Josh Bivens and Jori Kandra, "CEO Pay Has Skyrocketed 1,460% Since 1978," Economic Policy Institute, October 4, 2022.
21. See Domhoff 2006, Parenti 2010, and Silverstein 1998. As former US Supreme Court justice Louis Brandeis reportedly once put it, "We can either have democracy in this country or we can have great wealth concentrated in the hands of a few, but we can't have both."
22. Congressional Budget Office, "Trends in the Distribution of Family Wealth, 1989 to 2019," September 22, 2022, p. 8.
23. Inequality.org, "Wealth Inequality in the United States," https://inequality.org/facts/wealth-inequality/.
24. Chuck Collins, "Updates: Billionaire Wealth, U.S. Job Losses and Pandemic Profiteers," May 6, 2022, https://inequality.org/great-divide/updates-billionaire-pandemic/.
25. Nabil Ahmed, Anna Marriott, Nafkote Dabi, Megan Lowthers, Max Lawson, and Leah Mugehera, "Inequality Kills," Oxfam Briefing Paper, January 2022.

26. World Bank data cited by *Left Business Observer*, November 9, 2001, http://www.leftbusinessobserver.com/Stats_earns.html.
27. Economic Policy Institute, "The Productivity–Pay Gap," October 2022, https://www.epi.org/productivity-pay-gap/.
28. See Warren and Tyagi 2003. In the contemporary United States, "middle class" generally means neither rich nor poor, but most of those in this category count as workers in Marxist terms.
29. "When did our seasons become fiscal quarters?" asks a billboard slogan I saw some years ago. Of course, this too was selling something.
30. Schor 1991, p. 11.
31. See Rubin 1976.
32. Schor (1991, pp. 26–27) notes, "Not only are more of the nation's young people working, but they are working longer hours. A 1989 nationwide sweep by government inspectors uncovered wide-scale abuses of child labor laws. . . . In large urban centers . . . [i]nspectors have found nineteenth-century-style sweatshops where poor immigrants—young girls of twelve years and above—hold daytime jobs, missing out on school altogether. And a million to a million and a half migrant farmworker children—some as young as three and four years—are at work in the nation's fields."
33. See Foster 1999, Angus 2016, Camfield 2022.
34. For an introduction to *Capital*, Volume 1, see Gasper 2006.
35. See McNally 2011 and Roberts 2016.
36. See McNally 1998.
37. McNally 2011, p. 15.
38. See Sparks 1998 and Hoveman 1998.
39. Oxfam, "The Food System Summit Failed Hundreds of Millions Going Hungry Everyday–Oxfam Reaction," September 24, 2021.
40. For more on the "gravedigger thesis," see Vidal 2018. Vidal emphasizes that Marx and Engels were talking about a potential, not about something that is inevitable.
41. As Draper (2020, p. 234) points out, *unvermeidlich*, the word in the German original, often "conveys nothing more than high hope and confidence in a hortatory context. . . . In practice, the *unvermeidlich* is counterposed to the accidental, in order to stress that a phenomenon obeys definite laws and is the outcome of causes that can be examined; it implies a scientific attitude towards causation, not a metaphysical one."
42. Hobsbawm 1998, pp. 27–28.
43. *Los Angeles Times*, February 8, 1998. A common related criticism, also made by Enzensberger, is that the *Manifesto* incorrectly predicts "all intermediate strata are doomed to disappear." In fact, it is a myth that Marx and Engels claim in the *Manifesto* or elsewhere that the middle class (or middle classes) will eventually vanish. See Draper 1978, pp. 613–27, and Draper 2020, pp. 226 and 282.
44. U.S. Department of Commerce, Bureau of the Census, *Historical Statistics of the U.S., Colonial Times to 1970* (1975); U.S. Department of Labor, Bureau of Labor Statistics, "Employment by Major Industry Sector," September 8, 2022, https://www.bls.gov/emp/tables/employment-by-major-industry-sector.htm.
45. In a footnote to the English edition of 1888, Engels defines the proletariat as "the class of modern wage-laborers who, having no means of production of their own, are reduced to selling their labor power in order to live."
46. This process is discussed in detail in Braverman 1974, a classic study.
47. Moody 2021.
48. Hobsbawm 1998, p. 21.
49. Hobsbawm 1998, p. 22.
50. For the development of Marx's views on this question, see Mandel 1971, ch. 9.
51. To cite one striking example, compared with 1969, by 1991 "the average employed person [in the U.S.] is now on the job an additional 163 hours, or the equivalent of an extra month a year" (Schor 1991, p. 29).
52. Draper 1970, p. 209–10.
53. Since revolutions were about to break out across Europe, their optimism is surely understandable. Following the defeat of the revolutionary movements and the stabilization of the European economies, Marx argued that it would be decades before another revolutionary crisis would emerge.

54. Trotsky 1938, p. 142.
55. "Seventy-one percent of Americans now approve of labor unions . . . the highest Gallup has recorded on this measure since 1965." Justin McCarthy, "U.S. Approval of Labor Unions at Highest Point Since 1965," Gallup, August 30, 2022.
56. Birchall 1998, p. 119. For analysis of the events in France in 1968, Chile in 1972, Portugal in 1974–75, Iran in 1979, and Poland in 1980–81, see Barker 2002.
57. Zinn 2003 provides an excellent introduction to this tradition. Also see Brecher 2020.
58. The Palmer Raids—organized by Woodrow Wilson's attorney general A. Mitchell Palmer and future FBI director J. Edgar Hoover—rounded up more than sixteen thousand leftists and radicals, who were held without trial for long periods. Most of the charges were later dismissed.
59. Katsiaficas 1987, p. 135.
60. On the role of Black revolutionaries in the auto industry, see Georgakas and Surkin 1998.
61. Davis 1986 is a useful analysis of part of this history. Moody 2022 discusses perspectives for socialists in the United States today.
62. Ortiz et al. 2021.
63. Adam Taylor, "Why Is the World Protesting So Much? A New Study Claims to Have Some Answers," *Washington Post*, November 4, 2021.
64. *Washington Post*, November 4, 2021.
65. For a Marxist analysis of the Black Lives Matter protests, and for a more general discussion of the relationship between race and class, see Taylor 2021.
66. McNally 2020, p. 20.
67. McNally 2020.
68. For more on the recomposition of the working class in the United States in particular, see Moody 2017 and 2022.
69. See Callinicos 1991.
70. The embedded quotation is from Marx 1871.

APPENDIX A

Prefaces from Later Editions[1]

The 1872 German edition

The Communist League, an international association of workers, which could of course be only a secret one under conditions obtaining at the time, commissioned the undersigned, at the Congress held in London in November 1847, to draw up for publication a detailed theoretical and practical program of the Party. Such was the origin of the following *Manifesto*, the manuscript of which traveled to London to be printed a few weeks before the February Revolution.[2] First published in German, it has been republished in that language in at least twelve different editions in Germany, England, and America. It was published in English for the first time in 1850 in the *Red Republican*, London, translated by Miss Helen Macfarlane, and in 1871 in at least three different translations in America. A French version first appeared in Paris shortly before the June insurrection of 1848 and recently in *Le Socialiste* of New York. A new translation is in the course of preparation. A Polish version appeared in London shortly after it was first published in Germany. A Russian translation was published in Geneva in the sixties. It was also translated into Danish, shortly after its appearance.

However much the state of things may have altered during the last twenty-five years, the general principles laid down in this *Manifesto* are, on the whole, as correct today as ever. Here and there some detail might be improved. The practical application of the principles will depend, as the *Manifesto* itself states, everywhere and at all times, on the historical conditions that exist at the time, and, for that reason, no special stress is laid on the revolutionary measures proposed at the end of Section II. That passage would, in many respects, be very differently worded today. In view of the gigantic strides of Modern Industry in the last twenty-five years, and of the accompanying improved and extended party organization of the working class, in view of the practical experience gained, first in the February Revolution, and then, still more, in the Paris Commune, where the proletariat for the first time held political power for two whole months, this program has in some details become antiquated. One thing especially was proved by the Commune, viz., that "the working class cannot simply lay hold of the ready-made state machinery, and wield it for its own purposes." (See *The Civil War in France; Address of the General Council of the International Working Men's Association*, 1871, where this point is further developed.[3]) Further, it is self-evident that the criticism of socialist literature is deficient in relation to the present time, because it comes down only to 1847; also, that the remarks on the relation of the Communists to the various opposition parties (Section IV), although in principle still correct, yet in practice are antiquated, because the political situation has been entirely changed, and the progress of history has swept from off the earth the greater portion of the political parties there enumerated.

But then, the *Manifesto* has become a historical document, which we have no longer any right to alter. A subsequent edition may perhaps appear with an introduction bridging the gap from 1847 to the present day; this reprint was too unexpected to leave us time for that.

Karl Marx & Frederick Engels
June 24, 1872, London

The 1882 Russian edition

The first Russian edition of the *Manifesto of the Communist Party*, translated by Bakunin, was published early in the sixties by the printing office of the

Kolokol.[4] Then the West could see in it (the Russian edition of the *Manifesto*) only a literary curiosity. Such a view would be impossible today.

What a limited field the proletarian movement occupied at that time (December 1847) is most clearly shown by the last section of the *Manifesto*: the position of the Communists in relation to the various opposition parties in various countries. Precisely Russia and the United States are missing here.[5] It was the time when Russia constituted the last great reserve of all European reaction, when the United States absorbed the surplus proletarian forces of Europe through immigration. Both countries provided Europe with raw materials and were at the same time markets for the sale of its industrial products. At that time both were, therefore, in one way or another, pillars of the existing European order.

How very different today! Precisely European immigration fitted North America for a gigantic agricultural production, whose competition is shaking the very foundations of European landed property—large and small. In addition it enabled the United States to exploit its tremendous industrial resources with an energy and on a scale that must shortly break the industrial monopoly of Western Europe, and especially of England, existing up to now. Both circumstances react in revolutionary manner upon America itself. Step by step the small and middle land ownership of the farmers, the basis of the whole political constitution, is succumbing to the competition of giant farms; simultaneously, a mass proletariat and a fabulous concentration of capitals are developing for the first time in the industrial regions.

And now Russia! During the Revolution of 1848–49 not only the European princes, but the European bourgeois as well, found their only salvation from the proletariat, just beginning to awaken, in Russian intervention. The Tsar was proclaimed the chief of European reaction. Today he is a prisoner of war of the revolution, in Gatchina, and Russia forms the vanguard of revolutionary action in Europe.[6]

The Communist Manifesto had as its object the proclamation of the inevitably impending dissolution of modern bourgeois property. But in Russia we find, face to face with the rapidly developing capitalist swindle and bourgeois landed property, just beginning to develop, more than half the land owned in common by the peasants. Now the question is: can the Russian *obshchina*,[7] though greatly undermined, yet a form of primeval common ownership of land, pass directly to the higher form of communist common ownership? Or on the contrary, must it first pass through the same process of dissolution such as constitutes the historical evolution of the West?

The only answer to that possible today is this: If the Russian Revolution becomes the signal for a proletarian revolution in the West, so that both complement each other, the present Russian common ownership of land may serve as the starting point for a communist development.

Karl Marx & Frederick Engels
January 21, 1882, London

The 1883 German edition

The preface to the present edition I must, alas, sign alone. Marx, the man to whom the whole working class of Europe and America owes more than to any one else—rests at Highgate Cemetery and over his grave the first grass is already growing. Since his death,[8] there can be even less thought of revising or supplementing the *Manifesto.* All the more do I consider it necessary again to state here the following expressly:

The basic thought running through the *Manifesto*—that economic production and the structure of society of every historical epoch necessarily arising therefrom, constitute the foundation for the political and intellectual history of that epoch; that consequently (ever since the dissolution of the primeval communal ownership of land) all history has been a history of class struggles, of struggles between exploited and exploiting, between dominated and dominating classes at various stages of social development; that this struggle, however, has now reached a stage where the exploited and oppressed class (the proletariat) can no longer emancipate itself from the class which exploits and oppresses it (the bourgeoisie), without at the same time forever freeing the whole of society from exploitation, oppression, and class struggles—this basic thought belongs solely and exclusively to Marx.*

I have already stated this many times; but precisely now is it necessary that it also stand in front of the *Manifesto* itself.

Frederick Engels
June 28, 1883, London

The 1888 English edition

The *Manifesto* was published as the platform of the Communist League, a workingmen's association, first exclusively German, later on international, and under the political conditions of the Continent before 1848, unavoidably a secret society. At a Congress of the League, held in London in November 1847, Marx and Engels were commissioned to prepare for publication a complete theoretical and practical party program. Drawn up in German, in January 1848, the manuscript was sent to the printer in London a few weeks before the French revolution of February 24. A French translation was brought out in Paris, shortly before the insurrection of June 1848. The first English translation, by Miss Helen Macfarlane, appeared in George Julian Harney's *Red Republican*, London, 1850.[9] A Danish and a Polish edition had also been published.

The defeat of the Parisian insurrection of June 1848—the first great battle between proletariat and bourgeoisie—drove again into the background, for a time, the social and political aspirations of the European working class. Thenceforth, the struggle for supremacy was again, as it had been before the

---

*"This proposition," I wrote in the preface to the English translation, "which, in my opinion, is destined to do for history what Darwin's theory has done for biology, we, both of us, had been gradually approaching for some years before 1845. How far I had independently progressed toward it is best shown in my *Condition of the Working Class in England*. But when I again met Marx at Brussels, in spring, 1845, he had it ready worked out, and put it before me, in terms almost as clear as those in which I have stated it here." [Engels' note, 1890]

revolution of February, solely between different sections of the propertied class; the working class was reduced to a fight for political elbow-room, and to the position of extreme wing of the middle-class Radicals. Wherever independent proletarian movements continued to show signs of life, they were ruthlessly hunted down. Thus the Prussian police hunted out the Central Board of the Communist League, then located in Cologne. The members were arrested and, after eighteen months' imprisonment, they were tried in October 1852. This celebrated "Cologne Communist trial" lasted from October 4 till November 12; seven of the prisoners were sentenced to terms of imprisonment in a fortress, varying from three to six years. Immediately after the sentence, the League was formally dissolved by the remaining members. As to the *Manifesto*, it seemed thenceforth doomed to oblivion.

When the European working class had recovered sufficient strength for another attack on the ruling classes, the International Working Men's Association sprang up.[10] But this association, formed with the express aim of welding into one body the whole militant proletariat of Europe and America, could not at once proclaim the principles laid down in the *Manifesto*. The International was bound to have a program broad enough to be acceptable to the English trades unions, to the followers of Proudhon[11] in France, Belgium, Italy, and Spain, and to the Lassalleans[12] in Germany. Marx, who drew up this program to the satisfaction of all parties, entirely trusted to the intellectual development of the working class, which was sure to result from combined action and mutual discussion. The very events and vicissitudes of the struggle against capital, the defeats even more than the victories, could not help bringing home to men's minds the insufficiency of their various favorite nostrums, and preparing the way for a more complete insight into the true conditions of working-class emancipation. And Marx was right. The International, on its breaking up in 1874, left the workers quite different men from what it had found them in 1864. Proudhonism in France, Lassalleanism in Germany were dying out, and even the conservative English trades unions, though most of them had long since severed their connection with the International, were gradually advancing towards that point at which, last year at Swansea, their President could say in their name: "Continental socialism has lost its terror for us." In fact, the principles of the *Manifesto* had made considerable headway among the working men of all countries.

The *Manifesto* itself came thus to the front again. Since 1850, the German text had been reprinted several times in Switzerland, England, and America. In 1872, it was translated into English in New York, where the translation was published in *Woodhull and Claflin's Weekly*. From this English version, a French one was made in *Le Socialiste* of New York. Since then, at least two more English translations, more or less mutilated, have been brought out in America, and one of them has been reprinted in England. The first Russian translation, made by Bakunin, was published at Herzen's *Kolokol* office in Geneva, about 1863;[13] a second one, by the heroic Vera Zasulich, also in Geneva, in 1882.[14] A new Danish edition is to be found in *Social-demokratisk Bibliothek*, Copenhagen, 1885; a fresh French translation in *Le Socialiste*, Paris, 1885. From this latter, a Spanish version was prepared and published in Madrid, 1886. Not counting the German reprints, there have been at least twelve editions. An Armenian translation, which was to be published in Constantinople some months ago, did not see the light, I am told, because the publisher was afraid of bringing out a book with the name of Marx on it, while the translator declined to call it his own production. Of further translations into other languages I have heard, but have not seen. Thus the history of the *Manifesto* reflects the history of the modern working-class movement; at present, it is undoubtedly the most widespread, the most international production of all socialist literature, the common platform acknowledged by millions of working men from Siberia to California.

Yet, when it was written, we could not have called it a *socialist* manifesto. By socialists, in 1847, were understood, on the one hand, the adherents of the various Utopian systems: Owenites in England, Fourierists in France,[15] both of them already reduced to the position of mere sects, and gradually dying out; on the other hand, the most multifarious social quacks who, by all manner of tinkering, professed to redress, without any danger to capital and profit, all sorts of social grievances, in both cases men outside the working-class movement, and looking rather to the "educated" classes for support. Whatever portion of the working class had become convinced of the insufficiency of mere political revolutions, and had proclaimed the necessity of a total social change, that portion then called itself communist. It was a crude, rough-hewn, purely instinctive sort of communism; still, it touched the cardinal point and was powerful enough amongst the working class to produce the utopian communism of Cabet[16] in France, and in Germany, of Weitling.[17] Thus in 1847 socialism was a middle-class movement, communism a working-class movement. Socialism was, on the Continent at least, "respectable"; communism was the very opposite. And as our notion, from the very beginning, was that "the emancipation of the working class must be the act of the working class itself," there could be no doubt as to which of the two names we must take. Moreover, we have, ever since, been far from repudiating it.

The *Manifesto* being our joint production, I consider myself bound to state that the fundamental proposition, which forms its nucleus, belongs to Marx. That proposition is: that in every historical epoch, the prevailing mode of economic production and exchange, and the social organization necessarily following from it, form the basis upon which is built up, and from which alone can be explained, the political and intellectual history of that epoch; that consequently the whole history of mankind (since the dissolution of primitive tribal society, holding land in common ownership) has been a history of class struggles, contests between exploiting and exploited, ruling and oppressed classes; that the history of these class struggles forms a series of evolutions in which, nowadays, a stage has been reached where the exploited and oppressed class—the proletariat—cannot attain its emancipation from the sway of the exploiting and ruling class—the bourgeoisie—without, at the same time, and once and for all, emancipating society at large from all exploitation, oppression, class distinctions, and class struggles.

This proposition, which, in my opinion, is destined to do for history what Darwin's theory has done for biology, we, both of us, had been gradually approaching for some years before 1845. How far I had independently progressed towards it is best shown by my *Condition of the Working Class in England*. But when I again met Marx at Brussels, in spring 1845, he had it ready worked out and put it before me in terms almost as clear as those in which I have stated it here.

From our joint preface to the German edition of 1872, I quote the following:

> However much the state of things may have altered during the last twenty-five years, the general principles laid down in this *Manifesto* are, on the whole, as correct today as ever. Here and there some detail might be improved. The practical application of the principles will depend, as the *Manifesto* itself states, everywhere and at all times, on the historical conditions that exist at the time, and, for that reason, no special stress is laid on the revolutionary measures proposed at the end of Section II. That passage would, in many respects, be very differently worded today. In view of the gigantic strides of Modern Industry in the last twenty-five years, and of the accompanying improved and extended party organization of the working class, in view of the practical experience gained, first in the February Revolution, and then, still more, in the Paris Commune, where the proletariat for the first time held political power for two whole months, this program has in some details become antiquated. One thing especially was proved by the Commune, viz., that "the working class cannot simply lay hold of the ready-made state machinery, and wield it for its own purposes." (See *The Civil War in France; Address of the General Council of the International Working Men's Association*, 1871, where this point is further developed.) Further, it is self-evident that the criticism of socialist literature is deficient in relation to the present time, because it comes down only to 1847; also, that the remarks on the relation of the Communists to the various opposition parties (Section IV), although in principle still correct, yet in practice are antiquated, because the political situation has been entirely changed, and the progress of history has swept from off the earth the greater portion of the political parties there enumerated. But then, the *Manifesto* has become a historical document, which we have no longer any right to alter.

The present translation is by Mr. Samuel Moore, the translator of the greater portion of Marx's *Capital*. We have revised it in common, and I have added a few notes explanatory of historical allusions.

Frederick Engels
January 30, 1888, London

Notes

1. In addition to the four reprinted here, Engels also wrote prefaces for the German edition of 1890, the Polish edition of 1892, and the Italian edition of 1893. None of these, however, add anything new. All the prefaces are available online at http://www.marxists.org/archive/marx/works/1848/communist-manifesto/preface.htm.
2. The February Revolution in France, 1848.
3. See Appendix C.
4. *Kolokol* was a radical Russian newspaper published first in London and later in Geneva by Alexander Herzen and Nikolai Ogaryov. The (inaccurate) translation of the *Manifesto* produced by *Kolokol*'s Geneva printer (though not published by the newspaper itself) was actually issued in 1869 (not "early in the sixties") and the Russian anarchist Bakunin was not the translator. (For the origins of this myth, see Draper 1994, pp. 41–43.) The 1882 translation was prepared by Georgi Plekhanov, later known as the father of Russian Marxism.
5. Section IV of the *Manifesto* does mention "the Agrarian Reformers in America" (IV.1), but Marx and Engels classify them as a working-class party, not a non–working-class opposition party.
6. On March 1, 1881, Tsar Alexander II was assassinated by Russian populists. To protect himself, his son and successor, the reactionary Alexander III, hid in Gatchina Castle, south of the capital St. Petersburg.
7. Peasant communes, which held land in common and made collective decisions about what crops to plant.
8. Marx died on March 14, 1883.
9. Harney was a radical Chartist.
10. The International Working Men's Association (IWMA), founded in London in 1864, was a broad organization of trade unionists, socialists, anarchists, and other radicals, in which Marx and Engels played prominent roles. After sharp political disagreements, particularly with supporters of the Russian anarchist Mikhail Bakunin, the IWMA was formally dissolved in 1876. Following the creation of the Socialist International (a grouping of socialist political parties from around the world) in 1881, the IWMA was often referred to as the "First International."
11. Pierre-Joseph Proudhon (1809–65) was a French anarchist who advocated small-scale property ownership and workers' co-operatives in the context of a market economy as an alternative to capitalism.
12. Ferdinand Lassalle (1825–64) was a German socialist who believed that capitalism could be ended by state action without a revolution.
13. See note 4 above.
14. The translator of the 1882 Russian edition was Georgi Plekhanov, not Zasulich. See note 4 above, and Draper 1994, pp. 60–61.
15. Followers respectively of Robert Owen (1771–1851), who set up a model mill town in Britain, and Charles Fourier (1772–1837), who described a socially harmonious ideal society in elaborate detail.
16. Étienne Cabet (1788–1856) wrote a novel describing an ideal communist community, which he and his followers later unsuccessfully attempted to put into practice.
17. Wilhelm Weitling (1808–71) was a German tailor who played a leading role in the League of the Just (predecessor of the Communist League) before it was influenced by Marx and Engels' views.

APPENDIX B

The Principles of Communism

1. What is Communism?

Communism is the doctrine of the conditions of the liberation of the proletariat.

2. What is the proletariat?

Engels, *The Principles of Communism* (October–November 1847)

The proletariat is that class in society which lives entirely from the sale of its labor and does not draw profit from any kind of capital; whose weal and woe, whose life and death, whose sole existence depends on the demand for labor—hence, on the changing state of business, on the vagaries of unbridled competition. The proletariat, or the class of proletarians, is, in a word, the working class of the nineteenth century.

3. Proletarians, then, have not always existed?

No. There have always been poor and working classes; and the working class has mostly been poor. But there have not always been workers and poor people living under conditions as they are today; in other words, there have not always been proletarians, any more than there has always been free unbridled competition.

4. How did the proletariat originate?

The proletariat originated in the Industrial Revolution, which took place in England in the last half of the last (eighteenth) century, and which has since then been repeated in all the civilized countries of the world.

This Industrial Revolution was precipitated by the discovery of the steam engine, various spinning machines, the mechanical loom, and a whole series of other mechanical devices. These machines, which were very expensive and hence could be bought only by big capitalists, altered the whole mode of production and displaced the former workers, because the machines turned out cheaper and better commodities than the workers could produce with their inefficient spinning wheels and handlooms. The machines delivered industry wholly into the hands of the big capitalists and rendered entirely worthless the meager property of the workers (tools, looms, etc.). The result was that the capitalists soon had everything in their hands and nothing remained to the workers. This marked the introduction of the factory system into the textile industry.

Once the impulse to the introduction of machinery and the factory system had been given, this system spread quickly to all other branches of industry, especially cloth- and book-printing, pottery, and the metal industries.

Labor was more and more divided among the individual workers so that the worker who previously had done a complete piece of work now did only a part of that piece. This division of labor made it possible to produce things faster and cheaper. It reduced the activity of the individual worker to simple, endlessly repeated mechanical motions which could be performed not only as well but much better by a machine. In this way, all these industries fell, one after another, under the dominance of steam, machinery, and the factory system, just as spinning and weaving had already done.

But at the same time, they also fell into the hands of big capitalists, and their workers were deprived of whatever independence remained to them. Gradually, not only genuine manufacture but also handicrafts came within the province of the factory system as big capitalists increasingly displaced the small master craftsmen by setting up huge workshops, which saved many expenses and permitted an elaborate division of labor.

This is how it has come about that in civilized countries at the present time nearly all kinds of labor are performed in factories—and, in nearly all branches of work, handicrafts and manufacture have been superseded. This process has, to an ever greater degree, ruined the old middle class, especially the small handicraftsmen; it has entirely transformed the condition of the workers; and two new classes have been created which are gradually swallowing up all the others. These are:

(i) The class of big capitalists, who, in all civilized countries, are already in almost exclusive possession of all the means of subsistence and of the instruments (machines, factories) and materials necessary for the production of the means of subsistence. This is the bourgeois class, or the bourgeoisie.

(ii) The class of the wholly propertyless, who are obliged to sell their labor to the bourgeoisie in order to get, in exchange, the means of subsistence for their support. This is called the class of proletarians, or the proletariat.

5. Under what conditions does this sale of the labor of the proletarians to the bourgeoisie take place?

Labor is a commodity, like any other, and its price is therefore determined by exactly the same laws that apply to other commodities. In a regime of big industry or of free competition—as we shall see, the two come to the same thing—the price of a commodity is, on the average, always equal to its cost of production. Hence, the price of labor is also equal to the cost of production of labor.

But, the costs of production of labor consist of precisely the quantity of means of subsistence necessary to enable the worker to continue working, and to prevent the working class from dying out. The worker will therefore get no more for his labor than is necessary for this purpose; the price of labor, or the wage, will, in other words, be the lowest, the minimum, required for the maintenance of life.

However, since business is sometimes better and sometimes worse, it follows that the worker sometimes gets more and sometimes gets less for his commodities. But, again, just as the industrialist, on the average of good times and bad, gets no more and no less for his commodities than what they cost, similarly on the average the worker gets no more and no less than his minimum.

This economic law of wages operates the more strictly the greater the degree to which big industry has taken possession of all branches of production.

6. What working classes were there before the Industrial Revolution?

The working classes have always, according to the different stages of development of society, lived in different circumstances and had different relations to the owning and ruling classes.

In antiquity, the workers were the slaves of the owners, just as they still are in many backward countries and even in the southern part of the United States.

In the Middle Ages, they were the serfs of the land-owning nobility, as they still are in Hungary, Poland, and Russia. In the Middle Ages, and indeed right up to the industrial revolution, there were also journeymen in the cities who worked in the service of petty bourgeois masters. Gradually, as manufacture developed, these journeymen became manufacturing workers who were even then employed by larger capitalists.

7. In what way do proletarians differ from slaves?

The slave is sold once and for all; the proletarian must sell himself daily and hourly.

The individual slave, property of one master, is assured an existence, however miserable it may be, because of the master's interest. The individual proletarian, property as it were of the entire bourgeois class which buys his labor only when someone has need of it, has no secure existence. This existence is assured only to the class as a whole.

The slave is outside competition; the proletarian is in it and experiences all its vagaries.

The slave counts as a thing, not as a member of society. Thus, the slave can have a better existence than the proletarian, while the proletarian belongs to a higher stage of social development and, himself, stands on a higher social level than the slave.

The slave frees himself when, of all the relations of private property, he abolishes only the relation of slavery and thereby becomes a proletarian; the proletarian can free himself only by abolishing private property in general.

8. In what way do proletarians differ from serfs?

The serf possesses and uses an instrument of production, a piece of land, in exchange for which he gives up a part of his product or part of the services of his labor.

The proletarian works with the instruments of production of another, for the account of this other, in exchange for a part of the product.

The serf gives up, the proletarian receives. The serf has an assured existence, the proletarian has not. The serf is outside competition, the proletarian is in it.

The serf liberates himself in one of three ways: either he runs away to the city and there becomes a handicraftsman; or, instead of products and services, he gives money to his lord and thereby becomes a free tenant; or he overthrows his feudal lord and himself becomes a property owner. In short, by one route or another, he gets into the owning class and enters into competition. The proletarian liberates himself by abolishing competition, private property, and all class differences.

9. In what way do proletarians differ from handicraftsmen?

In contrast to the proletarian, the so-called handicraftsman, as he still existed almost everywhere in the past (eighteenth) century and still exists here and there at present, is a proletarian at most temporarily. His goal is to acquire capital himself wherewith to exploit other workers. He can often achieve this goal where guilds still exist or where freedom from guild restrictions has not yet led to the introduction of factory-style methods into the crafts nor yet to fierce competition. But as soon as the factory system has been introduced into the crafts and competition flourishes fully, this perspective dwindles away and the handicraftsman becomes more and more a proletarian. The handicraftsman therefore frees himself by becoming either bourgeois or entering the middle class in general, or becoming a proletarian because of competition (as is now more often the case). In which case he can free himself by joining the proletarian movement, i.e., the more or less communist movement.[1]

10. In what way do proletarians differ from manufacturing workers?

The manufacturing worker of the sixteenth to the eighteenth centuries still had, with but few exception, an instrument of production in his own possession

—his loom, the family spinning wheel, a little plot of land which he cultivated in his spare time. The proletarian has none of these things.

The manufacturing worker almost always lives in the countryside and in a more or less patriarchal relation to his landlord or employer; the proletarian lives, for the most part, in the city and his relation to his employer is purely a cash relation.

The manufacturing worker is torn out of his patriarchal relation by big industry, loses whatever property he still has, and in this way becomes a proletarian.

11. What were the immediate consequences of the Industrial Revolution and of the division of society into bourgeoisie and proletariat?

First, the lower and lower prices of industrial products brought about by machine labor totally destroyed, in all countries of the world, the old system of manufacture or industry based upon hand labor.

In this way, all semi-barbarian countries, which had hitherto been more or less strangers to historical development, and whose industry had been based on manufacture, were violently forced out of their isolation. They bought the cheaper commodities of the English and allowed their own manufacturing workers to be ruined. Countries which had known no progress for thousands of years—for example, India—were thoroughly revolutionized, and even China is now on the way to a revolution.

We have come to the point where a new machine invented in England deprives millions of Chinese workers of their livelihood within a year's time.

In this way, big industry has brought all the people of the Earth into contact with each other, has merged all local markets into one world market, has spread civilization and progress everywhere and has thus ensured that whatever happens in civilized countries will have repercussions in all other countries.

It follows that if the workers in England or France now liberate themselves, this must set off revolution in all other countries—revolutions which, sooner or later, must accomplish the liberation of their respective working class.

Second, wherever big industries displaced manufacture, the bourgeoisie developed in wealth and power to the utmost and made itself the first class of the country. The result was that wherever this happened, the bourgeoisie took political power into its own hands and displaced the hitherto ruling classes, the aristocracy, the guildmasters, and their representative, the absolute monarchy.

The bourgeoisie annihilated the power of the aristocracy, the nobility, by abolishing the entailment of estates—in other words, by making landed property subject to purchase and sale, and by doing away with the special privileges of the nobility. It destroyed the power of the guildmasters by abolishing guilds and handicraft privileges. In their place, it put competition—that is, a state of society in which everyone has the right to enter into any branch of industry, the only obstacle being a lack of the necessary capital.

The introduction of free competition is thus public declaration that from now on the members of society are unequal only to the extent that their capitals are unequal, that capital is the decisive power, and that therefore the capitalists, the bourgeoisie, have become the first class in society.

Free competition is necessary for the establishment of big industry, because it is the only condition of society in which big industry can make its way.

Having destroyed the social power of the nobility and the guildmasters, the bourgeois also destroyed their political power. Having raised itself to the actual position of first class in society, it proclaims itself to be also the dominant political class. This it does through the introduction of the representative system which rests on bourgeois equality before the law and the recognition of free competition, and in European countries takes the form of constitutional monarchy. In these constitutional monarchies, only those who possess a certain capital are voters—that is to say, only members of the bourgeoisie. These bourgeois voters choose the deputies, and these bourgeois deputies, by using their right to refuse to vote taxes, choose a bourgeois government.

Third, everywhere the proletariat develops in step with the bourgeoisie. In proportion, as the bourgeoisie grows in wealth, the proletariat grows in numbers. For, since the proletarians can be employed only by capital, and since capital extends only through employing labor, it follows that the growth of the proletariat proceeds at precisely the same pace as the growth of capital.

Simultaneously, this process draws members of the bourgeoisie and proletarians together into the great cities where industry can be carried on most profitably, and by thus throwing great masses in one spot it gives to the proletarians a consciousness of their own strength.

Moreover, the further this process advances, the more new labor-saving machines are invented, the greater is the pressure exercised by big industry on wages, which, as we have seen, sink to their minimum and therewith render the condition of the proletariat increasingly unbearable. The growing dissatisfaction of the proletariat thus joins with its rising power to prepare a proletarian social revolution.

12. What were the further consequences of the Industrial Revolution?

Big industry created in the steam engine, and other machines, the means of endlessly expanding industrial production, speeding it up, and cutting its costs. With production thus facilitated, the free competition, which is necessarily bound up with big industry, assumed the most extreme forms; a multitude of capitalists invaded industry, and, in a short while, more was produced than was needed.

As a consequence, finished commodities could not be sold, and a so-called commercial crisis broke out. Factories had to be closed, their owners went bankrupt, and the workers were without bread. Deepest misery reigned everywhere.

After a time, the superfluous products were sold, the factories began to operate again, wages rose, and gradually business got better than ever.

But it was not long before too many commodities were again produced and a new crisis broke out, only to follow the same course as its predecessor.

Ever since the beginning of this (nineteenth) century, the condition of industry has constantly fluctuated between periods of prosperity and periods of crisis; nearly every five to seven years, a fresh crisis has intervened, always with the greatest hardship for workers, and always accompanied by general revolutionary stirrings and the direct peril to the whole existing order of things.

13. What follows from these periodic commercial crises?

First: That, though big industry in its earliest stage created free competition, it has now outgrown free competition; that, for big industry, competition and generally the individualistic organization of production have become a fetter which it must and will shatter; that, so long as big industry remains on its present footing, it can be maintained only at the cost of general chaos every seven years, each time threatening the whole of civilization and not only plunging the proletarians into misery but also ruining large sections of the bourgeoisie; hence, either that big industry must itself be given up, which is an absolute impossibility, or that it makes unavoidably necessary an entirely new organization of society in which production is no longer directed by mutually competing individual industrialists but rather by the whole society operating according to a definite plan and taking account of the needs of all.

Second: That big industry, and the limitless expansion of production which it makes possible, bring within the range of feasibility a social order in which so much is produced that every member of society will be in a position to exercise and develop all his powers and faculties in complete freedom.

It thus appears that the very qualities of big industry which, in our present-day society, produce misery and crises are those which, in a different form of society, will abolish this misery and these catastrophic depressions.

We see with the greatest clarity:

(i) That all these evils are from now on to be ascribed solely to a social order which no longer corresponds to the requirements of the real situation; and

(ii) That it is possible, through a new social order, to do away with these evils altogether.

14. What will this new social order have to be like?

Above all, it will have to take the control of industry and of all branches of production out of the hands of mutually competing individuals, and instead institute a system in which all these branches of production are operated by society as a whole—that is, for the common account, according to a common plan, and with the participation of all members of society.

It will, in other words, abolish competition and replace it with association.

Moreover, since the management of industry by individuals necessarily implies private property, and since competition is in reality merely the manner and form in which the control of industry by private property owners expresses itself, it follows that private property cannot be separated from competition and the individual management of industry. Private property must, therefore, be abolished and in its place must come the common utilization of all instruments of production and the distribution of all products according to common agreement—in a word, what is called the communal ownership of goods.

In fact, the abolition of private property is, doubtless, the shortest and most significant way to characterize the revolution in the whole social order which has been made necessary by the development of industry—and for this reason it is rightly advanced by communists as their main demand.

15. Was not the abolition of private property possible at an earlier time?

No. Every change in the social order, every revolution in property relations, is the necessary consequence of the creation of new forces of production which no longer fit into the old property relations.

Private property has not always existed.

When, towards the end of the Middle Ages, there arose a new mode of production which could not be carried on under the then existing feudal and guild forms of property, this manufacture, which had outgrown the old property relations, created a new property form, private property. And for manufacture and the earliest stage of development of big industry, private property was the only possible property form; the social order based on it was the only possible social order.

So long as it is not possible to produce so much that there is enough for all, with more left over for expanding the social capital and extending the forces of production—so long as this is not possible, there must always be a ruling class directing the use of society's productive forces, and a poor, oppressed class. How these classes are constituted depends on the stage of development.

The agrarian Middle Ages give us the baron and the serf; the cities of the later Middle Ages show us the guildmaster and the journeyman and the day laborer; the seventeenth century has its manufacturing workers; the nineteenth has big factory owners and proletarians.

It is clear that, up to now, the forces of production have never been developed to the point where enough could be developed for all, and that private property has become a fetter and a barrier in relation to the further development of the forces of production.

Now, however, the development of big industry has ushered in a new period. Capital and the forces of production have been expanded to an unprecedented extent, and the means are at hand to multiply them without limit in the near future. Moreover, the forces of production have been concentrated in the hands of a few bourgeois, while the great mass of the people are more and more falling into the proletariat, their situation becoming more wretched and intolerable in proportion to the increase of wealth of the bourgeoisie. And finally, these mighty and easily extended forces of production have so far outgrown private property and the bourgeoisie, that they threaten at any moment to unleash the most violent disturbances of the social order. Now, under these conditions, the abolition of private property has become not only possible but absolutely necessary.

16. Will the peaceful abolition of private property be possible?

It would be desirable if this could happen, and the communists would certainly be the last to oppose it. Communists know only too well that all conspiracies are not only useless, but even harmful. They know all too well that revolutions are not made intentionally and arbitrarily, but that, everywhere and always, they have been the necessary consequence of conditions which were wholly independent of the will and direction of individual parties and entire classes.

But they also see that the development of the proletariat in nearly all civilized countries has been violently suppressed, and that in this way the opponents of communism have been working toward a revolution with all their strength. If the oppressed proletariat is finally driven to revolution, then we communists will defend the interests of the proletarians with deeds as we now defend them with words.

17. Will it be possible for private property to be abolished at one stroke?

No, no more than existing forces of production can at one stroke be multiplied to the extent necessary for the creation of a communal society.

In all probability, the proletarian revolution will transform existing society gradually and will be able to abolish private property only when the means of production are available in sufficient quantity.

18. What will be the course of this revolution?

Above all, it will establish a democratic constitution, and through this, the direct or indirect dominance of the proletariat. Direct in England, where the proletarians are already a majority of the people. Indirect in France and Germany, where the majority of the people consists not only of proletarians, but also of small peasants and petty bourgeois who are in the process of falling into the proletariat, who are more and more dependent in all their political interests on the proletariat, and who must, therefore, soon adapt to the demands of the proletariat. Perhaps this will cost a second struggle, but the outcome can only be the victory of the proletariat.

Democracy would be wholly valueless to the proletariat if it were not immediately used as a means for putting through measures directed against private property and ensuring the livelihood of the proletariat. The main measures, emerging as the necessary result of existing relations, are the following:

(i) Limitation of private property through progressive taxation, heavy inheritance taxes, abolition of inheritance through collateral lines (brothers, nephews, etc.), forced loans, etc.

(ii) Gradual expropriation of landowners, industrialists, railroad magnates, and shipowners, partly through competition by state industry, partly directly through compensation in the form of bonds.

(iii) Confiscation of the possessions of all emigrants and rebels against the majority of the people.

(iv) Organization of labor or employment of proletarians on publicly owned land, in factories and workshops, with competition among the workers being abolished and with the factory owners, in so far as they still exist, being obliged to pay the same high wages as those paid by the state.

(v) An equal obligation on all members of society to work until such time as private property has been completely abolished. Formation of industrial armies, especially for agriculture.

(vi) Centralization of money and credit in the hands of the state through a national bank with state capital, and the suppression of all private banks and bankers.

(vii) Increase in the number of national factories, workshops, railroads, ships; bringing new lands into cultivation and improvement of land already under cultivation—all in proportion to the growth of the capital and labor force at the disposal of the nation.

(viii) Education of all children, from the moment they can leave their mother's care, in national establishments at national cost. Education and production together.

(ix) Construction, on public lands, of great palaces as communal dwellings for associated groups of citizens engaged in both industry and agriculture and combining in their way of life the advantages of urban and rural conditions while avoiding the one-sidedness and drawbacks of each.

(x) Destruction of all unhealthy and badly built dwellings in urban districts.

(xi) Equal inheritance rights for children born in and out of wedlock.

(xii) Concentration of all means of transportation in the hands of the nation.

It is impossible, of course, to carry out all these measures at once. But one will always bring others in its wake. Once the first radical attack on private property has been launched, the proletariat will find itself forced to go ever further, to concentrate increasingly in the hands of the state all capital, all agriculture, all transport, all trade. All the foregoing measures are directed to this end; and they will become practicable and feasible, capable of producing their centralizing effects to precisely the degree that the proletariat, through its labor, multiplies the country's productive forces.

Finally, when all capital, all production, all exchange have been brought together in the hands of the nation, private property will disappear of its own accord, money will become superfluous, and production will so expand and man so change that society will be able to slough off whatever of its old economic habits may remain.

19. Will it be possible for this revolution to take place in one country alone?

No. By creating the world market, big industry has already brought all the peoples of the Earth, and especially the civilized peoples, into such close relation with one another that none is independent of what happens to the others.

Further, it has coordinated the social development of the civilized countries to such an extent that, in all of them, bourgeoisie and proletariat have become the decisive classes, and the struggle between them the great struggle of the day. It follows that the communist revolution will not merely be a national phenomenon but must take place simultaneously in all civilized countries—that is to say, at least in England, America, France, and Germany.

It will develop in each of these countries more or less rapidly, according as one country or the other has a more developed industry, greater wealth, a more significant mass of productive forces. Hence, it will go slowest and will meet most obstacles in Germany, most rapidly and with the fewest difficulties in England. It will have a powerful impact on the other countries of the world, and will radically alter the course of development which they have followed up to now, while greatly stepping up its pace.

It is a universal revolution and will, accordingly, have a universal range.

20. What will be the consequences of the ultimate disappearance of private property?

Society will take all forces of production and means of commerce, as well as the exchange and distribution of products, out of the hands of private capitalists and will manage them in accordance with a plan based on the availability of resources and the needs of the whole society. In this way, most important of all, the evil consequences which are now associated with the conduct of big industry will be abolished.

There will be no more crises; the expanded production, which for the present order of society is overproduction and hence a prevailing cause of misery, will then be insufficient and in need of being expanded much further. Instead of generating misery, overproduction will reach beyond the elementary requirements of society to assure the satisfaction of the needs of all; it will create new needs and, at the same time, the means of satisfying them. It will become the condition of, and the stimulus to, new progress, which will no longer throw the whole social order into confusion, as progress has always done in the past. Big industry, freed from the pressure of private property, will undergo such an expansion that what we now see will seem as petty in comparison as manufacture seems when put beside the big industry of our own day. This development of industry will make available to society a sufficient mass of products to satisfy the needs of everyone.

The same will be true of agriculture, which also suffers from the pressure of private property and is held back by the division of privately owned land into small parcels. Here, existing improvements and scientific procedures will be put into practice, with a resulting leap forward which will assure to society all the products it needs.

In this way, such an abundance of goods will be able to satisfy the needs of all its members.

The division of society into different, mutually hostile classes will then become unnecessary. Indeed, it will be not only unnecessary but intolerable in the new social order. The existence of classes originated in the division of labor, and the division of labor, as it has been known up to the present, will completely disappear. For mechanical and chemical processes are not enough to bring industrial and agricultural production up to the level we have described; the capacities of the men who make use of these processes must undergo a corresponding development.

Just as the peasants and manufacturing workers of the last century changed their whole way of life and became quite different people when they were impressed into big industry, in the same way, communal control over production by society as a whole, and the resulting new development, will both require an entirely different kind of human material.

People will no longer be, as they are today, subordinated to a single branch of production, bound to it, exploited by it; they will no longer develop one of their faculties at the expense of all others; they will no longer know only one branch, or one branch of a single branch, of production as a whole. Even industry as it is today is finding such people less and less useful.

Industry controlled by society as a whole, and operated according to a plan, presupposes well-rounded human beings, their faculties developed in balanced fashion, able to see the system of production in its entirety.

The form of the division of labor which makes one a peasant, another a cobbler, a third a factory worker, a fourth a stock-market operator, has already been undermined by machinery and will completely disappear. Education will enable young people quickly to familiarize themselves with the whole system of production and to pass from one branch of production to another in response to the needs of society or their own inclinations. It will, therefore, free them from the one-sided character which the present-day division of labor impresses upon every individual. Communist society will, in this way, make it possible for its members to put their comprehensively developed faculties to full use. But, when this happens, classes will necessarily disappear. It follows that society organized on a communist basis is incompatible with the existence of classes on the one hand, and that the very building of such a society provides the means of abolishing class differences on the other.

A corollary of this is that the difference between city and country is destined to disappear. The management of agriculture and industry by the same people rather than by two different classes of people is, if only for purely material reasons, a necessary condition of communist association. The dispersal of the agricultural population on the land, alongside the crowding of the industrial population into the great cities, is a condition which corresponds to an undeveloped state of both agriculture and industry and can already be felt as an obstacle to further development.

The general co-operation of all members of society for the purpose of planned exploitation of the forces of production, the expansion of production to the point where it will satisfy the needs of all, the abolition of a situation in which the needs of some are satisfied at the expense of the needs of others, the complete liquidation of classes and their conflicts, the rounded development of the capacities of all members of society through the elimination of the present division of labor, through industrial education, through engaging in varying activities, through the participation by all in the enjoyments produced by all, through the combination of city and country—these are the main consequences of the abolition of private property.

21. What will be the influence of communist society on the family?

It will transform the relations between the sexes into a purely private matter which concerns only the persons involved and into which society has no occasion to intervene. It can do this since it does away with private property and educates children on a communal basis, and in this way removes the two bases of traditional marriage—the dependence rooted in private property, of the women on the man, and of the children on the parents.

And here is the answer to the outcry of the highly moral philistines against the "community of women." Community of women is a condition which belongs entirely to bourgeois society and which today finds its complete expression in prostitution. But prostitution is based on private property and falls with it. Thus, communist society, instead of introducing community of women, in fact abolishes it.

22. What will be the attitude of communism to existing nationalities?

The nationalities of the peoples associating themselves in accordance with the principle of community will be compelled to mingle with each other as a result of this association and thereby to dissolve themselves, just as the various estate and class distinctions must disappear through the abolition of their basis, private property.[2]

23. What will be its attitude to existing religions?

All religions so far have been the expression of historical stages of development of individual peoples or groups of peoples. But communism is the stage of historical development which makes all existing religions superfluous and brings about their disappearance.[3]

24. How do communists differ from socialists?

The so-called socialists are divided into three categories.

The first category consists of adherents of a feudal and patriarchal society which has already been destroyed, and is still daily being destroyed, by big industry and world trade and their creation, bourgeois society. This category concludes, from the evils of existing society, that feudal and patriarchal society must be restored because it was free of such evils. In one way or another, all their proposals are directed to this end.

This category of reactionary socialists, for all their seeming partisanship and their scalding tears for the misery of the proletariat, is nevertheless energetically opposed by the communists for the following reasons:

(i) It strives for something which is entirely impossible.

(ii) It seeks to establish the rule of the aristocracy, the guildmasters, the small producers, and their retinue of absolute or feudal monarchs, officials, soldiers, and priests—a society which was, to be sure, free of the evils of present-day society but which brought it at least as many evils without even offering to the oppressed workers the prospect of liberation through a communist revolution.

(iii) As soon as the proletariat becomes revolutionary and communist, these reactionary socialists show their true colors by immediately making common cause with the bourgeoisie against the proletarians.

The second category consists of adherents of present-day society who have been frightened for its future by the evils to which it necessarily gives rise. What they want, therefore, is to maintain this society while getting rid of the evils which are an inherent part of it.

To this end, some propose mere welfare measures—while others come forward with grandiose systems of reform which, under the pretense of reorganizing society, are in fact intended to preserve the foundations, and hence the life, of existing society.

Communists must unremittingly struggle against these bourgeois socialists because they work for the enemies of communists and protect the society which communists aim to overthrow.

Finally, the third category consists of democratic socialists who favor some of the same measures the communists advocate, as described in Question 18, not as part of the transition to communism, however, but as measures which they believe will be sufficient to abolish the misery and evils of present-day society.

These democratic socialists are either proletarians who are not yet sufficiently clear about the conditions of the liberation of their class, or they are representatives of the petty bourgeoisie, a class which, prior to the achievement of democracy and the socialist measures to which it gives rise, has many interests in common with the proletariat.

It follows that, in moments of action, the communists will have to come to an understanding with these democratic socialists, and in general to follow as far as possible a common policy with them—provided that these socialists do not enter into the service of the ruling bourgeoisie and attack the communists.

It is clear that this form of cooperation in action does not exclude the discussion of differences.

25. What is the attitude of the communists to the other political parties of our time?

This attitude is different in the different countries.

In England, France, and Belgium, where the bourgeoisie rules, the communists still have a common interest with the various democratic parties, an interest which is all the greater the more closely the socialistic measures they champion approach the aims of the communists—that is, the more clearly and definitely they represent the interests of the proletariat and the more they depend on the proletariat for support. In England, for example, the working-class Chartists[4] are infinitely closer to the communists than the democratic petty bourgeoisie or the so-called Radicals.

In America, where a democratic constitution has already been established, the communists must make the common cause with the party which will turn this constitution against the bourgeoisie and use it in the interests of the proletariat—that is, with the agrarian National Reformers.[5]

In Switzerland, the Radicals, though a very mixed party, are the only group with which the communists can co-operate, and, among these Radicals, the Vaudois and Genevese are the most advanced.[6]

In Germany, finally, the decisive struggle now on the order of the day is that between the bourgeoisie and the absolute monarchy. Since the communists cannot enter upon the decisive struggle between themselves and the bourgeoisie until the bourgeoisie is in power, it follows that it is in the interest of the communists to help the bourgeoisie to power as soon as possible in order the sooner to be able to overthrow it.[7] Against the governments, therefore, the communists must continually support the radical liberal party, taking care to avoid the self-deceptions of the bourgeoisie and not fall for the enticing promises of benefits which a victory for the bourgeoisie would allegedly bring to the proletariat. The sole advantages which the proletariat would derive from a bourgeois victory would consist

(i) in various concessions which would facilitate the unification of the proletariat into a closely knit, battle-worthy, and organized class; and

(ii) in the certainty that, on the very day the absolute monarchies fall, the struggle between bourgeoisie and proletariat will start. From that day on, the policy of the communists will be the same as it now is in the countries where the bourgeoisie is already in power.

Notes

1. In the *Principles*, Engels left a blank. This answer is taken from his *Draft of the Communist Confession of Faith*, written a few months earlier in June 1847.
2. This response is from the *Draft*.
3. Also from the *Draft*.
4. The Chartists in Britain were the first mass working-class movement, pressing for a charter of electoral reforms, including annual parliaments and voting rights for all men.
5. Compare *Manifesto* IV.1.
6. Compare *Manifesto* IV.3.
7. Compare *Manifesto* IV.5–7.

APPENDIX C

Other Writings by Marx and Engels

Marx on Alienation

In his earlier writings, Marx forcefully condemns capitalism as an inhumane and alienating system. While the term "alienation" does not appear in the *Manifesto*, a similar critique is made in Section I.

From Marx, *Economic and Philosophic Manuscripts* (1844), First Manuscript

What constitutes the alienation of labor?

Firstly, the fact that labor is *external* to the worker—i.e., does not belong to his essential being; that he, therefore, does not confirm himself in his work, but denies himself, feels miserable and not happy, does not develop free mental and physical energy, but mortifies his flesh and ruins his mind. Hence, the worker feels himself only when he is not working; when he is working, he does not feel himself. He is at home when he is not working, and not at home when he is working. His labor is, therefore, not voluntary but forced, it is *forced labor*. It is, therefore, not the satisfaction of a need but a mere *means* to satisfy needs outside itself. Its alien character is clearly demonstrated by the fact that as soon as no physical or other compulsion exists, it is shunned like the plague. External labor, labor in which man alienates himself, is a labor of self-sacrifice, of mortification. Finally, the external character of labor for the worker is demonstrated by the fact that it belongs not to him but to another, and that in it he belongs not to himself but to another. Just as in religion the spontaneous activity of the human imagination, the human brain, and the human heart, detaches itself from the individual and reappears as the alien activity of a god or of a devil, so the activity of the worker is not his own spontaneous activity. It belongs to another, it is a loss of his self.

The result is that man (the worker) feels that he is acting freely only in his animal functions—eating, drinking, and procreating, or at most in his dwelling and adornment—while in his human functions, he is nothing more than animal.

It is true that eating, drinking, and procreating, etc., are also genuine human functions. However, when abstracted from other aspects of human activity, and turned into final and exclusive ends, they are animal.

We have considered the act of estrangement of practical human activity, of labor, from two aspects:

(1) The relationship of the worker to the product of labor as an alien object that has power over him. The relationship is, at the same time, the relationship to the sensuous external world, to natural objects, as an alien world confronting him, in hostile opposition.

(2) The relationship of labor to the *act of production* within labor. This relationship is the relationship of the worker to his own activity as something which is alien and does not belong to him, activity as passivity, power as impotence, procreation as emasculation, the worker's own physical and mental energy, his personal life—for what is life but activity?—as an activity directed against himself, which is independent of him and does not belong to him. Self-estrangement, as compared with the estrangement of the object mentioned above.

We now have to derive a third feature of estranged labor from the two we have already examined.

Man is a species-being, not only because he practically and theoretically makes the species—both his own and those of other things—his object, but also—and this is simply another way of saying the same thing—because he looks upon himself as the present, living species, because he looks upon himself as a universal and therefore free being.

Species-life, both for man and for animals, consists physically in the fact that man, like animals, lives from inorganic nature; and because man is more universal than animals, so too is the area of inorganic nature from which he lives more universal. Just as plants, animals, stones, air, light, etc., theoretically form a part of human consciousness, partly as objects of science and partly as objects of art—his spiritual inorganic nature, his spiritual means of life, which he must first prepare before he can enjoy and digest them—so, too, in practice they form a part of human life and human activity. In a physical sense, man lives only from these natural products, whether in the form of nourishment, heating, clothing, shelter, etc. The universality of man manifests itself in practice in that universality which makes the whole of nature his inorganic body, (1) as a direct means of life and (2) as the matter, the object, and the tool of his life activity. Nature is man's inorganic body—that is to say, nature insofar as it is not the human body. Man lives from nature—i.e., nature is his body—and he must maintain a continuing dialogue with it if he is not to die. To say that man's physical and mental life is linked to nature simply means that nature is linked to itself, for man is a part of nature.

Estranged labor not only (1) estranges nature from man and (2) estranges man from himself, from his own function, from his vital activity; because of this, it also estranges man from his species. It turns his species-life into a means for his individual life. Firstly, it estranges species-life and individual life, and, secondly, it turns the latter, in its abstract form, into the purpose of the former, also in its abstract and estranged form.

For in the first place labor, life activity, productive life itself, appears to man only as a means for the satisfaction of a need, the need to preserve physical existence. But productive life is species-life. It is life-producing life. The whole character of a species, its species-character, resides in the nature of its life activity, and free conscious activity constitutes the species-character of man. Life appears only as a means of life.

The animal is immediately one with its life activity. It is not distinct from that activity; it is that activity. Man makes his life activity itself an object of his will and consciousness. He has conscious life activity. It is not a determination with which he directly merges. Conscious life activity directly distinguishes man from animal life activity. Only because of that is he a species-being. Or, rather, he is a conscious being—i.e., his own life is an object for him, only because he is a species-being. Only because of that is his activity free activity. Estranged labor reverses the relationship so that man, just because he is a conscious being, makes his life activity, his *essential being*, a mere means for his *existence*.

The practical creation of an *objective world*, the fashioning of inorganic nature, is proof that man is a conscious species-being—i.e., a being which treats the species as its own essential being or itself as a species-being. It is true that animals also produce. They build nests and dwellings, like the bee, the beaver, the ant, etc. But they produce only their own immediate needs or those of their young; they produce only when immediate physical need compels them to do so, while man produces even when he is free from physical need and truly produces only in freedom from such need; they produce only themselves, while man reproduces the whole of nature; their products belong immediately to their physical bodies, while man freely confronts his own product. Animals produce only according to the standards and needs of the species to which they belong, while man is capable of producing according to the standards of every species and of applying to each object its inherent standard; hence, man also produces in accordance with the laws of beauty.

It is, therefore, in his fashioning of the objective that man really proves himself to be a species-being. Such production is his active species-life. Through it, nature appears as *his* work and his reality. The object of labor is, therefore, the objectification of the species-life of man: for man produces himself not only intellectually, in his consciousness, but actively and actually, and he can therefore contemplate himself in a world he himself has created. In tearing away the object of his production from man, estranged labor therefore tears away from him his species-life, his true species-objectivity, and transforms his advantage over animals into the disadvantage that his inorganic body, nature, is taken from him.

In the same way as estranged labor reduces spontaneous and free activity to a means, it makes man's species-life a means of his physical existence.

Consciousness, which man has from his species, is transformed through estrangement so that species-life becomes a means for him.

(3) Estranged labor, therefore, turns man's species-being—both nature and his intellectual species-power—into a being alien to him and a means of his indi-

vidual existence. It estranges man from his own body, from nature as it exists outside him, from his spiritual essence, his human existence.

(4) An immediate consequence of man's estrangement from the product of his labor, his life activity, his species-being, is the estrangement of man from man. When man confronts himself, he also confronts other men. What is true of man's relationship to his labor, to the product of his labor, and to himself, is also true of his relationship to other men, and to the labor and the object of the labor of other men.

In general, the proposition that man is estranged from his species-being means that each man is estranged from the others and that all are estranged from man's essence.

Man's estrangement, like all relationships of man to himself, is realized and expressed only in man's relationship to other men.

In the relationship of estranged labor, each man therefore regards the other in accordance with the standard and the situation in which he as a worker finds himself.

Demands of the Communist Party in Germany, March 1848

This document was issued by the Communist League in Paris in late March 1848 and reprinted in several German newspapers in the following month. It outlines the radical democratic demands advocated by Marx and Engels.

"Workers of all countries, unite!"

1. The whole of Germany shall be declared a single and indivisible republic.

2. Every German, having reached the age of 21, shall have the right to vote and to be elected, provided he has not been convicted of a criminal offence.

3. Representatives of the people shall receive payment so that workers, too, shall be able to become members of the German parliament.

4. Universal arming of the people. In the future the armies shall be simultaneously labor armies, so that the troops shall not, as formerly, merely consume, but shall produce more than is necessary for their upkeep.

This will moreover be conducive to the organization of labor.

5. Legal services shall be free of charge.

6. All feudal obligations, dues, corvées, tithes etc., which have hitherto weighed upon the rural population, shall be abolished without compensation.

7. Princely and other feudal estates, together with mines, pits, and so forth, shall become the property of the state. The estates shall be cultivated on a large scale and with the most up-to-date scientific devices in the interests of the whole of society.

8. Mortgages on peasant lands shall be declared the property of the state. Interest on such mortgages shall be paid by the peasants to the state.

9. In localities where the tenant system is developed, the land rent or the quitrent shall be paid to the state as a tax.

The measures specified in Nos. 6, 7, 8, and 9 are to be adopted in order to reduce the communal and other burdens hitherto imposed upon the peasants and small tenant farmers without curtailing the means available for defraying state expenses and without imperiling production.

The landowner in the strict sense, who is neither a peasant nor a tenant farmer, has no share in production. Consumption on his part is, therefore, nothing but abuse.

10. A state bank, whose paper issues are legal tender, shall replace all private banks.

This measure will make it possible to regulate the credit system in the interest of the people as a whole, and will thus undermine the dominion of the big financial magnates. Further, by gradually substituting paper money for gold and silver coin, the universal means of exchange (that indispensable prerequisite of bourgeois trade and commerce) will be cheapened, and gold and silver will be set free for use in foreign trade. Finally, this measure is necessary in order to bind the interests of the conservative bourgeoisie to the Government.

11. All the means of transport, railways, canals, steamships, roads, the posts, etc. shall be taken over by the state. They shall become the property of the state and shall be placed free at the disposal of the impecunious classes.

12. All civil servants shall receive the same salary, the only exception being that civil servants who have a family to support and who therefore have greater requirements, shall receive a higher salary.

13. Complete separation of Church and State. The clergy of every denomination shall be paid only by the voluntary contributions of their congregations.

14. The right of inheritance to be curtailed.

15. The introduction of steeply graduated taxes, and the abolition of taxes on articles of consumption.

16. Inauguration of national workshops. The state guarantees a livelihood to all workers and provides for those who are incapacitated for work.

17. Universal and free education of the people.

It is to the interest of the German proletariat, the petty bourgeoisie and the small peasants to support these demands with all possible energy. Only by the realization of these demands will the millions in Germany, who have hitherto been exploited by a handful of persons and whom the exploiters would like to keep in further subjection, win the rights and attain to that power to which they are entitled as the producers of all wealth.

The Committee:
K. Marx, K. Schapper, H. Bauer, F. Engels, J. Moll, W. Wolff

The Materialist Conception of History

Marx's most famous short summary of historical materialism was written in 1859.

From Marx, Preface to *A Contribution to the Critique of Political Economy* (1859)

The general conclusion at which I arrived [in the mid-1840s] and which, once reached, became the guiding principle of my studies can be summarized as follows. In the social production of their existence, men inevitably enter into definite relations, which are independent of their will, namely relations of production appropriate to a given stage in the development of their material forces of production. The totality of these relations of production constitutes the economic structure of society, the real foundation, on which arises a legal and political superstructure and to which correspond definite forms of social consciousness. The mode of production of material life conditions the general process of social, political, and intellectual life. It is not the consciousness of men that determines their existence, but their social existence that determines their consciousness. At a certain stage of development, the material productive forces of society come into conflict with the existing relations of production or—this merely expresses the same thing in legal terms—with the property relations within the framework of which they have operated hitherto. From forms of development of the productive forces these relations turn into their fetters. Then begins an era of social revolution. The changes in the economic foundation lead sooner or later to the transformation of the whole immense superstructure. In studying such transformations it is always necessary to distinguish between the material transformation of the economic conditions of production, which can be determined with the precision of natural science, and the legal, political, religious, artistic, or philosophic—in short, ideological forms in which men become conscious of this conflict and fight it out. Just as one does not judge an individual by what he thinks about himself, so one cannot judge such a period of transformation by its consciousness, but, on the contrary, this consciousness must be explained from the contradictions of material life, from the conflict existing between the social forces of production and the relations of production. No social order is ever destroyed before all the productive forces for which it is sufficient have been developed, and new superior relations of production never replace older ones before the material conditions for their existence have matured within the framework of the old society. Mankind thus inevitably sets itself only such tasks as it is able to solve, since closer examination will always show that the problem itself arises only when the material conditions for its solution are already present or at least in the course of formation. In broad outline, the Asiatic, ancient, feudal and modern bourgeois modes of production may be designated as epochs marking progress in the economic development of society. The bourgeois mode of production is the last antagonistic form of the social process of production—antagonistic not in the sense of individual antagonism but of an antagonism that emanates from the individuals' social conditions of existence—but the productive forces developing within bourgeois society create also the material conditions for a solution of this antagonism. The prehistory of human society accordingly closes with this social formation.

History and Revolution

Marx used the materialist conception of history to illuminate many significant events, including dramatic developments in France in the mid-nineteenth century. Following the defeat of the 1848 revolution, Napoleon Bonaparte's nephew, Louis Napoleon, seized power, eventually declaring himself Emperor Napoleon III. In the opening pages of his analysis, Marx makes clear that he does not see history as a deterministic process and contrasts bourgeois revolutions with workers' revolution.

From Marx, *The Eighteenth Brumaire of Louis Bonaparte* (1852)[1]

Hegel remarks somewhere that all the events and personalities of great importance in world history occur, as it were, twice. He forgot to add: the first time as tragedy, the second as farce. Caussidière for Danton, Louis Blanc for Robespierre, the Montagne of 1848–51 for the Montagne of 1793–95, the Nephew for the Uncle.[2] And the same caricature occurs in the circumstances attending the second edition of the *Eighteenth Brumaire*.[3]

Men make their own history, but they do not make it just as they please; they do not make it under circumstances chosen by themselves, but under given circumstances directly encountered and inherited from the past. The tradition of all the generations of the dead weighs like a nightmare on the brain of the living. And just when they seem involved in revolutionizing themselves and things, in creating something that has never before existed, it is precisely in such periods of revolutionary crisis that they anxiously conjure up the spirits of the past to their service and borrow names, battle cries, and costumes from them in order to act out the new scene of world history in this time-honored disguise and this borrowed language. Thus Luther donned the mask of the Apostle Paul, the Revolution of 1789–1814 draped itself alternately as the Roman republic and the Roman empire, and the Revolution of 1848 could do nothing better than parody 1789 one minute, and the revolutionary tradition of 1793–95 the next. In a similar way a beginner who has learned a new language always translates it back into his mother tongue, but he has assimilated the spirit of the new language and can freely express himself in it only when he can use it without recalling the old and forgets his native tongue in the use of the new.

If we consider this conjuring up of the dead of world history, a salient difference is revealed immediately. Camille Desmoulins,[4] Danton, Robespierre, Saint-Just,[5] Napoleon, the heroes as well as the parties and the masses of the old French Revolution, performed the task of their time in Roman costume and with Roman phrases, the task of unchaining and setting up modern bourgeois society. The first ones smashed the feudal basis to pieces and mowed down the feudal heads which had grown on it. The other created inside France the only conditions under which free competition could be developed, parceled landed property exploited and the unchained industrial productive power of the nation employed; and everywhere beyond the French borders he swept the feudal institutions away, to the extent necessary to provide bourgeois society in France with a suitable up-to-date environment on the European Continent. Once the new social formation was established, the antediluvian Colossi disappeared and with them the resurrected Romans—the Brutuses, Gracchi, Publicolas, the tribunes, the senators, and Caesar himself. Bourgeois society in its sober reality had begotten its true interpreters and mouthpieces in the Says, Cousins, Royer-Collards, Benjamin Constants, and Guizots[6]; its real military leaders sat behind the office desks, and the hog-headed Louis XVIII[7] was its political chief. Wholly absorbed in the production of wealth and in the peaceful struggle of competition, it no longer comprehended that the ghosts of Roman times had watched over its cradle. But unheroic as bourgeois society is, it nevertheless took heroism, sacrifice, terror, civil war, and the battles of nations to bring it into being. And in the classically austere traditions of the Roman republic its gladiators found the ideals and the art forms, the self-deceptions that they needed in order to conceal from themselves the bourgeois limitations of the content of their struggles and to keep their zeal on the high plane of the great historical tragedy. Similarly, at another stage of development, a century earlier, Cromwell and the English people had borrowed speech, passions, and illusions from the Old Testament for their bourgeois revolution.[8] When the real aim had been achieved, when the bourgeois transformation of English society had been accomplished, Locke supplanted Habakkuk[9]...

The social revolution of the nineteenth century cannot draw its poetry from the past, but only from the future. It cannot begin with itself before it has stripped off all superstition with regard to the past. Earlier revolutions required recollections of past world history in order to drug themselves against their own content. In order to arrive at its own content, the revolution of the nineteenth century must let the dead bury their dead. Then the words went beyond the content; now the content goes beyond the words . . .

Bourgeois revolutions, like those of the eighteenth century, storm swiftly from success to success; their dramatic effects outdo each other; men and things seem set in sparkling brilliants; ecstasy is the everyday spirit; but they are short-lived; soon they have attained their zenith, and a long crapulent depression lays hold of society before it learns soberly to assimilate the results of its storm-and-stress period. On the other hand, proletarian revolutions, like those of the nineteenth century, criticize themselves constantly, interrupt themselves continually in their own course, come back to the apparently accomplished in order to begin it afresh, deride with unmerciful thoroughness the inadequacies, weaknesses, and paltrinesses of their first attempts, seem to throw down their adversary only in order that he may draw new strength from the earth and rise before them again even more gigantic, recoil ever and anon from the indefinite prodigiousness of their own aims, until a situation has been created which makes all turning back impossible, and the conditions themselves cry out:

Hic Rhodus, hic salta![10]

Colonialism, Racism, Slavery, and the Origins of Capitalism

Marx and Engels wrote extensively about the relationship between capitalism, colonialism, racism, and slavery. The passage below is from Marx's lengthy account of the rise of capitalism.

From Marx, *Capital,* volume I, part VIII, chapter 31, "Genesis of the Industrial Capitalist" (1867)

The discovery of gold and silver in America, the extirpation, enslavement, and entombment in mines of the aboriginal population, the beginning of the conquest and looting of the East Indies, the turning of Africa into a warren for the commercial hunting of black-skins, signalized the rosy dawn of the era of capitalist production. These idyllic proceedings are the chief momenta of primitive accumulation. On their heels treads the commercial war of the European nations, with the globe for a theater. It begins with the revolt of the Netherlands from Spain,[11] assumes giant dimensions in England's Anti-Jacobin War,[12] and is still going on in the opium wars against China,[13] etc.

The different momenta of primitive accumulation distribute themselves now, more or less in chronological order, particularly over Spain, Portugal, Holland, France, and England. In England at the end of the seventeenth century, they arrive at a systematical combination, embracing the colonies, the national debt, the modern mode of taxation, and the protectionist system. These methods depend in part on brute force, e.g., the colonial system. But, they all employ the power of the State, the concentrated and organized force of society, to hasten, hot-house fashion, the process of transformation of the feudal mode of production into the capitalist mode, and to shorten the transition. Force is the midwife of every old society pregnant with a new one. It is itself an economic power.

Of the Christian colonial system, W. Howitt, a man who makes a specialty of Christianity, says: "The barbarities and desperate outrages of the so-called Christian race, throughout every region of the world, and upon every people they have been able to subdue, are not to be paralleled by those of any other race, however fierce, however untaught, and however reckless of mercy and of shame, in any age of the earth."[14] The history of the colonial administration of Holland—and Holland was the head capitalistic nation of the 17th century—"is one of the most extraordinary relations of treachery, bribery, massacre, and meanness."[15] Nothing is more characteristic than their system of stealing men, to get slaves for Java. The men stealers were trained for this purpose. The thief, the interpreter, and the seller were the chief agents in this trade, native princes the chief sellers. The young people stolen were thrown into the secret dungeons of Celebes, until they were ready for sending to the slave-ships. An official report says: "This one town of Macassar, e.g., is full of secret prisons, one more horrible than the other, crammed with unfortunates, victims of greed and tyranny fettered in chains, forcibly torn from their families." To secure Malacca, the Dutch corrupted the Portuguese governor. He let them into the town in 1641. They hurried at once to his house and assassinated him, to "abstain" from the payment of £21,875, the price of his treason. Wherever they set foot, devastation and depopulation followed. Banjuwangi, a province of Java, in 1750 numbered over 80,000 inhabitants, in 1811 only 18,000. Sweet commerce! . . .

The treatment of the aborigines was, naturally, most frightful in plantation-colonies destined for export trade only, such as the West Indies, and in rich and well-populated countries, such as Mexico and India, that were given over to plunder. But even in the colonies properly so called, the Christian character of primitive accumulation did not belie itself. Those sober virtuosi of Protestantism, the Puritans of New England, in 1703, by decrees of their assembly set a premium of £40 on every Indian scalp and every captured red-skin: in 1720 a premium of £100 on every scalp; in 1744, after Massachusetts Bay had proclaimed a certain tribe as rebels, the following prices: for a male scalp of 12 years and upwards £100 (new currency), for a male prisoner £105, for women and children prisoners £50, for scalps of women and children £50. Some decades later, the colonial system took its revenge on the descendants of the pious pilgrim fathers, who had grown seditious in the meantime. At English instigation and for English pay they were tomahawked by red-skins. The British Parliament proclaimed bloodhounds and scalping as "means that God and Nature had given into its hand.". . .

With the development of capitalist production during the manufacturing period, the public opinion of Europe had lost the last remnant of shame and conscience. The nations bragged cynically of every infamy that served them as a means to capitalistic accumulation. Read, e.g., the naïve *Annals of Commerce* of the worthy A. Anderson. Here it is trumpeted forth as a triumph of English statecraft that at the Peace of Utrecht,[16] England extorted from the Spaniards by the Asiento Treaty the privilege of being allowed to ply the negro trade, until then only carried on between Africa and the English West Indies, and between Africa and Spanish America as well. England thereby acquired the right of supplying Spanish America until 1743 with 4,800 negroes yearly. This threw, at the same time, an official cloak over British smuggling. Liverpool waxed fat on the slave trade. This was its method of primitive accumulation. And, even to the present day, Liverpool "respectability" is the Pindar[17] of the slave trade which—compare the work of Aikin [1795] already quoted—"has coincided with that spirit of bold adventure which has characterized the trade of Liverpool and rapidly carried it to its present state of prosperity; has occasioned vast employment for shipping and sailors, and greatly augmented the demand for the manufactures of the country" (p. 339).[18] Liverpool employed in the slave trade, in 1730, 15 ships; in 1751, 53; in 1760, 74; in 1770, 96; and in 1792, 132.

Whilst the cotton industry introduced child slavery in England, it gave in the United States a stimulus to the transformation of the earlier, more or less patriarchal slavery, into a system of commercial exploitation. In fact, the veiled slavery of the wage-workers in Europe needed, for its pedestal, slavery pure and simple in the new world.[19]

Tantae molis erat,[20] to establish the "eternal laws of Nature" of the capitalist mode of production, to complete the process of separation between laborers and conditions of labor, to transform, at one pole, the social means of production and subsistence into capital, at the opposite pole, the mass of the population into wage-laborers, into "free laboring poor," that artificial product of modern society. If money, according to Augier,[21] "comes into the world with a congenital blood-stain on one cheek," capital comes dripping from head to foot, from every pore, with blood and dirt.[22]

On the Irish Question

In their political maturity, Marx and Engels put increasing weight on the importance of national liberation struggles. In the letters below, Marx argues that the British occupation of Ireland harmed not just the Irish, but English workers, too. The analogy he draws to the relationship between "poor whites" and Blacks in the United States shows how the same kind of class analysis can be used to understand racism.

Marx to Engels in Manchester (December 11, 1869)

As to the Irish question . . . The way I shall put forward the matter next Tuesday is this: that quite apart from all phrases about "international" and "humane" *justice for Ireland*—which are to be taken for granted in the *International Council —it is in the direct and absolute interest of the English working class to get rid of their present connection with Ireland.* And this is my most complete conviction, and for reasons which in part I cannot tell the English workers themselves. For a long time I believed that it would be possible to overthrow the Irish regime by English working class ascendancy. I always expressed this point of view in the *New York Tribune.* Deeper study has now convinced me of the opposite. The English working class will *never accomplish anything* before it has got rid of Ireland. The lever must be applied in Ireland. That is why the Irish question is so important for the social movement in general.

Every industrial and commercial centre in England now possesses a working class divided into two *hostile* camps, English proletarians and Irish proletarians.

Marx to Sigfrid Meyer and August Vogt in New York (April 9, 1870)

The ordinary English worker hates the Irish worker as a competitor who lowers his standard of life. In relation to the Irish worker he regards himself as a member of the *ruling* nation and consequently he becomes a tool of the English aristocrats and capitalists against Ireland, thus strengthening their domination *over himself*. He cherishes religious, social, and national prejudices against the Irish worker. His attitude towards him is much the same as that of the "poor whites" to the Negroes in the former slave states of the U.S.A. The Irishman pays him back with interest in his own money. He sees in the English worker both the accomplice and the stupid tool of the *English rulers in Ireland.*

This antagonism is artificially kept alive and intensified by the press, the pulpit, the comic papers, in short, by all the means at the disposal of the ruling classes. *This antagonism* is the secret of the *impotence of the English working class*, despite its organization. It is the secret by which the capitalist class maintains its power. And the latter is quite aware of this.

The Paris Commune

Napoleon III was ousted from power after France's defeat in the Franco-Prussian war of 1870. In the chaos following the war, workers seized control of Paris for two months. Marx wrote a powerful defense of this brief experiment in workers' power.

On the dawn of March 18 [1871], Paris arose to the thunder-burst of "Vive la Commune!" What is the Commune, that sphinx so tantalizing to the bourgeois mind?

From Marx, *The Civil War in France* (1871)

"The proletarians of Paris," said the Central Committee in its manifesto of March 18, "amidst the failures and treasons of the ruling classes, have understood that the hour has struck for them to save the situation by taking into their own hands the direction of public affairs. . . . They have understood that it is their imperious duty, and their absolute right, to render themselves masters of their own destinies, by seizing upon the governmental power." But the working class cannot simply lay hold of the ready-made state machinery, and wield it for its own purposes.

The centralized state power, with its ubiquitous organs of standing army, police, bureaucracy, clergy, and judicature—organs wrought after the plan of a systematic and hierarchic division of labor—originates from the days of absolute monarchy, serving nascent middle class society as a mighty weapon in its struggle against feudalism. Still, its development remained clogged by all manner of medieval rubbish, seigniorial rights, local privileges, municipal and guild monopolies, and provincial constitutions. The gigantic broom of the French Revolution of the eighteenth century swept away all these relics of bygone times, thus clearing simultaneously the social soil of its last hindrances to the superstructure of the modern state edifice raised under the First Empire, itself the offspring of the coalition wars of old semi-feudal Europe against modern France.

During the subsequent regimes, the government, placed under parliamentary control—that is, under the direct control of the propertied classes—became not only a hotbed of huge national debts and crushing taxes; with its irresistible allurements of place, pelf [wealth], and patronage, it became not only the bone of contention between the rival factions and adventurers of the ruling classes; but its political character changed simultaneously with the economic changes of society. At the same pace at which the progress of modern industry developed, widened, intensified the class antagonism between capital and labor, the state power assumed more and more the character of the national power of capital over labor, of a public force organized for social enslavement, of an engine of class despotism.

After every revolution marking a progressive phase in the class struggle, the purely repressive character of the state power stands out in bolder and bolder relief. The Revolution of 1830, resulting in the transfer of government from the landlords to the capitalists, transferred it from the more remote to the more direct antagonists of the working men. The bourgeois republicans, who, in the name of the February Revolution, took the state power, used it for the June [1848] massacres, in order to convince the working class that "social" republic means the republic entrusting their social subjection, and in order to convince the royalist bulk of the bourgeois and landlord class that they might safely leave the cares and emoluments of government to the bourgeois "republicans."

However, after their one heroic exploit of June, the bourgeois republicans had, from the front, to fall back to the rear of the "Party of Order"—a combination formed by all the rival fractions and factions of the appropriating classes. The proper form of their joint-stock government was the parliamentary republic, with Louis Bonaparte for its president. Theirs was a regime of avowed class terrorism and deliberate insult towards the "vile multitude." If the parliamentary republic, as M. Thiers[23] said, "divided them [the different fractions of the ruling class] least," it opened an abyss between that class and the whole body of society outside their spare ranks. The restraints by which their own divisions had under former regimes still checked the state power, were removed by their union; and in view of the threatening upheaval of the proletariat, they now used that state power mercilessly and ostentatiously as the national war engine of capital against labor. In their uninterrupted crusade against the producing masses, they were, however, bound not only to invest the executive with continually increased powers of repression, but at the same time to divest their own parliamentary stronghold—the National Assembly—one by one, of all its own means of defense against the Executive. The Executive, in the person of Louis Bonaparte, turned them out. The natural offspring of the "Party of Order" republic was the Second Empire.

The empire, with the *coup d'état* for its birth certificate, universal suffrage for its sanction, and the sword for its scepter, professed to rest upon the peasantry, the large mass of producers not directly involved in the struggle of capital and labor. It professed to save the working class by breaking down parliamentarism, and, with it, the undisguised subserviency of government to the propertied classes. It professed to save the propertied classes by upholding their economic supremacy over the working class; and, finally, it professed to unite all classes by reviving for all the chimera of national glory. In reality, it was the only form of government possible at a time when the bourgeoisie had already lost, and the working class had not yet acquired, the faculty of ruling the nation. It was acclaimed throughout the world as the savior of society. Under its sway, bourgeois society, freed from political cares, attained a development unexpected even by itself. Its industry and commerce expanded to colossal dimensions; financial swindling celebrated cosmopolitan orgies; the misery of the masses was set off by a shameless display of gorgeous, meretricious, and debased luxury. The state power, apparently soaring high above society, was at the same time itself the greatest scandal of that society and the very hotbed of all its corruptions. Its own rottenness, and the rottenness of the society it had saved, were laid bare by the bayonet of Prussia, herself eagerly bent upon transferring the supreme seat of that regime from Paris to Berlin. Imperialism is, at the same time, the most prostitute and the ultimate form of the state power which nascent middle class society had commenced to elaborate as a means of its own emancipation from feudalism, and which full-grown bourgeois society had finally transformed into a means for the enslavement of labor by capital.

The direct antithesis to the empire was the Commune. The cry of "social republic," with which the February Revolution was ushered in by the Paris proletariat, did but express a vague aspiration after a republic that was not only to supercede the monarchical form of class rule, but class rule itself. The Commune was the positive form of that republic.

Paris, the central seat of the old governmental power, and, at the same time, the social stronghold of the French working class, had risen in arms against the attempt of Thiers and the Rurals to restore and perpetuate that old governmental power bequeathed to them by the empire. Paris could resist only because, in consequence of the siege, it had got rid of the army, and replaced it by a National Guard, the bulk of which consisted of working men. This fact was now to be transformed into an institution. The first decree of the Commune, therefore, was the suppression of the standing army, and the substitution for it of the armed people.

The Commune was formed of the municipal councilors, chosen by universal suffrage in the various wards of the town, responsible and revocable at short terms. The majority of its members were naturally working men, or acknowledged representatives of the working class. The Commune was to be a working, not a parliamentary body, executive and legislative at the same time. Instead of continuing to be the agent of the Central Government, the police were at once stripped of their political attributes, and turned into the responsible, and at all times revocable, agents of the Commune. So were the officials of all other branches of the administration. From the members of the Commune downwards, the public service had to be done at *workman's wage*. The vested interests and the representation allowances of the high dignitaries of state disappeared along with the high dignitaries themselves. Public functions ceased to be the private property of the tools of the Central Government. Not only municipal administration, but the whole initiative hitherto exercised by the state was laid into the hands of the Commune.

Having once got rid of the standing army and the police—the physical force elements of the old government—the Commune was anxious to break the spiritual force of repression, the "parson-power," by the disestablishment and disendowment of all churches as proprietary bodies. The priests were sent back to the recesses of private life, there to feed upon the alms of the faithful in imitation of their predecessors, the apostles. The whole of the educational institutions were opened to the people gratuitously, and at the same time cleared of all interference of church and state. Thus, not only was education made accessible to all, but science itself freed from the fetters which class prejudice and governmental force had imposed upon it.

The judicial functionaries were to be divested of that sham independence which had but served to mask their abject subserviency to all succeeding governments to which, in turn, they had taken, and broken, the oaths of allegiance. Like the rest of public servants, magistrates and judges were to be elective, responsible, and revocable.

The Paris Commune was, of course, to serve as a model to all the great industrial centers of France. The communal regime once established in Paris and the secondary centers, the old centralized government would in the provinces, too, have to give way to the self-government of the producers. In a rough sketch of national organization, which the Commune had no time to develop, it states clearly that the Commune was to be the political form of even the smallest country hamlet, and that in the rural districts the standing army was to be replaced by a national militia, with an extremely short term of service. The rural communities of every district were to administer their common affairs by an assembly of delegates in the central town, and these district assemblies were again to send deputies to the National Delegation in Paris, each delegate to be at any time revocable and bound by the *mandat imperatif* (formal instructions) of his constituents. The few but important functions which would still remain for a central government were not to be suppressed, as has been intentionally misstated, but were to be discharged by Communal and thereafter responsible agents.

The unity of the nation was not to be broken, but, on the contrary, to be organized by Communal Constitution, and to become a reality by the destruction of the state power which claimed to be the embodiment of that unity independent of, and superior to, the nation itself, from which it was but a parasitic excrescence. While the merely repressive organs of the old governmental power were to be amputated, its legitimate functions were to be wrested from an authority usurping preeminence over society itself, and restored to the responsible agents of society. Instead of deciding once in three or six years which member of the ruling class was to misrepresent the people in Parliament, universal suffrage was to serve the people, constituted in Communes, as individual suffrage serves every other employer in the search for the workmen and managers in his business. And it is well known that companies, like individuals, in matters of real business generally know how to put the right man in the right place, and, if they for once make a mistake, to redress it promptly. On the other hand, nothing could be more foreign to the spirit of the Commune than to supercede universal suffrage by hierarchical investiture.

It is generally the fate of completely new historical creations to be mistaken for the counterparts of older, and even defunct, forms of social life, to which they may bear a certain likeness. Thus, this new Commune, which breaks with the modern state power, has been mistaken for a reproduction of the medieval Communes, which first preceded, and afterward became the substratum of, that very state power. The Communal Constitution has been mistaken for an attempt to break up into the federation of small states, as dreamt of by Montesquieu and the Girondins,[24] that unity of great nations which, if originally brought about by political force, has now become a powerful coefficient of social production. The antagonism of the Commune against the state power has been mistaken for an exaggerated form of the ancient struggle against over-centralization. Peculiar historical circumstances may have prevented the classical development, as in France, of the bourgeois form of government, and may have allowed, as in England, to complete the great central state organs by corrupt vestries, jobbing councilors, and ferocious poor-law guardians in the towns, and virtually hereditary magistrates in the counties. The Communal Constitution would have restored to the social body all the forces hitherto absorbed by the state parasite feeding upon, and clogging the free movement of, society. By this one act, it would have initiated the regeneration of France.

The provincial French middle class saw in the Commune an attempt to restore the sway their order had held over the country under Louis Philippe, and which, under Louis Napoleon, was supplanted by the pretended rule of the country over the towns. In reality, the Communal Constitution brought the rural producers under the intellectual lead of the central towns of their districts, and there secured to them, in the working men, the natural trustees of their interests. The very existence of the Commune involved, as a matter of course, local municipal liberty, but no longer as a check upon the now superseded state power. It could only enter into the head of a Bismarck—who, when not engaged on his intrigues of blood and iron, always likes to resume his old trade, so befitting his mental caliber, of contributor to *Kladderadatsch* (the Berlin *Punch*)[25]—it could only enter into such a head to ascribe to the Paris Commune aspirations after the caricature of the old French municipal organization of 1791, the Prussian municipal constitution which degrades the town governments to mere secondary wheels in the police machinery of the Prussian state. The Commune made that catchword of bourgeois revolutions—cheap government—a reality by destroying the two greatest sources of expenditure: the standing army and state functionarism. Its very existence presupposed the nonexistence of monarchy, which, in Europe at least, is the normal encumbrance and indispensable cloak of class rule. It supplied the republic with the basis of really democratic institutions. But neither cheap government nor the "true republic" was its ultimate aim; they were its mere concomitants.

The multiplicity of interpretations to which the Commune has been subjected, and the multiplicity of interests which construed it in their favor, show that it was a thoroughly expansive political form, while all the previous forms of government had been emphatically repressive. Its true secret was this:

It was essentially a working class government, the product of the struggle of the producing against the appropriating class, the political form at last discovered under which to work out the economical emancipation of labor.

Except on this last condition, the Communal Constitution would have been an impossibility and a delusion. The political rule of the producer cannot coexist with the perpetuation of his social slavery. The Commune was therefore to serve as a lever for uprooting the economical foundation upon which rests the existence of classes, and therefore of class rule. With labor emancipated, every man becomes a working man, and productive labor ceases to be a class attribute.

It is a strange fact. In spite of all the tall talk and all the immense literature, for the last sixty years, about emancipation of labor, no sooner do the working men anywhere take the subject into their own hands with a will, than uprises at once all the apologetic phraseology of the mouthpieces of present society with its two poles of capital and wage-slavery (the landlord now is but the sleeping partner of the capitalist), as if the capitalist society was still in its purest state of virgin innocence, with its antagonisms still undeveloped, with its delusions still unexploded, with its prostitute realities not yet laid bare. The Commune, they exclaim, intends to abolish property, the basis of all civilization! Yes, gentlemen, the Commune intended to abolish that class property which makes the labor of the many the wealth of the few. It aimed at the expropriation of the expropriators. It wanted to make individual property a truth by transforming the means of production, land, and capital, now chiefly the means of enslaving and exploiting labor, into mere instruments of free and associated labor. But this is communism, "impossible" communism! Why, those members of the ruling classes who are intelligent enough to perceive the impossibility of continuing the present system—and they are many—have become the obtrusive and full-mouthed apostles of cooperative production. If cooperative production is not to remain a sham and a snare; if it is to supersede the capitalist system; if united cooperative societies are to regulate national production upon common plan, thus taking it under their own control, and putting an end to the constant anarchy and periodical convulsions which are the fatality of capitalist production—what else, gentlemen, would it be but communism, "possible" communism?

The working class did not expect miracles from the Commune. They have no ready-made utopias to introduce *par décret du people*.[26] They know that in order to work out their own emancipation, and along with it that higher form to which present society is irresistibly tending by its own economical agencies, they will have to pass through long struggles, through a series of historic processes, transforming circumstances and men. They have no ideals to realize, but to set free the elements of the new society with which old collapsing bourgeois society itself is pregnant. In the full consciousness of their historic mission, and with the heroic resolve to act up to it, the working class can afford to smile at the coarse invective of the gentlemen's gentlemen with pen and inkhorn, and at the didactic patronage of well-wishing bourgeois doctrinaires, pouring forth their ignorant platitudes and sectarian crotchets in the oracular tone of scientific infallibility.

When the Paris Commune took the management of the revolution in its own hands; when plain working men for the first time dared to infringe upon the governmental privilege of their "natural superiors," and, under circumstances of unexampled difficulty, performed it at salaries the highest of which barely amounted to one-fifth what, according to high scientific authority, is the minimum required for a secretary to a certain metropolitan school-board—the old world writhed in convulsions of rage at the sight of the Red Flag, the symbol of the Republic of Labor, floating over the Hôtel de Ville.[27]

And yet, this was the first revolution in which the working class was openly acknowledged as the only class capable of social initiative, even by the great bulk of the Paris middle class—shopkeepers, tradesmen, merchants—the wealthy capitalist alone excepted. The Commune had saved them by a sagacious settlement of that ever recurring cause of dispute among the middle class themselves—the debtor and creditor accounts. The same portion of the middle class, after they had assisted in putting down the working men's insurrection of June 1848, had been at once unceremoniously sacrificed to their creditors by the then-Constituent Assembly. But this was not their only motive for now rallying around the working class. They felt there was but one alternative—the Commune, or the empire—under whatever name it might reappear. The empire had ruined them economically by the havoc it made of public wealth, by the wholesale financial swindling it fostered, by the props it lent to the artificially accelerated centralization of capital, and the concomitant expropriation of their own ranks. It had suppressed them politically, it had shocked them morally by its orgies, it had insulted their Voltairianism[28] by handing over the education of their children to the *frères ignorantins*,[29] it had revolted their national feeling as Frenchmen by precipitating them headlong into a war which left only one equivalent for the ruins it made—the disappearance of the empire. In fact, after the exodus from Paris of the high Bonapartist and capitalist *bohème*, the true middle class Party of Order came out in the shape of the "Union Républicaine," enrolling themselves under the colors of the Commune and defending it against the willful misconstructions of Thiers. Whether the gratitude of this great body of the middle class will stand the present severe trial, time must show.

The Commune was perfectly right in telling the peasants that "its victory was their only hope.". . .

If the Commune was thus the true representative of all the healthy elements of French society, and therefore the truly national government, it was, at the same time, as a working men's government, as the bold champion of the emancipation of labor, emphatically international. Within sight of that Prussian army, that had annexed to Germany two French provinces, the Commune annexed to France the working people all over the world.

. . . The Commune made a German working man [Leo Frankel] its Minister of Labor. Thiers, the bourgeoisie, the Second Empire,[30] had continually deluded Poland by loud professions of sympathy, while in reality betraying her to, and doing the dirty work of, Russia. The Commune honored the heroic sons of Poland [J. Dabrowski and W. Wróblewski] by placing them at the head of the defenders of Paris. And, to broadly mark the new era of history it was conscious of initiating, under the eyes of the conquering Prussians on one side, and the Bonapartist army, led by Bonapartist generals, on the other, the Commune pulled down that colossal symbol of martial glory, the Vendôme Column.

The great social measure of the Commune was its own working existence. Its special measures could but betoken the tendency of a government of the people by the people. Such were the abolition of the nightwork of journeymen bakers; the prohibition, under penalty, of the employers' practice to reduce wages by levying upon their workpeople fines under manifold pretexts—a process in which the employer combines in his own person the parts of legislator, judge, and executor, and filches the money to boot. Another measure of this class was the surrender to associations of workmen, under reserve of compensation, of all closed workshops and factories, no matter whether the respective capitalists had absconded or preferred to strike work.

The financial measures of the Commune, remarkable for their sagacity and moderation, could only be such as were compatible with the state of a besieged town. Considering the colossal robberies committed upon the city of Paris by the great financial companies and contractors, under the protection of Haussmann,[31] the Commune would have had an incomparably better title to confiscate their property than Louis Napoleon had against the Orleans family. The Hohenzollern and the English oligarchs, who both have derived a good deal of their estates from church plunders, were, of course, greatly shocked at the Commune clearing but 8,000 *f* out of secularization.

While the Versailles government,[32] as soon as it had recovered some spirit and strength, used the most violent means against the Commune; while it put down the free expression of opinion all over France, even to the forbidding of meetings of delegates from the large towns; while it subjected Versailles and the rest of France to an espionage far surpassing that of the Second Empire; while it burned by its gendarme inquisitors all papers printed at Paris, and sifted all correspondence from and to Paris; while in the National Assembly the most timid attempts to put in a word for Paris were howled down in a manner unknown even to the *Chambre introuvable* of 1816;[33] with the savage warfare of Versailles outside, and its attempts at corruption and conspiracy inside Paris—would the Commune not have shamefully betrayed its trust by affecting to keep all the decencies and appearances of liberalism as in a time of profound peace? Had the government of the Commune been akin to that of M. Thiers, there would have been no more occasion to suppress Party of Order papers at Paris that there was to suppress Communal papers at Versailles. . . .

In every revolution there intrude, at the side of its true agents, men of different stamp; some of them survivors of and devotees to past revolutions, without insight into the present movement, but preserving popular influence by their known honesty and courage, or by the sheer force of tradition; others mere brawlers who, by dint of repeating year after year the same set of stereotyped declarations against the government of the day, have sneaked into the reputation of revolutionists of the first water. After March 18, some such men did also turn up, and in some cases contrived to play preeminent parts. As far as their power went, they hampered the real action of the working class, exactly as men of that sort have hampered the full development of every previous revolution. They are an unavoidable evil: with time they are shaken off; but time was not allowed to the Commune.

Wonderful, indeed, was the change the Commune had wrought in Paris! No longer any trace of the meretricious Paris of the Second Empire! No longer was Paris the rendezvous of British landlords, Irish absentees, American ex-slaveholders and shoddy men, Russian ex-serfowners, and Wallachian boyards.[34] No more corpses at the morgue, no nocturnal burglaries, scarcely any robberies; in fact, for the first time since the days of February 1848, the streets of Paris were safe, and that without any police of any kind. "We," said a member of the Commune, "hear no longer of assassination, theft, and personal assault; it seems indeed as if the police had dragged along with it to Versailles all its Conservative friends." The *cocottes*[35] had refound the scent of their protectors—the absconding men of family, religion, and, above all, of property. In their stead, the real women of Paris showed again at the surface—heroic, noble, and devoted, like the women of antiquity. Working, thinking, fighting, bleeding Paris—almost forgetful, in its incubation of a new society, of the cannibals at its gates—radiant in the enthusiasm of its historic initiative!

The Transition to Communism

In 1875, Marx's followers in Germany merged with the followers of Ferdinand Lassalle[36] to form a unified German Social Democratic Party. Marx wrote extensive critical comments on the party's draft program, later adopted with few changes at a congress in the town of Gotha. In his comments on paragraph 3, Marx makes some important remarks about post-capitalist society.

"3. The emancipation of labor demands the promotion of the instruments of labor to the common property of society and the cooperative regulation of the total labor, with a fair distribution of the proceeds of labor."

From Marx, *Critique of the Gotha Program* (1875)

"Promotion of the instruments of labor to the common property" ought obviously to read their "conversion into the common property"; but this is only passing.

What are the "proceeds of labor"? The product of labor, or its value? And in the latter case, is it the total value of the product, or only that part of the value which labor has newly added to the value of the means of production consumed?

"Proceeds of labor" is a loose notion which Lassalle has put in the place of definite economic conceptions.

What is "a fair distribution"?

Do not the bourgeois assert that the present-day distribution is "fair"? And is it not, in fact, the only "fair" distribution on the basis of the present-day mode of production? Are economic relations regulated by legal conceptions, or do not, on the contrary, legal relations arise out of economic ones? Have not also the socialist sectarians the most varied notions about "fair" distribution?

To understand what is implied in this connection by the phrase "fair distribution," we must take the first paragraph [of the Gotha Program] and this one together.[37] The latter presupposes a society wherein the instruments of labor are common property and the total labor is cooperatively regulated, and from the first paragraph we learn that "the proceeds of labor belong undiminished with equal right to all members of society."

"To all members of society"? To those who do not work as well? What remains then of the "undiminished" proceeds of labor? Only to those members of society who work? What remains then of the "equal right" of all members of society?

But "all members of society" and "equal right" are obviously mere phrases. The kernel consists in this, that in this communist society every worker must receive the "undiminished" Lassallean "proceeds of labor."

Let us take, first of all, the words "proceeds of labor" in the sense of the product of labor; then the co-operative proceeds of labor are the *total social product*.

From this must now be deducted: *First*, cover for replacement of the means of production used up. *Second*, additional portion for expansion of production. *Third*, reserve or insurance funds to provide against accidents, dislocations caused by natural calamities, etc.

These deductions from the "undiminished" proceeds of labor are an economic necessity, and their magnitude is to be determined according to available means and forces, and partly by computation of probabilities, but they are in no way calculable by equity.

There remains the other part of the total product, intended to serve as means of consumption.

Before this is divided among the individuals, there has to be deducted again, from it: *First*, the general costs of administration not belonging to production. This part will, from the outset, be very considerably restricted in comparison with present-day society, and it diminishes in proportion as the new society develops. *Second*, that which is intended for the common satisfaction of needs, such as schools, health services, etc. From the outset, this part grows considerably in comparison with present-day society, and it grows in proportion as the new society develops. *Third*, funds for those unable to work, etc., in short, for what is included under so-called official poor relief today.

Only now do we come to the "distribution" which the program, under Lassallean influence, alone has in view in its narrow fashion—namely, to that part of the means of consumption which is divided among the individual producers of the cooperative society.

The "undiminished" proceeds of labor have already unnoticeably become converted into the "diminished" proceeds, although what the producer is deprived of in his capacity as a private individual benefits him directly or indirectly in his capacity as a member of society.

Just as the phrase of the "undiminished" proceeds of labor has disappeared, so now does the phrase of the "proceeds of labor" disappear altogether.

Within the cooperative society based on common ownership of the means of production, the producers do not exchange their products; just as little does the labor employed on the products appear here as the *value* of these products, as a material quality possessed by them, since now, in contrast to capitalist society, individual labor no longer exists in an indirect fashion but directly as a component part of total labor. The phrase "proceeds of labor," objectionable also today on account of its ambiguity, thus loses all meaning.

What we have to deal with here is a communist society, not as it has *developed* on its own foundations, but, on the contrary, just as it *emerges* from capitalist society; which is thus in every respect, economically, morally, and intellectually, still stamped with the birthmarks of the old society from whose womb it emerges. Accordingly, the individual producer receives back from society—after the deductions have been made—exactly what he gives to it. What he has given to it is his individual quantum of labor. For example, the social working day consists of the sum of the individual hours of work; the individual labor time of the individual producer is the part of the social working day contributed by him, his share in it. He receives a certificate from society that he has furnished such-and-such an amount of labor (after deducting his labor for the common funds); and with this certificate, he draws from the social stock of means of consumption as much as the same amount of labor cost. The same amount of labor which he has given to society in one form, he receives back in another.

Here, obviously, the same principle prevails as that which regulates the exchange of commodities, as far as this is exchange of equal values. Content and form are changed, because under the altered circumstances no one can give anything except his labor, and because, on the other hand, nothing can pass to the ownership of individuals, except individual means of consumption. But as far as the distribution of the latter among the individual producers is concerned, the same principle prevails as in the exchange of commodity equivalents: a given amount of labor in one form is exchanged for an equal amount of labor in another form.

Hence, *equal right* here is still in principle—*bourgeois right*, although principle and practice are no longer at loggerheads, while the exchange of equivalents in commodity exchange exists only on the average and not in the individual case.

In spite of this advance, this equal right is still constantly stigmatized by a bourgeois limitation. The right of the producers is *proportional* to the labor they supply; the equality consists in the fact that measurement is made with an *equal standard*, labor.

But one man is superior to another physically, or mentally, and supplies more labor in the same time, or can labor for a longer time; and labor, to serve as a measure, must be defined by its duration or intensity, otherwise it ceases to be a standard of measurement. This *equal* right is an unequal right for unequal labor. It recognizes no class differences, because everyone is only a worker like everyone else; but it tacitly recognizes unequal individual endowment, and thus productive capacity, as a natural privilege. It is, therefore, a right of inequality, in its content, like every right. Right, by its very nature, can consist only in the application of an equal standard; but unequal individuals (and they would not be different individuals if they were not unequal) are measurable only by an equal standard insofar as they are brought under an equal point of view, are taken from one definite side only—for instance, in the present case, are regarded *only as workers* and nothing more is seen in them, everything else being ignored. Further, one worker is married, another is not; one has more children than another, and so on and so forth. Thus, with an equal performance of labor, and hence an equal in the social consumption fund, one will in fact receive more than another, one will be richer than another, and so on. To avoid all these defects, right, instead of being equal, would have to be unequal.

But these defects are inevitable in the first phase of communist society as it is when it has just emerged after prolonged birth pangs from capitalist society. Right can never be higher than the economic structure of society and its cultural development conditioned thereby.

In a higher phase of communist society, after the enslaving subordination of the individual to the division of labor, and therewith also the antithesis between mental and physical labor, has vanished; after labor has become not only a means of life but life's prime want; after the productive forces have also increased with the all-around development of the individual, and all the springs of cooperative wealth flow more abundantly—only then can the narrow horizon of bourgeois right be crossed in its entirety and society inscribe on its banners: From each according to his ability, to each according to his needs!

I have dealt more at length with the "undiminished" proceeds of labor, on the one hand, and with "equal right" and "fair distribution," on the other, in order to show what a crime it is to attempt, on the one hand, to force on our Party again, as dogmas, ideas which in a certain period had some meaning but have now become obsolete verbal rubbish, while again perverting, on the other, the realistic outlook, which it cost so much effort to instill into the Party but which has now taken root in it, by means of ideological nonsense about right and other trash so common among the democrats and French socialists.

Quite apart from the analysis so far given, it was in general a mistake to make a fuss about so-called distribution and put the principal stress on it.

Any distribution whatever of the means of consumption is only a consequence of the distribution of the conditions of production themselves. The latter distribution, however, is a feature of the mode of production itself. The capitalist mode of production, for example, rests on the fact that the material conditions of production are in the hands of non-workers in the form of property in capital and land, while the masses are only owners of the personal condition of production, of labor power. If the elements of production are so distributed, then the present-day distribution of the means of consumption results automatically. If the material conditions of production are the cooperative property of the workers themselves, then there likewise results a distribution of the means of consumption different from the present one. Vulgar socialism (and from it in turn a section of the democrats) has taken over from the bourgeois economists the consideration and treatment of distribution as independent of the mode of production and hence the presentation of socialism as turning principally on distribution. After the real relation has long been made clear, why retrogress again?

The Realm of Necessity and the Realm of Freedom

In the final volume of his economic masterpiece, *Capital*, Marx briefly argues that reducing necessary labor is a precondition for full freedom.

From Marx, *Capital*, volume III, chapter 48, "The Trinity Formula" (1894)[38]

Like all its predecessors, the capitalist process of production proceeds under definite material conditions, which are, however, simultaneously the bearers of definite social relations entered into by individuals in the process of reproducing their life. Those conditions, like these relations, are on the one hand prerequisites, on the other hand results and creations of the capitalist process of production; they are produced and reproduced by it. We saw also that capital—and the capitalist is merely capital personified and functions in the process of production solely as the agent of capital—in its corresponding social process of production, pumps a definite quantity of surplus-labor out of the direct producers, or laborers; capital obtains this surplus-labor without an equivalent, and in essence it always remains forced labor—no matter how much it may seem to result from free contractual agreement. This surplus-labor appears as surplus-value, and this surplus-value exists as a surplus-product. Surplus-labor in general, as labor performed over and above the given requirements, must always remain. In the capitalist as well as in the slave system, etc., it merely assumes an antagonistic form and is supplemented by complete idleness of a stratum of society. A definite quantity of surplus-labor is required as insurance against accidents, and by the necessary and progressive expansion of the process of reproduction in keeping with the development of the needs and the growth of population, which is called accumulation from the viewpoint of the capitalist. It is one of the civilizing aspects of capital that it enforces this surplus-labor in a manner and under conditions which are more advantageous to the development of the productive forces, social relations, and the creation of the elements for a new and higher form than under the preceding forms of slavery, serfdom, etc.

Thus it gives rise to a stage, on the one hand, in which coercion and monopolization of social development (including its material and intellectual advantages) by one portion of society at the expense of the other are eliminated; on the other hand, it creates the material means and embryonic conditions, making it possible in a higher form of society to combine this surplus-labor with a greater reduction of time devoted to material labor in general.

For, depending on the development of labor productivity, surplus-labor may be large in a small total working-day, and relatively small in a large total working-day. If the necessary labor-time = 3 and the surplus-labor = 3, then the total working-day = 6 and the rate of surplus-labor = 100%. If the necessary labor-time = 9 and the surplus-labor = 3, then the total working-day = 12 and the rate of surplus-labor only = 33 1/3%. In that case, it depends upon the labor productivity how much use-value shall be produced in a definite time, hence also in a definite surplus labor-time. The actual wealth of society, and the possibility of constantly expanding its reproduction process, therefore, do not depend upon the duration of surplus-labor, but upon its productivity and the more or less copious conditions of production under which it is performed.

In fact, the realm of freedom actually begins only where labor which is determined by necessity and mundane considerations ceases; thus in the very nature of things it lies beyond the sphere of actual material production. Just as the savage must wrestle with Nature to satisfy his wants, to maintain and reproduce life, so must civilized man, and he must do so in all social formations and under all possible modes of production. With his development this realm of physical necessity expands as a result of his wants; but, at the same time, the forces of production which satisfy these wants also increase. Freedom in this field can only consist in socialized man, the associated producers, rationally regulating their interchange with Nature, bringing it under their common control, instead of being ruled by it as by the blind forces of Nature; and achieving this with the least expenditure of energy and under conditions most favorable to, and worthy of, their human nature. But it nonetheless still remains a realm of necessity. Beyond it begins that development of human energy which is an end in itself, the true realm of freedom, which, however, can blossom forth only with this realm of necessity as its basis. The shortening of the working-day is its basic prerequisite.

Women's Oppression and Women's Liberation

In the *Manifesto*, Marx and Engels express their commitment "to do away with the status of women as mere instruments of production." Engels later argued at length that the oppression of women is a consequence of the development of class society and that women's liberation will require the abolition of classes.

From Engels, *The Origin of the Family, Private Property, and the State*, chapter II, "The Family" (1884)

The first class opposition that appears in history coincides with the development of the antagonism between man and woman in monogamous marriage, and the first class oppression coincides with that of the female sex by the male. Monogamous marriage was a great historical step forward; nevertheless, together with slavery and private wealth, it opens the period that has lasted until today in which every step forward is also relatively a step backward, in which prosperity and development for some is won through the misery and frustration of others. It is the cellular form of civilized society, in which the nature of the oppositions and contradictions fully active in that society can be already studied. . . .

In the great majority of cases today, at least in the possessing classes, the husband is obliged to earn a living and support his family, and that in itself gives him a position of supremacy, without any need for special legal titles and privileges. Within the family he is the bourgeois and the wife represents the proletariat. In the industrial world, the specific character of the economic oppression burdening the proletariat is visible in all its sharpness only when all special legal privileges of the capitalist class have been abolished and complete legal equality of both classes established. The democratic republic does not do away with the opposition of the two classes; on the contrary, it provides the clear field on which the fight can be fought out. And in the same way, the peculiar character of the supremacy of the husband over the wife in the modern family, the necessity of creating real social equality between them, and the way to do it, will only be seen in the clear light of day when both possess legally complete equality of rights. Then it will be plain that the first condition for the liberation of the wife is to bring the whole female sex back into public industry, and that this in turn demands the abolition of the monogamous family as the economic unit of society. . . .

With the transfer of the means of production into common ownership, the single family ceases to be the economic unit of society. Private housekeeping is transformed into a social industry. The care and education of the children becomes a public affair; society looks after all children alike, whether they are legitimate or not. This removes all the anxiety about the "consequences," which today is the most essential social—moral as well as economic—factor that prevents a girl from giving herself completely to the man she loves. Will not that suffice to bring about the gradual growth of unconstrained sexual intercourse and with it a more tolerant public opinion in regard to a maiden's honor and a woman's shame? And, finally, have we not seen that in the modern world monogamy and prostitution are indeed contradictions, but inseparable contradictions, poles of the same state of society? Can prostitution disappear without dragging monogamy with it into the abyss? . . .

What we can now conjecture about the way in which sexual relations will be ordered after the impending overthrow of capitalist production is mainly of a negative character, limited for the most part to what will disappear. But what will there be new? That will be answered when a new generation has grown up: a generation of men who never in their lives have known what it is to buy a woman's surrender with money or any other social instrument of power; a generation of women who have never known what it is to give themselves to a man from any other considerations than real love, or to refuse to give themselves to their lover from fear of the economic consequences. When these people are in the world, they will care precious little what anybody today thinks they ought to do; they will make their own practice and their corresponding public opinion about the practice of each individual—and that will be the end of it.

The Emergence of Classes and the State

Marx and Engels' confidence that class divisions and the state can eventually be dismantled was based on their belief that both were of fairly recent origin. Engels discussed these issues at length in some of his later writings. In the first extract below he discusses the primitive communist constitution of the Iroquois Indians in North America, in the second the development of class society, and in the third the origin of the state.

From Engels, *The Origin of the Family, Private Property, and the State,* chapter III, "The Iroquois Gens" (1884)

And a wonderful constitution it is, this gentile[39] constitution, in all its childlike simplicity! No soldiers, no gendarmes or police, no nobles, kings, regents, prefects, or judges, no prisons, no lawsuits—and everything takes its orderly course. All quarrels and disputes are settled by the whole of the community affected, by the gens or the tribe, or by the gentes among themselves; only as an extreme and exceptional measure is blood revenge threatened—and our capital punishment is nothing but blood revenge in a civilized form, with all the advantages and drawbacks of civilization. Although there were many more matters to be settled in common than today—the household is maintained by a number of families in common, and is communistic, the land belongs to the tribe, only the small gardens are allotted provisionally to the households—yet there is no need for even a trace of our complicated administrative apparatus with all its ramifications. The decisions are taken by those concerned, and in most cases everything has been already settled by the custom of centuries. There cannot be any poor or needy—the communal household and the gens know their responsibilities towards the old, the sick, and those disabled in war. All are equal and free—the women included. There is no place yet for slaves, nor, as a rule, for the subjugation of other tribes. When, about the year 1651, the Iroquois had conquered the Eries and the "Neutral Nation,"[40] they offered to accept them into the confederacy on equal terms; it was only after the defeated tribes had refused that they were driven from their territory. And what men and women such a society breeds is proved by the admiration inspired in all white people who have come into contact with unspoiled Indians, by the personal dignity, uprightness, strength of character, and courage of these barbarians. . . .

From Engels, *Anti-Dühring*, part II, chapter IV, "Theory of Force (Conclusion)" (1878)

As men originally made their exit from the animal world—in the narrower sense of the term—so they made their entry into history: still half animal, brutal, still helpless in face of the forces of nature, still ignorant of their own strength; and consequently as poor as the animals and hardly more productive than they. There prevailed a certain equality in the conditions of existence, and for the heads of families also a kind of equality of social position—at least an absence of social classes—which continued among the primitive agricultural communities of the civilized peoples of a later period. In each such community there were from the beginning certain common interests the safeguarding of which had to be handed over to individuals, true, under the control of the community as a whole: adjudication of disputes; repression of abuse of authority by individuals; control of water supplies, especially in hot countries; and finally when conditions were still absolutely primitive, religious functions. Such offices are found in aboriginal communities of every period—in the oldest German marks[41] and even today in India. They are naturally endowed with a certain measure of authority and are the beginnings of state power. The productive forces gradually increase; the increasing density of the population creates at one point common interests, at another conflicting interests, between the separate communities, whose grouping into larger units brings about in turn a new division of labor, the setting up of organs to safeguard common interests and combat conflicting interests. These organs which, if only because they represent the common interests of the whole group, hold a special position in relation to each individual community—in certain circumstances even one of opposition—soon make themselves still more independent, partly through heredity of functions, which comes about almost as a matter of course in a world where everything occurs spontaneously, and partly because they become increasingly indispensable owing to the growing number of conflicts with other groups. It is not necessary for us to examine here how this independence of social functions in relation to society increased with time until it developed into domination over society; how he who was originally the servant, where conditions were favorable, changed gradually into the lord; how this lord, depending on the conditions, emerged as an Oriental despot or satrap,[42] the dynast[43] of a Greek tribe, chieftain of a Celtic clan, and so on; to what extent he subsequently had recourse to force in the course of this transformation; and how finally the individual rulers united into a ruling class. Here we are only concerned with establishing the fact that the exercise of a social function was everywhere the basis of political supremacy; and further that political supremacy has existed for any length of time only when it discharged its social functions. However great the number of despotisms which rose and fell in Persia and India, each was fully aware that above all it was the entrepreneur responsible for the collective maintenance of irrigation throughout the river valleys, without which no agriculture was possible there. It was reserved for the enlightened English to lose sight of this in India; they let the irrigation canals and sluices fall into decay, and are now at last discovering, through the regularly recurring famines, that they have neglected the one activity which might have made their rule in India at least as legitimate as that of their predecessors.

But alongside this process of formation of classes another was also taking place. The spontaneously evolved division of labor within the family cultivating the soil made possible, at a certain level of well-being, the incorporation of one or more strangers as additional labor forces. This was especially the case in countries where the old common ownership of the land had already disintegrated or at least the former joint cultivation had given place to the separate cultivation of parcels of land by the respective families. Production had developed so far that the labor-power of a man could now produce more than was necessary for its mere maintenance; the means of maintaining additional labor forces existed; likewise the means of employing them; labor-power acquired a *value.* But the community itself and the association to which it belonged yielded no available, superfluous labor forces. On the other hand, such forces were provided by war, and war was as old as the simultaneous existence alongside each other of several groups of communities. Up to that time one had not known what to do with prisoners of war, and had therefore simply killed them; at an even earlier period, eaten them. But at the stage of "economic situation" which had now been attained, the prisoners acquired value; one therefore let them live and made use of their labor. Thus force, instead of controlling the economic situation, was on the contrary pressed into the service of the economic situation. *Slavery* had been invented. It soon became the dominant form of production among all peoples who were developing beyond the old community, but in the end was also one of the chief causes of their decay. It was slavery that first made possible the division of labor between agriculture and industry on a larger scale, and thereby also Hellenism,[44] the flowering of the ancient world. Without slavery, no Greek state, no Greek art and science, without slavery, no Roman Empire. . . .

We may add at this point that all historical antagonisms between exploiting and exploited, ruling and oppressed classes to this very day find their explanation in this same relatively undeveloped human labor. So long as the really working population were so much occupied with their necessary labor that they had no time left for looking after the common affairs of society—the direction of labor, affairs of state, legal matters, art, science, etc.—so long was it necessary that there should constantly exist a special class, freed from actual labor, to manage these affairs; and this class never failed, for its own advantage, to impose a greater and greater burden of labor on the working masses. Only the immense increase of the productive forces attained by modern industry has made it possible to distribute labor among all members of society without exception, and thereby to limit the labor-time of each individual member to such an extent that all have enough free time left to take part in the general—both theoretical and practical—affairs of society. It is only now, therefore, that every ruling and exploiting class has become superfluous and indeed a hindrance to social development, and it is only now, too, that it will be inexorably abolished, however much it may be in possession of "direct force."

From Engels, *The Origin of the Family, Private Property, and the State,* chapter IX, "Barbarism and Civilization" (1884)

As the state arose from the need to keep class antagonisms in check, but also arose in the thick of the fight between the classes, it is normally the state of the most powerful, economically ruling class, which by its means becomes also the politically ruling class, and so acquires new means of holding down and exploiting the oppressed class. The ancient state was, above all, the state of the slave-owners for holding down the slaves, just as the feudal state was the organ of the nobility for holding down the peasant serfs and bondsmen, and the modern representative state is the instrument for exploiting wage-labor by capital. . . .

The state . . . has not existed from all eternity. There have been societies which have managed without it, which had no notion of the state or state power. At a definite stage of economic development, which necessarily involved the cleavage of society into classes, the state became a necessity because of this cleavage. We are now rapidly approaching a stage in the development of production at which the existence of these classes has not only ceased to be a necessity, but becomes a positive hindrance to production. They will fall as inevitably as they once arose. The state inevitably falls with them. The society which organizes production anew on the basis of free and equal association of the producers will put the whole state machinery where it will then belong—into the museum of antiquities, next to the spinning wheel and the bronze ax.

Marx's Legacy

Marx died on March 14, 1883, and was buried three days later in Highgate cemetery in London. Engels gave the following speech, summarizing Marx's legacy.

Engels' Speech at Marx's Funeral (1883)

On the 14th of March, at a quarter to three in the afternoon, the greatest living thinker ceased to think. He had been left alone for scarcely two minutes, and when we came back we found him in his armchair, peacefully gone to sleep—but forever.

An immeasurable loss has been sustained both by the militant proletariat of Europe and America, and by historical science, in the death of this man. The gap that has been left by the departure of this mighty spirit will soon enough make itself felt.

Just as Darwin discovered the law of development of organic nature,[45] so Marx discovered the law of development of human history: the simple fact, hitherto concealed by an overgrowth of ideology, that mankind must first of all eat, drink, have shelter and clothing, before it can pursue politics, science, art, religion, etc.; that therefore the production of the immediate material means, and consequently the degree of economic development attained by a given people or during a given epoch, form the foundation upon which the state institutions, the legal conceptions, art, and even the ideas on religion, of the people concerned have been evolved, and in the light of which they must, therefore, be explained, instead of vice versa, as had hitherto been the case.

But that is not all. Marx also discovered the special law of motion governing the present-day capitalist mode of production, and the bourgeois society that this mode of production has created. The discovery of surplus value suddenly threw light on the problem, in trying to solve which all previous investigations, of both bourgeois economists and socialist critics, had been groping in the dark.

Two such discoveries would be enough for one lifetime. Happy the man to whom it is granted to make even one such discovery. But in every single field which Marx investigated—and he investigated very many fields, none of them superficially—in every field, even in that of mathematics, he made independent discoveries.

Such was the man of science. But this was not even half the man. Science was for Marx a historically dynamic, revolutionary force. However great the joy with which he welcomed a new discovery in some theoretical science whose practical application perhaps it was as yet quite impossible to envisage, he experienced quite another kind of joy when the discovery involved immediate revolutionary changes in industry, and in historical development in general. For example, he followed closely the development of the discoveries made in the field of electricity and recently those of Marcel Deprez.[46]

For Marx was before all else a revolutionist. His real mission in life was to contribute, in one way or another, to the overthrow of capitalist society and of the state institutions which it had brought into being, to contribute to the liberation of the modern proletariat, which he was the first to make conscious of its own position and its needs, conscious of the conditions of its emancipation. Fighting was his element. And he fought with a passion, a tenacity, and a success such as few could rival. His work on the first *Rheinische Zeitung* (1842), the Paris *Vorwarts* (1844), the *Deutsche Brusseler Zeitung* (1847), the *Neue Rheinische Zeitung* (1848–49), the *New York Tribune* (1852–61), and, in addition to these, a host of militant pamphlets, work in organizations in Paris, Brussels, and London, and finally, crowning all, the formation of the great International Working Men's Association—this was indeed an achievement of which its founder might well have been proud even if he had done nothing else.

And, consequently, Marx was the best hated and most calumniated man of his time. Governments, both absolutist and republican, deported him from their territories. Bourgeois, whether conservative or ultra-democratic, vied with one another in heaping slanders upon him. All this he brushed aside as though it were a cobweb, ignoring it, answering only when extreme necessity compelled him. And he died beloved, revered, and mourned by millions of revolutionary fellow workers—from the mines of Siberia to California, in all parts of Europe and America—and I make bold to say that, though he may have had many opponents, he had hardly one personal enemy.

His name will endure through the ages, and so also will his work.

Notes

1. The French Revolution of 1789 changed the names of the months. The eighteenth Brumaire was the day on which Napoleon Bonaparte seized power.
2. Louis Marc Caussidière (1808–61) was a member of the republican *Réformiste* current (see *Manifesto* III.57 and IV.2), elected to the Constituent Assembly following the February 1848 revolution and forced into exile after the suppressions of the workers' uprising in June. Georges Jacques Danton (1759–94) was one of the principal leaders of the French Revolution of 1789, executed in 1794 after advocating moderation. Louis Blanc (1811–82) was a utopian socialist who helped establish national workshops after the 1848 revolution, but who fled to England after June. Maximilien François Marie Isidore de Robespierre (1758–94) was leader of the radical Jacobin faction in the 1789 revolution, eventually executed a few months after Danton. The "Montagne" (mountain) was originally the name given to the radicals (including Danton and Robespierre) who occupied the highest benches in the French Assembly in the early 1790s, and reclaimed by radicals and socialists in the 1848 revolution. The nephew was Louis Bonaparte (Napoleon III), the uncle, Napoleon Bonaparte (Napoleon I).
3. Louis Bonaparte's seizure of power in December 1851.
4. Camille Desmoulins (1760–94) was a close ally of Danton, executed along with him.
5. Louis Antoine de Saint-Just (1767–94) was a close ally of Robespierre, executed on the same day as his friend.
6. Bourgeois French thinkers and politicians in the first half of the nineteenth century.
7. Louis XVIII was placed on the French throne by the main European powers after Napoleon's defeat. He was succeeded in 1824 by his brother, Charles X, who was overthrown in 1830.
8. The seventeenth-century English Revolution.
9. John Locke (1632–1704) was the principal political philosopher of the new bourgeois regime in England. Habakkuk was a minor Old Testament prophet.
10. "This is Rhodes, jump here!" This is a reference to one of Aesop's fables, in which an athlete boasts that witnesses can confirm that he once made an amazing jump in Rhodes. A skeptical onlooker tells him to give an immediate demonstration of his abilities.
11. Between 1568 and 1648, the Netherlands fought a long war for independence from Spain, sometimes referred to as the first bourgeois revolution, which turned it into a world power in the second half of the seventeenth century.
12. Britain's war against France in the period following the French Revolution of 1789. The Jacobins were the most radical wing of the Revolution's leadership.
13. From 1839 to 1842 and 1856 to 1860, western powers fought two wars against China to force open its markets to imports, including opium.
14. *{Marx's footnote in the original.}* William Howitt, "Colonisation and Christianity: A Popular History of the Treatment of the Natives by the Europeans in all their Colonies." London, 1838, p. 9. On the treatment of the slaves there is a good compilation in Charles Comte, "Traité de la Législation." 3me éd., Bruxelles, 1837. This subject one must study in detail, to see what the bourgeoisie makes of itself and of the laborer, wherever it can, without restraint, model the world after its own image.
15. *{Marx's footnote in the original.}* Thomas Stamford Raffles, late Lieutenant Governor of that island: "The History of Java." London, 1817.
16. A series of treaties signed by the major European powers from 1713 to 1714, putting an end to the War of the Spanish Succession begun in 1701 after the death of the childless Charles II of Spain.
17. Greek lyric poet (522–443 BC).
18. Page number refers to a work cited in a chapter XXIV footnote: Dr. Aikin: "Description of the Country from 30 to 40 miles round Manchester." London, 1795.
19. *{Marx's footnote in the original.}* In 1790, there were in the English West Indies ten slaves for one free man, in the French fourteen for one, in the Dutch

twenty-three for one. (Henry Brougham, "An Inquiry into the Colonial Policy of the European Powers." Edinburgh, 1803, vol. II., p. 74.)

20. A reference to a line from the Roman poet Virgil: *"Tantae molis erat Romanam condere gentem." (The Aeneid*: Book 1, Line 33) "So massive was the effort to found the Roman nation."
21. *{Marx's footnote in the original.}* Marie Angier, "Du Crédit Public." Paris, 1842.
22. *{Marx's footnote in the original. The reference is to Dunning's "Trades' Unions and Strikes." Lond., 1860. Dunning was a British trade unionist, secretary to the London Society of Bookbinders.}* "Capital is said by a Quarterly Reviewer to fly turbulence and strife, and to be timid, which is very true; but this is very incompletely stating the question. Capital eschews no profit, or very small profit, just as Nature was formerly said to abhor a vacuum. With adequate profit, capital is very bold. A certain 10 percent. will ensure its employment anywhere; 20 percent. certain will produce eagerness; 50 percent., positive audacity; 100 percent. will make it ready to trample on all human laws; 300 percent., and there is not a crime at which it will scruple, nor a risk it will not run, even to the chance of its owner being hanged. If turbulence and strife will bring a profit, it will freely encourage both. Smuggling and the slave trade have amply proved all that is here stated." (T. J. Dunning, l.c., pp. 35, 36.)
23. Louis Adolphe Thiers (1797–1877) was French prime minister in the 1830s and reemerged as provisional president in early 1871, after Louis Bonaparte's fall. In May he sent troops to crush the Paris Commune, killing tens of thousands of workers.
24. The Baron de Montesquieu (1689–1755) was the Enlightenment philosopher who devised the political doctrine of separation of powers. The Girondins formed the more moderate wing of the French Revolution of 1789.
25. *Punch* was a British satirical magazine.
26. By decree of the people.
27. Town Hall.
28. Voltaire (1694–1778) was the leading French enlightenment philosopher, a champion of reason and opponent of established religion.
29. Ignorant brothers—a reference to conservative religious educators.
30. The regime of Louis Bonaparte, who declared himself Emperor Napoleon III.
31. Baron Haussmann (1809–91) was the French official who redesigned Paris under Louis Bonaparte, with the explicit aim of making it more difficult to set up revolutionary barricades in the streets.
32. The French bourgeoisie moved its government to Versailles during the period of the Commune.
33. The ultra-conservative French parliament convened after the fall of Napoleon Bonaparte.
34. Aristocrats from southeast Romania.
35. Prostitutes.
36. See note 12 of Appendix A above.
37. The first paragraph of the program states: "Labor is the source of wealth and all culture, and since useful labor is possible only in society and through society, the proceeds of labor belong undiminished with equal right to all members of society."
38. Marx died in 1883. Engels published volume II of *Capital* in 1885 and volume III in 1894, based on Marx's unfinished manuscripts and notes.
39. Engels is using this word in an old sense in which it means "pagan."
40. Indian tribes neutral in the conflict between the Iroquois and the Hurons in the seventeenth century.
41. Tracts of land held in common by medieval communities.
42. A ruler or official.
43. A hereditary ruler.
44. Ancient Greek civilization.
45. Charles Darwin (1809–1882) established the modern theory of biological evolution by natural selection in *The Origin of Species* (1859) and subsequent works.
46. Marcel Deprez (1843–1918) was a French engineer who pioneered the transmission of electrical power over long distances.

Study and Discussion Questions

Section I: Bourgeois and Proletarians

Study Questions

1. "[T]he modern bourgeoisie is . . . the product of a long course of development, of a series of revolutions in the modes of production and of exchange." What were the most important stages in this development?

2. "The bourgeoisie, historically, has played a most revolutionary part." Why do Marx and Engels say this?

3. How does the bourgeoisie create "a world after its own image"?

4. Marx and Engels claim that feudal society ended because "the feudal relations of property became no longer compatible with the already developed productive forces." What evidence do they offer for a similar incompatibility in bourgeois society?

5. What do Marx and Engels mean by "the proletariat"? What divides the proletariat from the bourgeoisie?

6. How does the proletariat unite as a class?

7. "The bourgeoisie itself, therefore, supplies the proletariat with its own elements of political and general education, in other words, it furnishes the proletariat with weapons for fighting the bourgeoisie." Why does the bourgeoisie do this?

8. "Of all the classes that stand face to face with the bourgeoisie today, the proletariat alone is a genuinely revolutionary class," while all other non-bourgeois classes are "not revolutionary, but conservative. Nay, more, they are reactionary." Why do Marx and Engels think that only the proletariat has revolutionary potential? Why are the other classes described not merely as conservative, but as reactionary?

9. "All the preceding classes that got the upper hand sought to fortify their already acquired status by subjecting society at large to their conditions of appropriation." Why won't the proletariat do the same if it gets the upper hand?

10. Why do Marx and Engels say that the bourgeoisie has become unfit to rule?

Discussion Questions

1. If the history of all class societies is the history of class struggle, how should we understand pre-class societies? Was there conflict in such societies? What caused them to change?

2. What are examples of class struggle where you live? Would you say that class struggle is increasing, decreasing, or staying about the same? Is class struggle inevitable in capitalist society?

3. It is sometimes said that Marx and Engels attempt to explain everything in society in terms of class. Are Marx and Engels "class reductionists"? What does this mean? Is there anything in society that is (sometimes) more important than class, or equally important as class, or that cannot be explained in terms of class? What about divisions based on race, gender, nationality, or religion?

4. How would you categorize your own class position in Marxist terms? How should students be classified? What about teachers, professors, full-time union officials, people who work for "nonprofit" organizations? Is class structure today more complicated or less complicated than in the nineteenth century?

5. Was the victory of the bourgeoisie against feudalism inevitable?

6. "The executive of the modern state is but a committee for managing the common affairs of the whole bourgeoisie." Do you agree or disagree? How can a minority control the state in a modern democracy such as the United States? Do governments ever act against the interests of the bourgeoisie? If so, why?

7. Is exploitation under capitalism more "naked, shameless, direct, [and] brutal" than in earlier forms of society?

8. Has the family become a "mere money relation" in capitalist society?

9. Marx and Engels claim that in bourgeois society "all that is solid melts into air." What do they mean by this? Can you think of any examples? Can you think of any counterexamples?

10. The bourgeoisie "creates a world after its own image." What do Marx and Engels mean by this? Are they correct? Do they think this is a good thing, a bad thing, both, or neither?

11. According to Marx and Engels, "feudal relations of property became no longer compatible with the already developed productive forces." What do they mean by this? Can you think of specific examples?

12. "For many a decade past, the history of industry and commerce is but the history of the revolt of modern productive forces against modern conditions of production, against the property relations that are the conditions for the existence of the bourgeoisie and of its rule." If this was true in the mid-nineteenth century, why is capitalism still here?

13. Are economic crises inevitable under capitalism?

14. "Owing to the extensive use of machinery and to the division of labor, the work of the proletarians has lost all individual character and, consequently, all charm for the workman." Is this true? Don't some people enjoy their work?

15. Marx and Engels argue that the "various interests and conditions of life within the ranks of the proletariat are more and more equalized, in proportion as machinery obliterates all distinctions of labor, and nearly everywhere reduces wages to the same low level." Is this an accurate description of modern capitalism?

16. As capitalism develops, Marx and Engels believe that it will produce an "ever expanding union of the workers." Does the fact unionization levels in the United States have been falling for several decades show that they were wrong?

17. "This organization of the proletarians into a class, and consequently into a political party, is continually being upset again by the competition between the workers themselves." Can you think of any examples of this? Do they mean economic competition, or are they talking about other forms of competition too? If so, what other forms?

18. Do you think that workers are a "genuinely revolutionary class" in modern capitalist societies such as the United States? If yes, why? If no, why not?

19. "All revolutions lead to tyranny." How would Marx and Engels respond to this claim? How would you respond?

20. Is a socialist revolution possible in the United States? Is it likely? Is it desirable?

Section II: Proletarians and Communists

Study Questions

1. What, according to Marx and Engels, is the relationship between Communists and the working class?

2. How does bourgeois private property differ from other forms of property?

3. "Capital is, therefore, not only a personal, it is a social power." Why?

4. Why do Marx and Engels criticize "bourgeois freedom"?

5. How do Marx and Engels respond to the charge that communism will abolish the family?

6. Why do Marx and Engels argue that it is hypocritical for the bourgeoisie to accuse communists of intending to establish a "community of women"?

7. Why do Marx and Engels think, "National divisions and antagonisms between peoples are daily more and more vanishing"?

8. Why do Marx and Engels argue that "the social consciousness of past ages, despite all the multiplicity and variety it displays, moves within certain common forms, or general ideas"?

9. What do Marx and Engels think the proletariat will use its political supremacy to do?

10. Why do Marx and Engels believe that eventually "the public power will lose its political character"?

Discussion Questions

1. Communists "do not set up any special principles of their own, by which to shape and mold the proletarian movement." In that case, why is there any need for communists to set up their own organization?

2. Sometimes groups with different political ideas call themselves "socialist" or "communist" and claim to understand "the line of march, the conditions, and the ultimate general results of the proletarian movement." If the groups disagree, how is it possible to tell which, if any, knows what it is talking about?

3. Marx and Engels say that by "freedom," the bourgeoisie means free trade. Is this a fair criticism? How would you define freedom?

4. Do you think that Marx and Engels give a convincing response to the objection "that upon the abolition of private property all work will cease and universal laziness will overtake us"? If capitalism were abolished, what incentive would people have to work?

5. Do Marx and Engels believe that there are any "eternal laws of nature and of reason"? Do you?

6. According to Marx and Engels, capitalism destroys the family. Do you agree? Should we support the "traditional" family? Do we need new kinds of family? Should the family be abolished altogether?

7. Is women's liberation possible in a capitalist society? Why or why not?

8. Marx and Engels argue that international solidarity is necessary for a successful workers' revolution. Is there any evidence to think that national rivalries can be overcome? Is there any evidence to think otherwise?

9. What are the ruling ideas in our society? Do they reflect the interests of capitalists? If so, why do other people accept them? What might lead people to challenge such ideas?

10. If Marx and Engels were writing the *Manifesto* today, how might they have modified their list of immediate aims after a workers' revolution?

11. Is it possible to abolish class divisions? If class conflict were abolished, would some other form of conflict replace it?

12. Is communism compatible with human nature? What is human nature? How do you think Marx and Engels would have answered this question?

Section III: Socialist and Communist Literature

Study Questions

1. What is "feudal socialism"?

2. Why do Marx and Engels criticize the positive goals of petty-bourgeois socialism?

3. What class interests did the German "true" socialists represent?

4. How does "bourgeois socialism" differ from "reactionary socialism"?

5. Why do the critical-utopian socialists "search after a new social science"?

6. Why do Marx and Engels describe the followers of the original utopian socialists as "reactionary"?

Discussion Questions

1. "Nothing is easier than to give Christian asceticism a socialist tinge." Is it possible to be a religious communist? What do you think Marx and Engels' view was? What is your view?

2. Should socialists represent the interests of the working class, all (or most) of humanity, both, or neither? Does the majority of humanity have the same interests? Do all workers have the same interests?

3. Marx and Engels argue that capitalism's problems cannot be solved by reforms. Do you agree? If they are right, what attitude should socialists or communists have toward reforms?

4. Is there any value in constructing detailed models of how a socialist or communist society might function? Why do Marx and Engels call such models "castles in the air"? Is what they say about postcapitalist society equally utopian?

5. In the nineteenth and twentieth centuries, there were many attempts to establish alternative, "utopian" communities on a small scale. Is this a good way to try to bring about change on a larger scale? Is the fact that all of these experiments failed evidence that socialism is impossible?

Section IV: Position of the Communists in Relation to the Various Existing Opposition Parties

Study Questions

1. What is the relation of communists to non–working-class opposition parties?

2. Why do Marx and Engels view developments in Germany as having special importance?

Discussion Questions

1. Where should socialists or communists look for allies today? Are there still progressive sections of the bourgeoisie with whom they should unite around specific issues?

2. Do you agree that if there is a socialist revolution, workers will have nothing to lose but their chains?

3. Do workers in economically advanced countries such as the United States have the same interests as workers in much poorer countries?

4. Marx and Engels envisage socialism as a genuinely democratic form of society. How does socialism differ from capitalism in this respect? Is the sort of democracy that Marx defends a workable system in the modern world? Is the claim that the state will eventually wither away believable?

A Note on the Translation

The Communist Manifesto was first published in German in 1848. Helen Macfarlane produced the first English translation in 1850, but the translation used almost universally today was made by Samuel Moore in 1888, under Engels' close supervision. This edition uses Moore's translation. However, Moore's translation differs from the German original in many small ways. Most of the differences are either inconsequential or make small improvements on the original text. In a few places, however, I am persuaded by Hal Draper's detailed analysis (1994) that the Moore translation is confusing or misleading. In these places, I have altered Moore's text slightly. These changes are explained below. I have also Americanized the spelling and modernized punctuation and capitalization.

Changes to Samuel Moore's translation

I.17: 1st sentence & I.20 2nd sentence: "reactionaries" replaces the archaic "reactionists"

I.22 2nd sentence: "isolation" (a better translation of the German "Idiotismus") replaces "idiocy"

I.42 2nd sentence: "educational elements" replaces "fresh elements of enlightenment and progress."

I.44 2nd sentence: "go under" replaces "finally disappear" (which gives support to the mistaken view that Marx and Engels believed that the middle classes would eventually vanish under capitalism)

I.45 1st sentence: "ruin" replaces "extinction"

I.51: "forcible" replaces "violent" (since force may be threatened but not used)

II.2: "are not a special party in relation to the" replaces "do not form a separate party opposed to" (Draper points out that Moore's translation is at best confusing. Communists had already established a separate political organization—the Communist League—with political differences from other tendencies in the workers' movement.)

II.4: "special" replaces "sectarian"

II.18 1st sentence: "position" replaces "status"

II.37 2nd sentence: "but" deleted preceding "the outgrowth"

II.51 2nd sentence: "official and unofficial" replaces "public and private"

II.53 2nd sentence: "workers" replaces "working men"

II.54: "divisions" replaces "differences" (Marx and Engels' point is not that distinctive cultures will vanish, but that hostile national rivalries will disappear.)

II.57: "detailed" replaces "serious"

II.73 3rd sentence: "when" replaces "if" twice

III.9: "fidelity" replaces "truth"

III.10: "feudalist" replaces "landlord"

III.11 4th sentence: "Religious" replaces "Christian"

III.13 2nd sentence: "labor overseers and stewards" replaces "overlookers, bailiffs and shopmen"

III.15 3rd sentence: "small burghers and peasants" replaces "petty bourgeois and peasant" (since it is not the petty bourgeoisie as a whole that is ruined)

III.20 3rd sentence: Moore omits this whole sentence. This is Draper's translation.

III.35 4th sentence: "(1847)" deleted before "circulate"

III.45 1st sentence: "these attempts" deleted before "necessarily failed"

III.49 1st sentence: "social" replaces "historical"

III.49 1st sentence: "fanciful" replaces "fantastic"

III.51 1st sentence: "status" replaces "surroundings"

III.53: "fanciful" replaces "fantastic" twice

III.55 2nd sentence: "fanciful" replaces "fantastic" twice

III.55 6th sentence: "individual" replaces "isolated"

III.55 7th sentence: "or" added before "conservative"

IV.2 1st sentence: "momentary" deleted before "interests"

IV.4: "Among the Poles" replaces "In Poland" (since many Poles were living in exile)

IV.12: "Workers" replaces "Working men"

Further Reading

1. Other works by Marx and Engels

The best single-volume collection of Marx's writings is David McLellan, ed., *Karl Marx: Selected Writings*, 2nd ed. (New York: Oxford University Press, 2000). Another good collection, which also includes material by Engels, is Robert C. Tucker, ed., *The Marx-Engels Reader*, 2nd ed. (New York: W. W. Norton, 1978). Many works by Marx and Engels, including most of the works I cite in the References section, are available online at the Marxists Internet Archive: https://www.marxists.org/.

After *The Communist Manifesto*, I suggest reading Engels' *Socialism: Utopian and Scientific* (1880). This is an extract from a longer work, *Anti-Dühring: Herr Eugen Dühring's Revolution in Science* (1878), a polemic against a German academic that provides a systematic exposition of Marxist ideas.

For Marx's early writings, which condemn capitalism as inhumane, the best source is the *Economic and Philosophic Manuscripts* (1844). Marx and Engels set out their materialist view of history in part 1 of *The German Ideology* (1846). Marx's *The Eighteenth Brumaire of Louis Bonaparte* (1852) and Engels' *The Origin of the Family, Private Property, and the State* (1884) provide examples of the materialist method in practice.

Marx wrote two short introductions to his basic economic ideas—*Wage Labor and Capital* (1847) and *Value, Price, and Profit* (1865)—which are worth reading before tackling volume 1 of *Capital* (1867).

Finally, Marx wrote little about what a future socialist society might look like, preferring to leave that to the democratic decisions of a future workers' state, but in *The Civil War in France* (1871), he draws important lessons from the short-lived Paris Commune of 1871, in which workers ran the city for about two months, and he makes some general comments on the transition to a classless society in *Critique of the Gotha Program* (1875).

2. Books and articles about Marx and Engels

A. Introductory

Alex Callinicos, *The Revolutionary Ideas of Karl Marx* (Chicago: Haymarket Books, 2010).

Clear introduction by a British academic and activist.

Hal Draper, "The Two Souls of Socialism," *New Politics* 5, no.1 (Winter 1966). Reprinted in *Socialism from Below* (Chicago: Haymarket Books, 2019). Contrasts Marx and Engels' vision of "socialism from below" with various versions of "socialism from above."

Terry Eagleton, *Why Marx Was Right*, 2nd ed. (New Haven: Yale University Press, 2018). Eagleton replies to ten common criticisms of Marx's ideas.

Ernst Fischer, *How to Read Karl Marx* (New York: Monthly Review Press, 1996). Includes generous quotations from Marx's writings.

Mary Gabriel, *Love and Capital: Karl and Jenny Marx and the Birth of a Revolution* (New York: Little, Brown, 2011). Excellent biography that discusses Marx's work in the context of his family life.

Duncan Hallas, *The Meaning of Marxism* (London: Pluto Press, 1971). Good brief introduction.

Chris Harman, *How Marxism Works*, 6th ed. (London: Bookmarks, 1999). Another good short guide.

David Smith, *Marx's Capital Illustrated* (Chicago: Haymarket Books, 2014). A graphic guide to Marx's *Capital* with illustrations by the socialist cartoonist Phil Evans.

Hadas Thier, *A People's Guide to Capitalism* (Chicago: Haymarket Books, 2020). The best introduction to Marxist economics.

Howard Zinn, *Marx in Soho: A Play on History* (Chicago: Haymarket Books, 2012). Entertaining and informative one-man play about Marx's life and ideas by the radical historian best known for his book *A People's History of the United States*. (Haymarket also distributes the audio CD of a performance of the play by Brian Jones.)

B. More advanced

Kevin B. Anderson, *Marx at the Margins: On Nationalism, Ethnicity, and Non-Western Societies*, 2nd ed. (Chicago: University of Chicago Press, 2016). Anderson shows that Marx was a global thinker, concerned with nationality, race, and ethnicity as well as class.

Marshall Berman, *Adventures in Marxism* (New York: Verso, 1999). Wonderful collection of essays, including "Unchained Melody," Berman's reflections on the *Manifesto*.

Paul Blackledge, *Friedrich Engels and Modern Social and Political Theory* (Albany: SUNY Press, 2019). Comprehensive study that rejects the claim that there were significant differences between Marx and Engels or that Engels distorted Marx's ideas.

Heather A. Brown, *Marx on Gender and the Family* (Chicago: Haymarket Books, 2013). Valuable discussion of Marx's analysis of women's oppression.

Hal Draper, *Karl Marx's Theory of Revolution* Vol. 1, *State and Bureaucracy* (1977); Vol. 2, *The Politics of Social Classes* (1978); Vol. 3, *The "Dictatorship of the Proletariat"* (1986); Vol. 4, *Critique of Other Socialisms* (1990); Vol. 5, *War and Revolution* (2005) (New York: Monthly Review Press). Far and away the best overall account of Marx's social and political views. Volume 5 was constructed from Draper's notes after his death by E. Haberkern.

John Bellamy Foster, *Marx's Ecology* (New York: Monthly Review Press, 2000). Important study that shows that ecological ideas were central to Marx's thought.

Michael Löwy, *The Theory of Revolution in the Young Marx* (Chicago: Haymarket Books, 2005). A Marxist analysis of the origins of Marxism. Originally published in French in 1970.

Richard W. Miller, *Analyzing Marx: Morality, Power and History* (Princeton: Princeton University Press, 1984). Particularly good discussion of Marx's theory of history.

August H. Nimtz Jr., *Marx and Engels: Their Contribution to the Democratic Breakthrough* (Albany: SUNY Press, 2000). Detailed study of Marx and Engels' political activity.

August H. Nimtz, Jr. *The Ballot, the Streets—or Both: From Marx and Engels to Lenin and the October Revolution* (Chicago: Haymarket Books, 2019). Extensive look at the classical Marxist approach to elections.

Lise Vogel, *Marxism and the Oppression of Women* (Chicago: Haymarket Books, 2014). Originally published in 1983, Vogel uses Marx's work to develop a materialist theory of gender oppression.

Allen Wood, *Karl Marx*, 2nd ed. (New York: Routledge, 2004). Discusses Marx's philosophical ideas.

Ellen Meiksins Wood, *The Retreat from Class: A New "True" Socialism*, 2nd ed. (New York: Verso, 1999). Defends the continuing relevance of class politics. Originally published in 1986, this edition has a new introduction.

C. Surveys

Alex Callinicos, Stathis Kouvelakis, and Lucia Pradella, eds., *Routledge Handbook of Marxism and Post-Marxism* (New York: Routledge, 2020). A wide-ranging survey of Marxist ideas.

Marcello Musto, ed., *The Marx Revival* (New York: Cambridge University Press, 2020). A contemporary survey of what Marx actually wrote, grouped by twenty-two key concepts.

Matt Vidal et al. eds., *The Oxford Handbook of Karl Marx* (Oxford University Press, 2018). Intended both as an introduction to Marx's central ideas and as an original contribution to Marxist theory and research.

3. Books specifically about the *Manifesto*

Frederic L. Bender, ed., *The Communist Manifesto* (New York: W. W. Norton, 1988). A critical edition, with background material and commentaries by several authors.

Terrell Carver and James Farr, eds., *The Cambridge Companion to* The Communist Manifesto (New York: Cambridge University Press, 2015). Extensive historical and interpretative analysis by several scholars and a new English translation of the first edition by Carver.

Hal Draper, *The Adventures of* The Communist Manifesto (Chicago: Haymarket Books, 2020). Contains (1) a lengthy history of the *Manifesto*; (2) the text of the first German edition in parallel with the first English translation (produced by Helen Macfarlane in 1850), Samuel Moore's translation, and a new translation by Draper intended to complement Moore's; and (3) a detailed paragraph-by-paragraph analysis of the entire text. (This is a reprint of an edition published after Draper's death by the Center for Socialist History. Unfortunately, Draper was not well served by his editors. In particular, the text of the Moore translation contains numerous errors.)

Prakash Karat, *A World to Win: Essays on* The Communist Manifesto (New Delhi: LeftWord Books, 1999). Commentary by Indian Marxists.

Peter Lamb, *Marx and Engels'* Communist Manifesto*: A Reader's Guide* (New York: Bloomsbury, 2015). Includes historical background, a summary of the *Manifesto*, an extensive commentary (longer than the *Manifesto* itself), and discussion of the pamphlet's reception and influence.

China Miéville, *A Spectre, Haunting: On* The Communist Manifesto (Chicago: Haymarket Books, 2022). A multifaceted interpretation of the *Manifesto* that argues for its continued relevance.

Leo Panitch and Colin Leys, eds., *Socialist Register 1998:* The Communist Manifesto *Now* (New York: Monthly Review Press, 1998). A collection of essays published on the *Manifesto*'s 150th anniversary.

Dirk J. Struik, *Birth of the Communist Manifesto* (New York: International Publishers, 1971). Includes a long essay by Struik on the *Manifesto*'s historical background as well as supplementary material by Marx and Engels.

4. Periodicals and online resources

Climate and Capitalism: https://climateandcapitalism.com/. An ecosocialist journal, reflecting the viewpoint of ecological Marxism.

Lux: https://lux-magazine.com/. The world's first socialist-feminist glossy magazine.

Marxist Left Review: https://marxistleftreview.org/. Journal produced by socialists in Australia.

Marxists Internet Archive: https://www.marxists.org/. Large collection of works by Marx, Engels, and later Marxist writers.

New Politics: https://newpol.org/. Independent socialist journal, published since 1961.

REDS–Die Roten: http://www.marxists.de/. Links to books and articles in English and German on Marxist theory and contemporary issues.

Spectre: https://spectrejournal.com/. A biannual journal of Marxist theory, strategy, and analysis.

Tempest: https://www.tempestmag.org/. An online magazine published by revolutionary socialists in the United States.

We Are Many: https://wearemany.org/. Audio and video recordings of hundreds of radical talks. Sponsored by the Center for Economic Research and Social Change, which publishes Haymarket Books.

Glossary

Absolute monarchy: A form of rule in which the sovereign (king or queen) is unconstrained by law or parliament. In medieval Europe, absolutism developed in the late feudal period, from the fifteenth century onward, as states became more centralized, although in practice few rulers were truly absolute. Absolute monarchy was generally defended with the doctrine of the divine right of kings, which claimed that monarchs were chosen to rule by God.

Accumulated labor: Wealth created by previously performed work.

Agrarian Reformers in America: A reference to the New York–based National Reform Association (NRA), founded in 1844 by George Henry Evans (1805–56), an important US labor leader in the first half of the nineteenth century. Organizing under the slogan "Vote yourself a farm," the NRA called for the free distribution of public land to those without property, an end to the seizure of small farms to settle debts, and a limit to the total amount of land any individual could own. The first of these demands was eventually achieved with the passage of the 1862 Homestead Act during the Civil War. The NRA also worked with utopian socialists to support experiments in collective ownership of land, campaigned for a shorter workday, opposed the US invasion of Mexico in 1846, opposed the extension of slavery, and supported women's equality. After the Civil War, former members of the NRA were active in the US sections of the International Working Men's Association, an organization of trade unionists, socialists, and other radicals, in which Marx played a leading role (see Appendix A, note 10).

Alienation: A condition in which people are separated from the products of their labor, other people, the natural world, and their own humanity. Marx used the term extensively in some early writings but not in his later work. However, it is clear that he continued to see alienation as one consequence of class division and capitalist development.

Babeuf, François-Noël "Gracchus" (1760–97): French political activist who has been called the first revolutionary communist. Babeuf advocated economic as well as political equality and believed the ideals of the 1789 revolution had been betrayed after the defeat of the radical Jacobin faction in 1794. He took the name "Gracchus" from two brothers in ancient Rome, Tiberius and Gaius, who championed the interests of the lower classes in the second century BC. Babeuf formed the secret Society of the Pantheon, later known as the Conspiracy of Equals, which planned an uprising against the French government in May 1796. The plot was betrayed, and Babeuf was arrested and executed the following year.

Bourgeoisie: "By bourgeoisie is meant the class of modern capitalists, owners of the means of social production and employers of wage labor." (Engels)

Burgher: A merchant or citizen of a medieval European city.

Capital: Money or wealth invested in economic activity with the aim of making a profit. Capital depends on wage labor because profits are created by paying workers less than the value of what they produce. Sometimes used to refer to the capitalist class as a whole.

Capitalist: Someone who makes a living through ownership or control of capital.

Chartism: The Chartist movement was launched in 1838 by working-class leaders in Britain to campaign for a charter of political reforms, which they hoped would also make it easier to win social and economic demands. The Chartists' main demands were (1) voting rights for all men, (2) electoral districts of equal size, (3) abolition of property ownership requirements for Members of Parliament (MPs), (4) salaries for MPs, (5) secret ballots, and (6) annual parliamentary elections. The Chartist leaders ranged from moderates like William Lovett (1800–77), who thought the demands could be won by peaceful means, and radicals like Feargus O'Connor (1795–1856), who thought that force would be necessary. The Chartists organized huge demonstrations that were sometimes met with brutal repression. They played a leading role in a wave of strikes in the 1840s that raised both political and economic demands. In 1839, 1842, and 1848, they gathered millions of signatures on petitions to Parliament in support of their demands. After the last of these petitions was rejected, the movement gradually declined. Engels made contact with the Chartists in 1843 and contributed to their newspaper, the *Northern Star*. The first five of the Chartists' demands were eventually granted in the Reform Acts of 1867 and 1884.

Class: As Marx and Engels understand it, a person's class position is defined by their relationship to the process of production in society. Moreover, since production in class societies is based on exploitation, the relationship between those who actually produce society's wealth and those who control it is essentially antagonistic. The direct producers (enslaved people, peasants, wage laborers) are compelled to work not only to meet their own needs but also to meet the needs of the owner of the means of production, whether this is an enslaver, a feudal lord, or a capitalist. The rest of a society's class structure fits in around this relationship between the direct producers and the economically dominant class.

Because class relations are antagonistic, they give rise to resistance and class struggle, which Marx identifies as "the immediate driving power of history."

Commodity: An item that is bought or sold or that is produced to be bought or sold on the market.

Communism: A form of society in which the means of production are communally owned and in which class divisions have been abolished. According to Marx, communist society will operate according to the principle "From each according to their ability, to each according to their need."

Community of women: Communists were falsely charged with planning to introduce a system in which, instead of monogamous relationships, men would have access to any woman of their choice. Marx and Engels respond that communism aims "to do away with the status of women as mere instruments of production" and that the bourgeoisie has in effect already instituted a community of women through prostitution, sexual exploitation in the workplace, and adultery. (Also see Engels, *The Principles of Communism.* question 21, in Appendix B.)

Cracow insurrection: During the nineteenth century, Poland was occupied by Austria, Prussia, and Russia. In February 1846, an uprising against foreign rule, led by Edward Dembowski (1822–46), a young miner, took place in the city of Cracow, with the hope that it would spark insurrection across the country. The insurgents promised freedom for the peasantry, abolition of feudal taxes, redistribution of land, and the establishment of national workshops paying high wages. The rebellion failed to spread and was crushed by Austrian troops the following month, but it sparked enormous sympathy for the Polish cause across the rest of Europe.

Critical-utopian socialism/communism: A set of ideas associated with Claude-Henri de Saint-Simon (1760–1825), Robert Owen (1771–1858), Charles Fourier (1772–1837), Étienne Cabet (1788–1856), and others who made incisive criticisms of the brutality of early capitalism but whose alternatives consisted in constructing blueprints for an ideal society (or actually setting up small-scale communities based on such plans). Marx and Engels criticized critical-utopians for failing to have a realistic strategy for transforming society and for viewing workers as passive victims rather than as agents capable of fighting for their own emancipation.

Dialectical/dialectics: A dialectical approach is one that looks to explain change as typically the result of internal tensions, conflicts, and contradictions and is open to the idea of small quantitative changes accumulating to the point where significant and often sudden qualitative change occurs. Marx and Engels learned dialectical thinking from the writings of the German idealist philosopher Georg Hegel, while rejecting his idealism. As Marx later wrote, with Hegel, dialectic "is standing on its head. It must be turned right side up again, if you would discover the rational kernel within the mystical shell."

Division of labor: The distribution of tasks within the process of production, often for purposes of efficiency. Some division of labor is a necessary feature of every economy, but under capitalism the division tends to go to extremes, with complex jobs broken down into their simplest and most monotonous components and a sharp line drawn between mental and manual (or creative and uncreative) work. There is also an international dimension to the division of labor, with jobs increasingly being shifted to countries where workers can be paid much less than their counterparts in the richer economies.

English Restoration: The period following the collapse of the Commonwealth (1649–60). In 1660, Charles II (son of Charles I, who was executed in 1649) was restored to the throne. In December 1688, the Dutch prince William of Orange overthrew Charles' brother, James II, in the so-called Glorious Revolution, ending the Stuart dynasty. In early 1689, William and his wife, Mary (James' eldest daughter), were crowned king and queen, and the power of the monarchy was reduced.

Exchange value: The value of goods or services for which a commodity can be traded in the marketplace, roughly equivalent to its price. In *Capital*, Marx contrasts an item's exchange value with its use value—that is, its capacity to satisfy human needs or wants.

Exploitation: In Marxist economics, a measure of the amount of surplus value (or wealth) extracted by the ruling class from the direct producers. Workers in capitalist societies are exploited because they are paid less than the value of the goods and services that they produce.

Feudalism: The social system in Europe before the rise of capitalism. In its classic form, which emerged in the eighth century, feudalism was based on lords granting land (or fiefs) to peasants in exchange for military service and a portion of the peasants' crops. Peasants were initially legally bound to the land as serfs, but after the abolition of serfdom, feudalism became a more fluid system. A surplus continued to be extracted from the immediate producers by direct military and political means rather than by indirect economic mechanisms, as under capitalism. There is much debate about whether precapitalist modes of production in other parts of the world were also varieties of feudalism.

Forces of production: *See* Productive forces.

Fourier, Charles (1772–1837): French utopian socialist who described an ideal community (called a "phalanx"), based on a central building known as a *phalanstère*, in great detail. Marx and Engels particularly admired Fourier's progressive views on women's rights (he invented the term "feminism") and sexual liberation.

French Legitimists: Ultraconservative monarchists in the first half of the nineteenth century who defended the divine right of kings and believed that the Bourbon dynasty—overthrown following the French Revolution of 1789 and temporarily reinstated from 1815 to 1830—was France's legitimate ruling family.

French Radicals: Despite their name, a group of moderate French republicans in the 1840s, grouped around the newspaper *Le National*. (More radical republicans, known as Réformistes, were associated with *La Réforme.*) Following the overthrow of the monarchy in February 1848, many of the "Radicals" joined the new government and attempted to crush the popular movement.

French Restoration: The period following the defeat of Napoleon I, in which the Bourbon dynasty was restored to the French throne. In 1814, Louis XVIII (brother of Louis XVI, who was executed in 1792) was declared king. In 1830, Louis Philippe, the Duke of Orleans, overthrew Louis' brother, Charles X (who had succeeded him in 1824), with the support of the French bourgeoisie, and the power of the monarchy was reduced.

French Revolution (1789): One of the most important events in modern European history, the French Revolution of 1789 began as an attempt by the bourgeois leaders of the Third Estate in the French Assembly to limit the authority of King Louis XVI and the nobility and to increase their own power. Pushed on by the lower classes in Paris, however, it led in 1793 to the execution of the king, along with thousands of supporters of the old regime, in the Reign of Terror. The radical phase of the revolution ended in 1794. Then, after several years of weak conservative rule, Napoleon Bonaparte seized power in a coup in 1799, eventually declaring himself emperor. The revolution marked the end of French feudalism and the emergence of the bourgeoisie as the new ruling class. Just as importantly, the radical ideas of its early phase—calling for liberty, equality, and fraternity—had an enormous political impact in Europe and other parts of the world.

French Revolution (1830): The overthrow of Charles X (last of the Bourbon kings) by a popular uprising in Paris after he attempted to restrict freedom of the press and reduce the power of the legislature. Charles was replaced by the "Citizen King," Louis Philippe, the Duke of Orleans, who repudiated the divine right of kings and reigned as a constitutional monarch. Initially popular, Louis increasingly favored the interests of the bourgeoisie as the condition of French workers got worse and was himself overthrown in February 1848, following a sharp economic crisis.

Grün (or Gruen), Karl (1813–84): German "true" socialist allied with Proudhon in the 1840s.

Guild-master: In feudalism, the head of an association of merchants or artisans that was often granted a royal charter or monopoly.

Guizot, François (1787–1874): French historian and politician. Guizot was a moderate royalist who served in the government of the constitutional monarch Louis Philippe in the 1830s and 1840s. He became prime minister in 1847, shortly before the revolution of February 1848. Ousted from power, Guizot spent the rest of his life as a writer, producing a multivolume history of the English Revolution, among other works.

Haxthausen, Baron August von (1792–1866): Conservative German landowner who claimed to have found evidence for a tradition of common ownership of land in Russia during his travels there in the 1840s.

Home Colonies: Robert Owen's name for his

proposed utopian socialist communities in Britain.

Ideology: In the Marxist sense, a system of ideas that systematically distorts the nature of reality to protect certain class interests.

Instruments of production: Tools and technology used in production. Part of the means of production, which are in turn part of the productive forces.

Journeyman: In feudalism, a skilled worker or master craftsman who had completed an apprenticeship but remained employed by someone else.

Labor power: An individual's ability to perform work. While workers themselves are not commodities in capitalist societies, their labor power is.

Little Icaria: Icaria was the name of the utopian communist society described by the French political activist and writer Étienne Cabet (1788–1856) in his 1840 novel *Travels in Icaria*. (Icaria is the Greek island where, according to ancient Greek mythology, Icarus fell to earth after flying too close to the sun.) Little Icaria refers to the kind of small-scale utopian community that Cabet and his followers attempted to establish in various parts of the United States.

Materialism: The view that the world consists only of material phenomena. Applied to human history in particular, the view that the way in which a society produces to meet the material needs of its members decisively shapes its cultural, political, legal, artistic, religious, and philosophical institutions and ideas.

Maurer, Georg Ludwig von (1790–1872): German politician and academic who wrote several books on the early history of the Germans.

Means of production: Nonhuman physical inputs used in production, including raw materials, animals, land, buildings, tools, and technology.

Metternich, Prince Klemens Wenzel von (1773–1858): Austria's reactionary foreign minister for nearly four decades. Metternich played a key role at the Congress of Vienna (1814–15), which redrew Europe's political map following Napoleon's defeat, including reinstating the Bourbon monarchy in France. An opponent of democracy and popular sovereignty, Metternich was finally forced to resign by mass demonstrations in Vienna during the revolutionary wave of 1848.

Middle Ages: The period of about one thousand years following the collapse of the Roman Empire in Western Europe in the fifth century AD. Roughly synonymous with feudalism.

Mode of appropriation: The particular way in which surplus wealth is extracted from the immediate producers in any given class society.

Mode of production: The combination of a society's productive forces and relations of production. Feudalism represents one mode of production, capitalism another, communism a third, and so on. A mode of production begins to break down when its productive forces and relations of production come into conflict with each other, either because the relations hold back the development of the forces or because the existing forces are not adequate to sustain the relations.

Morgan, Lewis Henry (1818–81): Influential US anthropologist who conducted pioneering studies of the social structures and kinship systems of Native American societies.

Owen, Robert (1771–1858): An enlightened Welsh textile manufacturer and early socialist. Owen constructed a factory town in New Lanark, Scotland, in the early nineteenth century, which he attempted to run for the benefit of workers. The experiment survived with the contributions of social philanthropists, but his attempts to set up less paternalistic model communities in the United States and England failed.

Patrician: An aristocrat in ancient Rome.

Pauper: A very poor person, dependent on charity or public assistance.

Peasantry: The class of agricultural producers who are either small farmers or tenants.

Petty bourgeoisie: Literally the "small bourgeoisie"—small farmers, shopkeepers, small business owners, doctors, lawyers, and the self-employed. More generally, people who are not wage laborers (because they own some means of production or have some special professional skill) but who nevertheless must work to make a living, even if they employ some wage labor themselves. In capitalist society, the petty bourgeoisie forms part of the middle class (or middle classes) between labor and capital, which at different times may be pulled in either direction.

Phalanstères: The central buildings in Charles Fourier's ideal socialist communities. The term is also often used to refer to the communities themselves.

Plebeian: A member of the lower classes in ancient Rome.

Productive forces: The means of production (nonhuman physical inputs in production) together with human labor power and knowledge.

Proletariat: "By proletariat [is meant] the class of modern wage laborers who, having no means of production of their own, are reduced to selling their labor power in order to live." (Engels)

Property relations: The legal expression of a society's relations of production.

Proudhon, Pierre-Joseph (1803–65): Self-identified French anarchist (an opponent of all government and authority) who opposed capitalism and declared, "Property is theft," but who advocated "individual possession" rather than common ownership of economic resources. Proudhon envisaged a market economy without wage labor in which the self-employed and workers' cooperatives would trade with each other. Although the *Manifesto* classifies him as a "bourgeois socialist," Marx had earlier described Proudhon's ideas as reflecting the interests of the petty bourgeoisie.

Reactionary: An ultraconservative. Someone who opposes progress and wishes to turn the clock back to an earlier time.

Réformistes: Radical French republicans in the 1840s grouped around the newspaper *La*

Réforme, including moderate socialists such as Louis Blanc (1811–82). Marx and Engels gave this current critical support (see III.57 and IV.2), but the Réformistes moved to the right and discredited themselves after the February 1848 revolution. *See also* French Radicals.

Relations of production: The network of relations that exists between individuals and groups in the production and reproduction of material life. Of particular importance is the question of which group controls society's surplus wealth (over and above what is needed to provide for the basic needs of the population) and which group is responsible for producing it. The relations of production thus define a society's class structure and the relations between classes. The relations of production are real material relations but are typically codified in a legal system. Ruling classes, for instance, not only have material control of the surplus but are generally given legal ownership of it as well. It is possible, however, to have the former without the latter.

Ruling class: The economically dominant class in society, which directly or indirectly controls the state.

Saint-Simon, Claude-Henri de Rouvroy, Comte de (1760–1825): French utopian socialist who argued that society should be organized to improve the situation of the poorest class and who advocated a system of planning informed by modern science. An opponent of revolution, he once appealed to the reactionary Louis XVIII to implement his ideas by decree.

Serf: A peasant bound to the land who must perform work for a feudal lord in return for protection.

Sismondi, Jean-Charles-Léonard Simonde de (1773–1842): Swiss historian and political economist who became an early critic of capitalism. Sismondi argued that crises were endemic to capitalism because of insufficient demand. He advocated government intervention to regulate competition and protect small businesses.

Social relations of production: *See* Relations of production.

Socialism: Marx and Engels sometimes use this term in a very broad sense to mean any concern for the social problems generated by capitalism. More narrowly, it refers to a society in which the working class is dominant and there is some significant degree of social ownership or state control of the economy, perhaps as a transition to a fully communist, classless society.

Third Estate: In feudal France, those members of the population who were not members of the clergy (the First Estate) or the nobility (the Second Estate). All three estates were represented in the Estates-General, the politically weak national assembly. In 1789, when the assembly was reconvened after a gap of 175 years to address the country's financial crisis, the bourgeois leaders of the Third Estate demanded more power, thus precipitating the French Revolution.

"True" socialism: A socialist current in Germany in the 1840s, associated with the philosopher Moses Hess (1812–75) and others, that rejected a class perspective in favor of an abstract commitment to justice and humanity. They regarded themselves as "true" socialists because they rejected an alliance with the bourgeoisie against German feudalism, seeing capitalism as the main enemy. Marx and Engels criticized these ideas as playing into the hands of the feudal ruling class and of failing to appreciate the importance of democratic reforms in the struggle for social and economic change. Ultimately, they saw "true" socialism as reflecting the interests of a section of the German middle class.

Utopian socialism/communism: *See* Critical-utopian socialism/communism.

Vassals: Serfs.

Wage labor: Workers who own no means of production and must sell their labor power (ability to work) to make a living.

Young England: An aristocratic faction of the British Tory (later Conservative) Party in the 1840s, led by the future prime minister Benjamin Disraeli (1804–81). Young England deplored the brutality of the Industrial Revolution but offered in its place a return to a paternalistic and romanticized version of feudalism. Young England disintegrated after Disraeli left the group in the late 1840s.

References

Angus, Ian. 2016. *Facing the Anthropocene: Fossil Capitalism and the Crisis of the Earth System.* New York: Monthly Review Press.

Arnove, Anthony. 2000. "The Fall of Stalinism: Ten Years On." *International Socialist Review* 10.

Bakan, Joel. 2004. *The Corporation: The Pathological Pursuit of Profit and Power.* New York: Free Press.

Barker, Colin, ed. 2002. *Revolutionary Rehearsals.* Chicago: Haymarket Books.

Bender, Frederic L., ed. 1988. *The Communist Manifesto.* New York: W. W. Norton.

Berman, Marshall. 1998. "Unchained Melody," *The Nation* (May 11). Reprinted in 1999, *Adventures in Marxism.* London: Verso.

Binns, Peter, et al. 2003. *Russia: From Workers' State to State Capitalism.* Chicago: Haymarket Books.

Birchall, Ian. 1998. "The Manifesto Remains a Guide." *New Politics* 24.

Bowles, Samuel, and Herbert Gintis. 2011. *Schooling in Capitalist America: Educational Reform and the Contradictions of Economic Life.* Chicago: Haymarket Books.

Braverman, Harry. 1974. *Labor and Monopoly Capital.* New York: Monthly Review Press.

Brecher, Jeremy. 2020. *Strike!* 50th anniversary ed. Oakland: PM Press.

Burkett, Paul. 2014. *Marx and Nature: A Red and Green Perspective.* Chicago: Haymarket Books.

Callinicos, Alex. 1991. *The Revenge of History: Marxism and the East European Revolutions.* University Park, PA: Penn State University Press.

Camfield, David. 2022. *Future on Fire: Capitalism and the Politics of Climate Change.* Oakland: PM Press.

Davis, Mike. 1986. *Prisoners of the American Dream.* New York: Verso.

Dickens, Charles. 1842. "Philadelphia, and Its Solitary Prison." *American Notes*, chapter 7. Available online at http:// www.victorianweb.org/authors/dickens/ pva/pva344.html.

Domhoff, G. William. 2006. *Who Rules America? Power, Politics, and Social Change.* 5th ed. New York: McGraw Hill.

Draper, Hal. 1966. "The Two Souls of Socialism." *New Politics* 5, no. 1. Reprinted in 2019, *Socialism from Below.* Chicago: Haymarket Books.

———. 1970. "Marx, 'Marxism,' and Trade Unions." Reprinted in 2019, *Socialism from Below.* Chicago: Haymarket Books.

———. 1977. *Karl Marx's Theory of Revolution, Vol. I: State and Bureaucracy.* New York:

Monthly Review Press.
———. 1978. *Karl Marx's Theory of Revolution, Vol. II: The Politics of Social Classes.* New York: Monthly Review Press.
———. 2020. *The Adventures of the Communist Manifesto.* Chicago: Haymarket Books.
Ehrenreich, Barbara. 2001. *Nickel and Dimed: On (Not) Getting By in America.* New York: Metropolitan Books.
Engels, Frederick. 1842a. *Schelling and Revelation: Critique of the Latest Attempt of Reaction Against the Free Philosophy.* Marxists Internet Archive. https://marxists.architexturez.net/archive/marx/works/1841/anti-schelling/ch02.htm.
———. 1842b. *Schelling, Philosopher in Christ.* Marxists Internet Archive. https://marxists.architexturez.net/archive/marx/works/1841/anti-schelling/ch06.htm.
———. 1844. "Outlines of a Critique of Political Economy." Marxists Internet Archive. https://www.marxists.org/archive/marx/works/1844/df-jahrbucher/outlines.htm.
———. 1845. *Condition of the Working Class in England.* Marxists Internet Archive. https://www.marxists.org/archive/marx/works/download/pdf/condition-working-class-england.pdf.
———. 1847a. *Draft of a Communist Confession of Faith.* Marxists Internet Archive. https://www.marxists.org/archive/marx/works/1847/06/09.htm.
———. 1847b. *The Principles of Communism.* Reprinted in Appendix B.
———. 1878. *Anti-Dühring: Herr Eugen Dühring's Revolution in Science.* Marx-Engels Archive. https://www.marxists.org/archive/marx/works/download/pdf/anti_duhring.pdf.
———. 1880. *Socialism: Utopian and Scientific.* Marxists Internet Archive. https://www.marxists.org/archive/marx/works/download/Engels_Socialism_Utopian_and_Scientific.pdf.
Finn, Daniel. 2023. "Two Centuries of the National Question." *Jacobin* 48 (Winter).
Foster, John Bellamy. 1999. *The Vulnerable Planet: A Short Economic History of the Environment.* Rev. ed. New York: New York University Press.
———. 2000. *Marx's Ecology: Materialism and Nature.* New York: Monthly Review Press.
Gasper, Phil. 1998. "A Manifesto for Today." *International Socialist Review* 5.
———. 2004. "Genes, Evolution and Human Nature: Is Biology Destiny?" *International Socialist Review* 38.
———. 2005. "Genes, Evolution and Human Nature, Part Two." *International Socialist Review* 40.
———. 2006. "Classics of Marxism: *Capital* Volume 1." *International Socialist Review* 49.
———, ed. 2017. *Imperialism and War: Classic Writings by V. I. Lenin and Nikolai Bukharin.* Chicago: Haymarket Books.
Georgakas, Dan, and Marvin Surkin. 2012: *Detroit, I Do Mind Dying.* 3rd ed. Chicago: Haymarket Books.
Gould, Stephen Jay. 1977. "Biological Potentiality vs. Biological Determinism." In *Ever Since Darwin: Reflections in Natural History.* New York: W. W. Norton.
Harman, Chris. 1967. "How the Revolution Was Lost." *International Socialism* 1, no. 30. Reprinted in Binns 2003.
———. 1992. "The Return of the National Question." *International Socialism* 2, no. 56.
Herman, Edward S. 1998. "The Reopening of Marx's System." *New Politics* 24.

Hill, Christopher. 1972. *The World Turned Upside Down: Radical Ideas During the English Revolution*. New York: Viking.

Hobsbawm, Eric. 1998. Introduction to *The Communist Manifesto: A Modern Edition*. London: Verso.

Hoveman, Rob. 1998. "Financial Crises and the Real Economy." *International Socialism* 2, no. 78.

Hudis, Peter. 2013. *Marx's Concept of the Alternative to Capitalism*. Chicago: Haymarket Books.

Kamin, Leon J., Richard C. Lewontin, and Steven Rose. 2017. *Not in Our Genes: Biology, Ideology, and Human Nature*. Chicago: Haymarket Books.

Katsiaficas, George. 1987. *The Imagination of the New Left*. Boston: South End.

Loewen, James W. 2018. *Lies My Teacher Told Me: Everything Your American History Textbook Got Wrong*. Rev. ed. New York: New Press.

Löwy, Michael. 1976. "Marxism and the National Question." *New Left Review* 1 no. 96 (March/April).

Mandel, Ernest. 1971. *The Formation of The Economic Thought of Karl Marx*. New York: Monthly Review Press.

Marx, Karl. 1841. *The Difference Between the Democritean and Epicurean Philosophy of Nature*. Marxists Internet Archive. https://www.marxists.org/archive/marx/works/1841/dr-theses/index.htm.

———. 1844a. "A Contribution to the Critique of Hegel's *Philosophy of Right*: Introduction." Marxists Internet Archive. https://www.marxists.org/archive/marx/works/1843/critique-hpr/intro.htm.

———. 1847. *The Poverty of Philosophy*. Marxists Internet Archive. https://www.marxists.org/archive/marx/works/1847/poverty-philosophy/index.htm.

———. 1859. Preface to *A Contribution to the Critique of Political Economy*. (An extract is reprinted in Appendix C.)

———. 1867. *Capital*, Volume I. Marxists Internet Archive. https://www.marxists.org/archive/marx/works/1867-c1/.

———. 1871. *The Civil War in France*. (An extract is reprinted in Appendix C.)

———. 1874. *Conspectus of Bakunin's* Statism and Anarchy. Marxists Internet Archive. https://www.marxists.org/archive/marx/works/1874/04/bakunin-notes.htm.

———. 1875. *Critique of the Gotha Program*. (An extract is reprinted in Appendix C.)

Marx, Karl, and Frederick Engels. 1845. *The Holy Family*. Marxists Internet Archive. https://www.marxists.org/archive/marx/works/download/Marx_The_Holy_Family.pdf.

———. 1845–46. *The German Ideology*. Marxists Internet Archive. https://www.marxists.org/archive/marx/works/1845/german-ideology/.

———. 1850. "Address of the Central Committee to the Communist League" (March). Marxists Internet Archive. https://www.marxists.org/archive/marx/works/1847/communist-league/1850-ad1.htm.

McNally, David. 1998. "Globalization on Trial: Crisis and Class Struggle in East Asia." *Monthly Review* 50, no. 4.

———. 2011. *Global Slump: The Economics and Politics of Crisis and Resistance*. Oakland: PM Press.

———. 2020. "The Return of the Mass Strike: Teachers, Students, Feminists, and the New Wave of Popular Upheavals." *Spectre* 1, no. 1.

Molyneux, John. 2003. *Marxism and the Party*. Chicago: Haymarket Books.

———. 2021. "State Capitalism Today." *Irish*

Marxist Review 10, no. 31.

Moody, Kim. 2017. *On New Terrain: How Capital Is Reshaping the Battleground of Class War.* Chicago: Haymarket Books.

———. 2021. "Workers of the World: Growth, Change, and Rebellion." *New Politics* 18, no. 2, whole no. 70 (Winter).

———. 2022. *Breaking the Impasse: Electoral Politics, Mass Action, the New Socialist Movement in the United States.* Chicago: Haymarket Books.

Ortiz, Isabel, Sara Burke, Mohamed Berrada, and Hernán Saenz Cortés. 2021. *World Protests: A Study of Key Protest Issues in the 21st Century.* New York: Palgrave Macmillan.

Parenti, Michael. 2010. *Democracy for the Few.* 9th ed. Boston: Wadsworth/Cengage Learning.

Prinz, Jesse J. 2012. *Beyond Human Nature: How Culture and Experience Shape the Human Mind.* New York: W. W. Norton.

Rippa, S. Alexander. 1997. *Education in a Free Society: An American History.* 8th ed. New York: Allyn and Bacon.

Roberts, Michael. 2016. *The Long Depression: How It Happened, Why It Happened, and What Happens Next.* Chicago: Haymarket Books.

Rubin, Lillian Breslow. 1976. *Worlds of Pain: Life in the Working-Class Family.* New York: Basic Books.

Schor, Juliet. 1991. *The Overworked American.* New York: Basic Books.

Scialabba, George. 2005. "Zippie World!" *The Nation.* June 13.

Silverstein, Ken. 1998. *Washington on $10 Million a Day: How Lobbyists Plunder the Nation.* Monroe, ME: Common Courage.

Singer, Peter. 1983. *Hegel.* New York: Oxford University Press.

Sparks, Colin. 1998. "The Eye of the Storm," *International Socialism* 2, no. 78.

Struik, Dirk J. 1971. *Birth of the Communist Manifesto.* New York: Monthly Review Press.

Taylor, Keeanga-Yamahtta. 2021. *From #BlackLivesMatter to Black Liberation.* 2nd ed. Chicago: Haymarket Books.

Trotsky, Leon. 1924. *The First Five Years of the Communist International*, Volume 2. Marxists Internet Archive. https://www.marxists.org/archive/trotsky/1924/ffyci-1/index.htm.

———. 1930. *The History of the Russian Revolution.* Marxists Internet Archive. https://www.marxists.org/archive/trotsky/1930/hrr/.

———. 1938. "Ninety Years of the *Communist Manifesto.*" Marxists Internet Archive. https://www.marxists.org/archive/trotsky/1937/10/90manifesto.htm.

Tucker, Robert C., ed. 1978. *The Marx-Engels Reader.* 2nd ed. New York: W. W. Norton.

Vidal, Matt. 2018. "Was the Gravedigger Thesis Central to Marx's Theory of the Working Class?" Marxist Sociology Blog, October 12, 2018. https://marxistsociology.org/2018/10/was-the-gravedigger-thesis-central-to-marxs-theory-of-the-working-class.

Warren, Elizabeth, and Amelia Warren Tyagi. 2003. *The Two-Income Trap: Why Middle-Class Mothers and Fathers Are Going Broke.* New York: Basic Books.

Wolff, Edward N. 2000. *Recent Trends in Wealth Ownership, 1983–1998.* Working Paper, No. 300. Annandale-on-Hudson, NY: Levy Economics Institute of Bard College.

Zinn, Howard. 1980. *A People's History of the United States.* New York: HarperCollins.

Index

Also Available from Haymarket Books

The Adventures of The Communist Manifesto
by Hal Draper

The Ballot, the Streets—or Both: From Marx and Engels to Lenin and the October Revolution
by August H. Nimtz

Blood and Money: War, Slavery, Finance, and Empire by David McNally

A Brief History of Commercial Capitalism
by Jairus Banaji

Care: The Highest Stage of Capitalism
by Premilla Nadasen

C. L. R. James and Revolutionary Marxism Selected Writings of C. L. R. James 1939–1949
edited by Paul Le Blanc and Scott McLemee

From Marx to Gramsci: A Reader in Revolutionary Marxist Politics edited by Paul Le Blanc

Imperialism and War: Classic Writings by V. I. Lenin and Nikolai Bukharin by Nikolai Bukharin and V. I. Lenin, edited by Phil Gasper

Karl Marx by Karl Korsch

Marx and Nature: A Red and Green Perspective
by Paul Burkett

Marxism and the Oppression of Women: Toward a Unitary Theory by Lise Vogel, introduction by Susan Ferguson and David McNally

Marx's Capital Illustrated: An Illustrated Introduction by David Smith, illustrated by Phil Evans

Marx, Women, and Capitalist Social Reproduction: Marxist Feminist Essays by Martha E. Giménez

A People's Guide to Capitalism: An Introduction to Marxist Economics by Hadas Thier

Revolutions by Michael Löwy

Revolutionary Democracy: Emancipation in Classical Marxism by Soma Marik

Socialism from Below by Hal Draper

A Spectre, Haunting: On the Communist Manifesto
by China Miéville

Socialism . . . Seriously: A Brief Guide to Surviving the 21st Century by Danny Katch

State and Revolution: Fully Annotated Edition
by V. I. Lenin, introduction and annotations by Todd Chretien

About Haymarket Books

Haymarket Books is a radical, independent, nonprofit book publisher based in Chicago. Our mission is to publish books that contribute to struggles for social and economic justice. We strive to make our books a vibrant and organic part of social movements and the education and development of a critical, engaged, and internationalist Left.

We take inspiration and courage from our namesakes, the Haymarket Martyrs, who gave their lives fighting for a better world. Their 1886 struggle for the eight-hour day—which gave us May Day, the international workers' holiday—reminds workers around the world that ordinary people can organize and struggle for their own liberation. These struggles—against oppression, exploitation, environmental devastation, and war—continue today across the globe.

Since our founding in 2001, Haymarket has published more than nine hundred titles. Radically independent, we seek to drive a wedge into the risk-averse world of corporate book publishing. Our authors include Angela Y. Davis, Arundhati Roy, Keeanga-Yamahtta Taylor, Eve L. Ewing, Aja Monet, Mariame Kaba, Naomi Klein, Rebecca Solnit, Olúfẹ́mi O. Táíwò, Mohammed El-Kurd, José Olivarez, Noam Chomsky, Winona LaDuke, Robyn Maynard, Leanne Betasamosake Simpson, Howard Zinn, Mike Davis, Marc Lamont Hill, Dave Zirin, Astra Taylor, and Amy Goodman, among many other leading writers of our time. We are also the trade publishers of the acclaimed Historical Materialism Book Series.

Haymarket also manages a vibrant community organizing and event space in Chicago, Haymarket House, the popular Haymarket Books Live event series and podcast, and the annual Socialism Conference.

About the Author

Phil Gasper is Emeritus Professor of Philosophy, Notre Dame de Namur University. He is coeditor of the independent socialist journal *New Politics* and a member of the Tempest Collective. Gasper edited *Imperialism and War: Classic Writings by V. I. Lenin and Nikolai Bukharin.* He lives and works in Madison, Wisconsin, where he is a member of AFT Local 243.